THE CHERKASSY INCIDENT

First edition, published in 2001 by

WOODFIELD PUBLISHING
Woodfield House, Babsham Lane, Bognor Regis
West Sussex PO21 5EL, England.

© Hunter Carlyle, 2001

All rights reserved.
No part of this publication may be reproduced
or transmitted in any form or by any means,
electronic or mechanical, nor may it be stored
in any information storage and retrieval system,
without prior permission from the publisher.

The right of Hunter Carlyle
to be identified as Author of this work
has been asserted by him in accordance with
the Copyright, Designs and Patents Act 1988

ISBN 1-903953-05-7

THE
Cherkassy
INCIDENT

Hunter Carlyle

Woodfield Publishing
~ WEST SUSSEX • ENGLAND ~

Contents

About the author 7
Prologue 9
1   Russia : Barents Sea 15
2   Russia : St Petersburg 30
3   Ireland : Belfast 40
4   Pakistan : Gwadar 48
5   United States : Colorado 58
6   Russia : Kola Peninsula 71
7   Iran : Tehran 81
8   Russia : St Petersburg 91
9   Israel : Jerusalem 99
10 Denmark : Esbjerg 107
11 Iran : Gulf of Oman 113
12 United States : Washington 125
13 England : London 133

14	Ireland : Belfast	142
15	United States : Colorado	149
16	Israel : Haifa	157
17	Iran : Gulf of Oman	166
18	Esbjerg : The Norwegian Sea	175
19	Russia : Kola Peninsula	185
20	Pakistan : Gwadar	195
21	Iran : Dasht-e Kavir	206
22	United States : Washington	215
23	England : London	223
24	Russia : St Petersburg	233
25	Russia : Barents Sea	243
26	The High Seas	254
27	Ireland : Mayo	267
28	Russia : St Petersburg	282
29	Israel : Tel Aviv	292
30	USA : Washington & Colorado	301
31	Northern Ireland - Belfast	312
32	England - London	322

About the Author

HUNTER CARLYLE ran his own group of companies for twenty-three years, operating from four offices within the United Kingdom and one in St. Petersburg. He has worked with many well-known political figures and multinational organisations throughout the world, especially in Russia.

His professional and personal acquaintances within Russia have included Mikhail Gorbachev, Anatoly Sobchak (Mayor of St. Petersburg), Michael Gubkin (Vice Mayor), Vladimir Putin (President), Pyotr Aven (Minister of Foreign Trade), Anatoly Chubais (Deputy Prime Minister), Sergei Filatov (First Deputy Chairman of the Supreme Soviet) and many others, including senior members within the Russian Navy and Admiralty.

The storyline of *The Cherkassy Incident* has proved remarkably prophetic. Written *before* the tragic sinking of the *Kursk* hit international headlines, it is a truly international novel, featuring the possible consequences of the sinking of a Russian nuclear submarine. Although written as fiction, it is very much based on fact and upon the author's personal experiences – including visits to American and Russian nuclear submarines. He says:

> "It is a very sobering thought when one tries to comprehend the full extent of Russia's nuclear problems. They still have a further 113 nuclear submarines (plus another 61 nuclear warships and ice-breakers) rotting away in their Northern Fleet."

Prologue

Armageddon was only a hair's breath away. One bleak and blustery January morning in 1995, mankind came within minutes of total annihilation. Norway had just launched their latest multi-stage research rocket into the upper atmosphere from a remote test range to the northwest of the mainland where the Norwegian and Barents Seas merge.

Twenty four hours earlier, a US Defence Support Programme satellite had gently manoeuvred into geo-synchronous orbit 22,300 miles above the earth's curvature and deployed the petals of its eight thousand cell detector array. The satellite's infra-red telescope silently came into focus as it dipped in the vacuum of space and looked down upon the isolated launch site. Having detected the rocket's first stage of ignition, an endless stream of encrypted data was instantly beamed back from the space sentinel to its masters at the North American Aerospace Defence Command in Colorado. Meanwhile, back in Northern Europe, the earth shook and vibrated with an ear-splitting roar as the rocket's engines reached maximum thrust and the umbilicals withdrew to the service tower. The inertial guidance system took over and stabilised , as the vehicle gave an involuntary shudder and rose smoothly from its exhaust shrouded launch pad and began its journey towards the heavens.

Several times zones to the west, a Duty Officer at NORAD's Command Centre, deep inside Cheyenne Mountain, put down his coffee and went over to the secure laser printer as it buzzed into life and gently deposited a series of classified documents into its collection tray. He picked up the authenticating yellow sheets and casually shuffled through them. Everything seemed to be in order. He verified the launch with his orders for the day – and entered it into the log. All Nations had been notified about the rocket's deployment and more importantly, its purpose:

It was a routine procedure.

Although committed to an entirely peaceful scientific programme, the Norwegians had nevertheless become increasingly sensitive when launching rockets so close to the Russian borders. As a consequence, they had always been meticulous about advising the Russians well in advance of any intended launch. Some four weeks before this particular launch, a carefully written protocol and notification had been dispatched through the usual Diplomatic channels to the Russian Foreign Ministry.

But somehow the Russians had misplaced the vital message...

Ever since the rapid and unexpected collapse of Communism in the early nineteen nineties, secure communications had become chaotic and were fraught with endless difficulties. Many disillusioned Russians were totally bewildered when they found themselves out of work and with no income for the first time within living memory. Morale and commitment were at an all time low. The muddy streets of Russia's once proud cities were now crowded with hungry and dispossessed people. Even her privileged top scientists, technicians and engineers were reduced to jostling amidst the growing piles of refuse as they scrambled to offer a few pathetic possessions ... and all just for the price of their next meal. Most high-ranking officials had managed to escape these everyday hardships which had to be endured by the ordinary citizens. However, it was becoming clearer by the day that desperate people might do desperate things.

A more significant consequence of this insidious malaise had been a systematic breakdown in morale which permeated throughout every branch of the Russian military – including the entire Command structure. Most conscripts either deserted or were stripped of their basic dignity and self-respect by being reduced to scavenging for the bare essentials of life. Meanwhile, many of their superiors were actively engaged in more sinister and audacious schemes to secure their own futures.

At a secluded Black Sea airbase near the outskirts of Oktyabr'skoye, a small group of disillusioned high-ranking Generals had decided to act swiftly to secure their own doubtful futures. They had brazenly ordered the loading of four giant *Antanov An-22 Antheus* freighter aircraft with *Mi-24 HIND-D* troop carrying helicopters and *MiL Mi-28 Havoc* gunships, plus millions of dollars worth of assorted weapons and supplies from the vast army stockpile. A hand-picked squad of elite *Spetsnaz* troops then captured the world's imagination by carrying out an audacious operation to fly the illicit cargo eastwards for final delivery to a much favoured 'client' in South East Asia.

The defensive radar system encircling the former Soviet Union may be old and poorly maintained, but it nevertheless still functions as the only means of providing early warning of an impending attack.

Colonel Vladimir Kusminov sighed with boredom as he leant back in his chair at the radar control centre near Murmansk. He crossed his feet up on the huge desk in front of him and laced his fingers behind his bald head. Kusminov casually glanced across at the slowly rotating radar traces on a bank of luminescent instruments which lined the opposite wall: everything seemed to be in order.

The Colonel quietly hummed the *'March Slave'* to himself as he took his feet off the desk and began to shuffle through the latest batch of routine orders and requisitions which had found their way into his pending tray.

Kusminov's concentration was suddenly interrupted as a bright blip appeared on one of the radar screens to the left of his peripheral vision. He dropped the papers on to his desk and dashed over to study the antiquated equipment more closely. He swallowed hard and his mouth went dry as he rapidly went through the various check procedures: there was no mistake. Even though the Cold War had ended several years ago, Russia remained on constant twenty-four hour alert and was still regarded as a formidable nuclear superpower. Kusminov wasted no time. The Radar Control Centre came alive as he flashed urgent encrypted news of an unidentified rocket launch back to the nuclear Command and Control Centre in Moscow: the countdown had started. In less than thirty minutes, everyone assumed, the hostile missile would re-enter the earth's atmosphere and fall on Russian territory. Missile headquarters immediately contacted all launch centres throughout the length and breadth of the Motherland, including all her ballistic missile submarines already deployed at sea.

Twelve hundred miles away, to the north west of Moscow, the Norwegian scientists were busily congratulating themselves on yet another successful launch. However, before returning to the comparative warmth and comfort of their command bunker, the scientists briefly remained in a huddled group behind the blast wall and shielded their eyes as they took one last admiring look at the rapidly vanishing space vehicle. Handshakes were exchanged and a lot of back slapping ensued as the rocket's white hot shaft of flame shortened and diminished to a bright point of light when the second stage booster took over and thrust it through the stratosphere. Three minutes had elapsed since launch. At his northern underground missile warning bunker, Colonel Kusminov and his colleagues were still intently watching their radar screens as the mysterious rocket shot higher into space.

It was immediately classified as a threat.

Some elder statesmen within the Russian high-command structure still clung to the possibility of a surprise nuclear attack from a United States submarine patrolling in Arctic waters. After eight agonising minutes of flight, it finally became clear that the rocket was actually heading northwards – out over the Arctic Ocean and away from the mainland.

But Russia had come within minutes of retaliating. She was on the brink of launching a massive full-scale nuclear strike at the United States and Western Europe.

❖ ❖ ❖

Six years later, nothing had changed. Having just completed an extensive refit, the Russian nuclear submarine *Cherkassy* was in to the third day of a shakedown cruise from Severodvinsk. Her giant black shape had just levelled off at three hundred feet below the choppy surface of the Barents Sea.

Captain Valentin Tarasov came over from the navigation plot and climbed on to an elevated platform surrounded by a stainless steel handrail in the centre of the control room. Behind him, the attack periscope had been lowered into its well, two decks below. The control room was hot and claustrophobic. Space within a nuclear submarine was always at a premium, but on this occasion the whole situation had become further exacerbated as a result of taking an Iranian naval delegation on board. Colour coded valves, piping and cables ran in all directions: green for water, brown for fuel, red for safety and blue for high-pressure air. Extra test equipment for her sea trials had also been hooked up to the various consoles. The cramped and vaulted chamber hummed with a low growl from the ventilation system and a dull red glow from the overhead lighting and control consoles filled the room.

A series of violent manoeuvres during the past few hours had caused one of the reactor's primary cooling circuits to malfunction. A massive gate valve, essential to seal off the port coolant loop, had also failed. Her exhausted engineers had been battling with this problem for more than two hours, before finally having to make up a jury rig to provide pure coolant water directly from the submarine's storage tanks and her desalination plant. They were fast running out of options. As a last desperate measure, they decided to hook up a seperate supply hose to force seawater into the coolant system ... despite the knowledge that this would probably corrode the pressure vessel in a matter of hours.

Rem Bukato, the Executive Officer, looked over an engineer's shoulder and quickly scanned the twinkling warning lights on the reactor plant's control panel. Power had just been reduced by driving the main fusion control rods into the highly enriched uranium fuel modules contained within the two reactor cores in compartment 7. The sub's engineers were still concerned about the latest modifications to the control rod power systems as they continued to nurse her ageing nuclear reactors, already made brittle by radiation. Even at two-thirds power, there were intermittent problems with the secondary cooling circuit and radiation levels in the main reactor room had risen well above normal.

❖ ❖ ❖

On 6th October 1986 the world had held its breath when the Russians had lost their Yankee Class nuclear submarine K219 just to the east of Bermuda. This was followed nearly two and a half years later when their Mike-class nuclear submarine *Komsomolets* went down on the 7th April 1989 some 180 kilometers south west of Bear Island. Now they were about to lose another...

CHAPTER 1

RUSSIA : BARENTS SEA

"FIRE! FIRE!" THE ALARM CALL CAME from the Russian nuclear submarine's hot and cramped main propulsion battery storage area situated directly underneath her forward torpedo room. It was quickly followed by the urgent and rasping sound of klaxons reverberating throughout every compartment. The sinister and shadowy form of the 11,500-ton titanium hull of the *Cherkassy* was gliding silently through the icy blackness of the Barents Sea, close to the Kola Peninsula, just four hundred feet over the featureless bottom. This post cold war leviathan had just completed the surface portion of her sea trials, which had included a series of crash-dive exercises, followed by sonar and radar calibration tests while pulling tight radius turns to port and starboard. During the past forty-eight hours of this latest exercise, they had endured an endless bombardment of simulated attacks from the Russian Air Force and other submarines of the Northern Fleet. Such intensive exercises were designed to probe the full operational capabilities of these search-and-strike underwater killers ... and could make or break any submariner's career. Captain Valentin Tarasov pulled himself across the control centre's sloping deck and made his way towards the main engineering console. He switched to the number three closed-circuit monitor.

"Get it under control!" Tarasov screamed as he tried to make himself heard above the high pitched whine of the inertial navigation equipment and the constant low roar rushing through the ventilation ducts. The monitor displayed a flickering grey image of the Fire Officer being joined in the torpedo room by several enlisted men from Blue Watch. They were doing everything they could to get the blaze under control – but the sharp fifteen degree angles of the latest manoeuvre had made them slip and slide all over the greasy metal floor plates.

The old familiar smell of an operational submarine permeated throughout the vessel. It was a volatile concoction of diesel oil, cigarette smoke, stale sweat, cooking fat and raw sewage backing-up from the heads. Curtains remained tightly drawn across the entrance to the Officers wardroom, situated at the far end of a narrow passageway on the middle deck. Four of the off-duty officers from the previous watch were sprawled about on the banquette seating and appeared to be completely indifferent to the insistent rasping of the klaxon. One Lieutenant tried to focus through his half-drunken stupor and reached out to steady a bottle of vodka as it slid towards him across the table. He gave an irritated grunt when he noticed the liquid in his glass kept changing angles with the submarines latest erratic moves.

As fires go, it wasn't really that serious. Sudden flare-ups and power surges from the batteries were a common occurrence and even after her extensive modifications, this latest Yankee Notch class submarine was still not the best maintained in the Russian Navy. She wasn't fully operational – and she wasn't ready for sea. Under normal circumstances, the crew would have been able to treat such a fire-fighting exercise as routine, but with two of the half-dozen Iranian naval observers standing by his side, Tarasov's face began to tighten with frustration. Walled in by his own enforced sense of duty, he began to reflect upon the real prospect of failure and imminent death. His growing agitation travelled down the intercom right to the scene of the blaze. The Fire Officer instinctively repeated his Captain's muffled commands as the enlisted men crashed into each other in their eagerness to respond.

This minor emergency was rapidly developing into a major catastrophe.

"Captain..." The exhausted voice of Boris Lukin, the Weapons Officer, sounded urgent. Tarasov quickly scanned the twinkling lights of the engineering console before turning back to monitor number two. He took a deep breath and slowly let it out as he watched Lukin's anxious face intermittently breaking up on the screen "...it must be kept away from the Torpedo Room," gasped Lukin.

"I know!" snapped Tarasov in terse reply. He was a Commander of the old school. From the very start of his naval career in the former Soviet Union, he had developed an ability to instantly grasp the most intricate of details – and quickly.

He had made his name as a tough battle line strategist, an expert submariner and a deadly tactician. Under combat pressure he always remained cautious, but was nevertheless absolutely decisive, an essential quality in any submarine's operational centre.

It was stifling hot in the cramped control centre, and the subdued lighting glistened from the faces of their bemused Iranian guests. Tarasov hadn't wanted them on board in the first place, and certainly not on such a critical mission intended to test the submarine to its limits of endurance. Every spare inch was crammed with machinery or test equipment for this shake-down cruise. It was impossible to stretch out an arm, without touching racks of glowing monitors and oscilloscopes. The suffocating and claustrophobic atmosphere of the *Cherkassy* was no place for trying to impress his foreign visitors. The main longitudinal corridor was no more than three feet wide at the widest point, and there was barely enough headroom to get through the heavy-duty water tight hatches which separated each compartment. If the Iranians had wanted to learn about submarines, they should have been placed aboard another vessel. But no, the big brass in St Petersburg had reluctantly succumbed to the constant stream of diplomatic pressure coming from Tehran.

The Ayatollahs had been emphatic. They wanted their men to observe Russia's latest nuclear submarine at full stretch. And because the Ayatollahs were in the market place to spend millions of US dollars on a wide range of military equipment – Moscow had willingly bowed to the colour of their money.

"Shall we continue with the exercise, Captain?" Rem Bukato asked quietly, as he tried to keep his footing on the canted deck by hooking his arm around the base of the number two periscope. Bukato was the *Cherkassy's* youthful, blue-eyed Executive Officer. He was a stocky, medium height Adonis, with a shock of fair-hair and a thick bull neck that seemed to disappear into his huge shoulders. Although a career officer, he nevertheless still loved athletics and particularly enjoyed representing the Russian Naval Academy at Ice Hockey on an international level. Some believed his privileged status for foreign travel and rapid rise through the ranks was as a result of being caught in bed with the Admiral's daughter – and her mother. When Bukato reported to the *Cherkassy* just a few days ago, his enviable reputation as a national athletics hero and ladies man preceded him.

"No!" snapped Tarasov, as he tried to clear his head and take stock of the rapidly deteriorating situation. He didn't want the Iranians to become unduly alarmed, or for them to become directly involved with his current problem. Valentin Tarasov was only too well aware that Iran had recently taken delivery of three Russian attack submarines of similar design and performance to his latest command.

He also knew that Iran was actively in the marketplace to buy more, and especially keen to acquire a nuclear capability to match that of the *Cherkassy*.

Neither St Petersburg nor Moscow would forgive him if he screwed up the deal. Before her hasty departure from Severodvinsk just a few days ago, this deadly Russian behemoth had been fully equipped with a compliment of nuclear torpedoes, and sixteen of the latest sub-sonic, long-range SS-N-21 Sampson cruise missiles – complete with nuclear warheads.

The main propulsion battery compartment and the forward torpedo room were rapidly filling with smoke. The exhausted fire-fighters could hardly be seen on the control room monitor, as a wild hissing curtain of steam suddenly billowed around them. Fatigue was beginning to dull their judgement.

"What do you propose to do now?" a concerned Sharif Hamad enquired of the Captain, as he wedged himself against the hull.

Tarasov ignored the Iranian officer. He remained calm and focused on their current situation as beads of grimy perspiration trickled down their worried faces. It began to glisten in the eerie dull red glow created by endless banks of brightly coloured controls pulsating intermittently within the command centre's subdued environment of attack-operational lighting.

"Captain…" Rem Bukato spoke with cool and detached precision, but realised their latest manoeuvre would have to be abandoned.

"What?"

"The exercise?"

"Captain!" Boris Lukin had managed to fight his way through the panic stricken crew and made his way into to the forward Torpedo Room. His frantic cries now came through on monitor number four "The flames are licking at the Torpedo Room floor!"

The intense heat from the deck plates seemed to sear the very soles of their feet, even through the navy's standard issue boots. Portable oxygen masks were proving to be equally ineffective. The rubber face pieces were melting from the rapidly developing firestorm, causing terrible burns to the unfortunate fire-fighters. Within just a few minutes, the compartment temperature had risen to 200°C, and their only option left was to fill the compartment with freon gas to smother the flames.

"Get more hands to the battery compartment... Immediately!" Tarasov ordered.

"Swing Watch are still off-duty... in the Forward Crew Quarters" Lukin advised, in exhausted gasps.

"Then get them out of their bunks!" screamed the Captain.

Swing Watch had only been cat-napping. The worst part of this watch was not just the tedium and loneliness. It was the relentless boredom. However, they were soon galvanised into action and quickly responded to the tremors and changes. The subtle alteration of motion and speed had brought them instantly awake – as they instinctively began to lock onto the immediate crisis. Blood curdling screams could be heard coming from the battery compartment between them and the command centre. Vivid blue flames leapt from terminal to terminal in spluttering arcs of fire, and a thin film of blood could be seen dripping from the lens of a closed circuit camera in the immediate vicinity. One of the main sea-water valves within the salt-water ballast system had blown, and the enormous pressure had now vaporised the gushing flood into an opaque fog. The ghoulish shapes of the fire control team gasped and wretched at the fetid air as they struggled and sloshed through the rising oily waters in their attempts to contain the flow.

Valentin Tarasov briefly stared at the deck, expecting it to yield up inspiration or solution. None was forthcoming. He remained totally resolute, even though his options were rapidly diminishing. His mind was in unrelenting turmoil, trying to balance the lives of a few seamen against the very survival of his submarine... and more importantly, the rest of his crew.

If things didn't improve, would Tarasov react like a seasoned submariner and unwittingly jeopardise both crew and vessel in an attempt to complete the mission? He took a calculated gamble and suppressed his personal feelings. He gave orders for the freon gas valves to be opened. However, Tarasov was unaware the intense heat had already melted some critical high-pressure lines in the forward torpedo room. Instead of releasing the freon gas, the blazing compartment was instantly filled with pure oxygen. Suddenly, a deep muffled series of explosions sent a terrifying shudder rippling throughout the length of the submarine as several oxygen tanks erupted. The blast ripped a gaping hole in the chequer-plate floor of the torpedo room.

Boris Lukin had been thrown against the steel hull where he slumped to the floor, bathed in the clammy sweat of mild shock. He staggered back onto his feet, holding his head in his hands, with a steady stream of blood flowing down the right side of his blackened face. The explosion had severed some of the main torpedo fixing straps, which were used to secure the weapons in their tiered racks. Two of the torpedoes had crashed down upon the ruptured floor, whilst a third hung precariously by its rear fixing.

"The exercise!" Bukato screamed, as he made eye contact with Tarasov.

"Level off! Level off!" roared the Captain.

The *Cherkassy* suddenly lurched to starboard, throwing Bukato and the Iranians to the floor of the control room like a pile of discarded rag dolls.

"Fire Officer!" screamed Tarasov down the intercom.

"It's no use. He's dead, Sir," came the harsh rasping reply from a smoke dazed Watch Engineer, up to his knees in water, gasping for air and clutching his ears to relieve the intolerable pressure.

"Captain, the torpedoes!" Boris Lukin's blood-stained and distorted face reappeared on the grainy screen of monitor number four. "We must stabilise."

The fractured image of the Weapons Officer suddenly disappeared from the screen and was instantly replaced by a series of crazy intermittent test patterns.

Another severe lurch took everyone by surprise as the submarine suffered a dramatic loss of underwater stability. This latest violent manoeuvre was too much for the frayed remains of the strap still holding the swinging torpedo: it snapped apart like a pistol shot. The weapon rolled off the rack and crashed to the floor, crushing two hapless seamen against the other nuclear warheads below. Boris Lukin recoiled in horror, raising his hands instinctively to protect his face – but there was no explosion.

"Radiation!" whispered Rem Bukato as he remained transfixed at his post, staring into the torpedo room monitor.

"Take a dosimeter reading!" Tarasov ordered Lukin over the intercom.

"8.16 milliroentgens ... and rising," came the panic-stricken response.

"Get the men out of there!" screamed the Captain, as he punched his balled fist down onto the chart table in front of him. "Get them out of there – now!"

"What about those below, in the battery compartment?"

"Get them out too!"

"No time ..." the Executive Officer's brows were knit in furious concentration.

"How many left down there?" Monitor number three began to clear from the smoke and sea-water mist. Valentin Tarasov didn't need a reply. He could see for himself that about eight men from Swing Watch were still alive and struggling to contain the flow of water.

"Make turns for five knots!" the Captain ordered.

"We must seal the area ... *now*." Bukato's voice was cold and unemotional.

"Make your course two-seven-zero." Tarasov ignored Bukato's last remark as he gave further orders to the navigating officer. "Steady on the bow planes."

"We must seal the battery compartment immediately – and the torpedo room," Bukato repeated.

THE CHERKASSY INCIDENT · 21

"There are men down there..." The Captain shot a knowing glance towards the Executive Officer, as he ran a sweaty hand through his hair, trying to sort out the possibilities. He knew Rem Bukato was right. The water they had shipped was already at a critical level and the radiation leak in the torpedo room had now compounded their problems.

Tarasov had no way of knowing if Boris Lukin was out or not ... "I can't."

"You must, comrade Captain," whispered Bukato as he moved closer.

"I ..."

"Now!" hissed the XO.

After an agonising deliberation, Valentin Tarasov reluctantly gave orders to seal the main propulsion battery compartment and the torpedo room. His eyes never left the monitors as the water-tight doors were closed and dogged; sealing his men into their salt-water tomb. Tarasov's face tightened in grim determination as he saw his doomed men panic when they realised what was happening.

All discipline disappeared, as they stumbled over each other like demented animals, frantically clawing at the steel doors with their fingernails. The Captain bowed his head and solemnly reached over to shut off the sound system, ending the torment of their incoherent cries. His final image was the contorted and pleading face of his watch engineer, pressed up against the camera lens.

"Where are the rest of your people?" Tarasov turned and enquired of the petrified Sharif Hamad.

"Two are down in the engine room – and two others forward with Swing Watch."

"You may have lost the two forward," Bukato coldly informed him.

"And him?" Sharif Hamad's shaking finger pointed towards his companion, lying slumped on the floor of the control room. Blood trickled from a deep gash beneath the man's scalp and ran down the tilt, to disappear into a meshed floor grating further along. Rem Bukato knelt beside the Iranian's prostrate figure and felt for a pulse. There was none. The Executive Officer cast his eyes down in resignation and shook his head. The electric bulkhead clock confirmed the finality of the event at 0810 zulu time.

"Rig for surfacing! Rig for surfacing!" Tarasov's chilling orders echoed throughout every compartment of the submarine, galvanising the remaining crew into action. His senior career officers were strategically placed throughout the boat and were accustomed to achieving exacting teamwork in such close quarters situations.

"Bow planes and stern planes manned," came a sharp reply from the Chief Petty Officer.

"Emergency blow forward ballast tanks!" ordered the Captain as he anxiously scanned the control console.

"Blow forward aye," confirmed the Chief Engineer, as he reached for a large lever and pushed it right up to the stop. Almost instantaneously, the floor shook and vibrated as a loud roar filled the control room when high-pressure air began pumping into the ship's ballast tanks to blow out the water. The Chief grabbed another small lever and pulled it to sound the alarm for an emergency surface.

"The reducer valves will be too slow!" snapped Rem Bukato when his eyes finally met those of the Captain. Both men knew that even a modern nuclear submarine still required an adequate power source – and forward propulsion – if it was to regain the surface: The main reducer valves were critical.

"It will be enough," Tarasov assured him with an authoritative nod.

The Chief Engineer hesitated, gathering his thoughts, before reaching over and grabbing a hand-held microphone from the panel in front of him:

"SURFACE, SURFACE, SURFACE."

Boris Lukin had somehow pulled himself up the sloping deck and now staggered into the control room, with blood still pouring from his head wound.

"We must get her up," he croaked.

"We're blowing the main forward ballast," the steady voice of the XO confirmed, as he systematically scanned the controls. The noise became intolerable. It was a sustained high-pitched scream and the forward tanks went dry just twenty-five seconds after the emergency blow. The *Cherkassy* had suddenly become several hundred tons lighter.

"Secure the blow," ordered Tarasov.

"Will it be enough? Surely we must blow *all* tanks?" gasped the Weapon's Officer. Lukin's face appeared pale and death-like in the flickering spectral light of the submarine, as he shot another nervous glance towards the Captain.

"Not yet." Tarasov reached out and restrained Lukin by grabbing his arm. The control room went quiet, except for the reassuring click of the depth gauge.

Both men instinctively looked up towards the curved roof as they felt the *Cherkassy* shudder and began to rise slowly through the freezing waters of the Barents Sea.

"Stand by!" Tarasov ordered the XO. "We must be ready to abandon ship when she surfaces."

"If she surfaces..." hissed Rem Bukato as he braced himself for the ride.

Valentin Tarasov moved from his command position, handing over control of the submarine to his Executive Officer. The Captain quietly signalled for Boris Lukin to follow, and both men left Bukato anxiously watching the depth meters as he monitored the *Cherkassy's* slow and painful rise towards the surface. Tarasov made his way to the radio room, where a young and frightened Petty Officer tore a sheet from his notepad and gave him their position.

"Fifty kilometres due north of Kolskiy Zaliv," the Officer confirmed, swallowing hard to hide his fear.

"Are we in radio contact with any shipping in the immediate vicinity?"

"No inwards traffic, Sir. We've lost it."

"Can we signal out?"

"I think so, Sir."

"Don't just *think*! Get out an emergency rescue message immediately *and keep repeating it!* Do you hear me?"

"Aye, aye, Sir!" the nervous officer replied, "I will keep repeating it!"

Tarasov left the terrified officer tuning into the emergency frequency and made his way back through the narrow passageways and gangways, re-assuring the young and raw conscript crew desperately clutching at his every word of encouragement. With a continuing shortage of skilled manpower from within the former Soviet Union, the navy had been forced to press an uncomfortably disproportionate number of young and inexperienced recruits into the submarine service. Many were little more than teenaged peasants from the vast collective farms stretching away to the east of the Urals – and most were probably away from home for the very first time. This was one of those decisive moments they had trained for; it was hoped that all the intensive battle training of the past few weeks would transform the boat and her entire crew into a well disciplined force. With such a crisis, Tarasov could not afford any weak links in his chain of command. The Captain nodded and maintained a confident smile as he passed through the various compartments. He knew these nervous men were only inches away from the intense pressure and arctic cold embracing the *Cherkassy.*'s insulated steel hull.

Boris Lukin tumbled through the watertight doorways as he tried to keep up.

"What about the missiles, Captain?"

"What about them, Boris?"

"Surely we must disarm them, even if we can't bring the ship in."

"Can they swim?"

"Of course not."

"Then they will go *down* if the vessel goes *down*."

"But..."

Valentin Tarasov's eyes met those of the Weapons Officer as he raised a hand to indicate the finality of his last statement.

"We must save lives now Boris – that's our number one priority. Let the Admiralty in St. Petersburg worry about the missiles. We're just outside of Russian waters, but nevertheless still over the continental shelf. If she goes down she won't sink more than six hundred feet. At that depth they'll at least be salvageable – won't they?" Without waiting for a reply, Tarasov continued his tour of duty, grinning and saluting – with an occasional reassuring slap on the back for some of the petrified crew. Rem Bukato tore his gaze from the controls and was visibly relieved to be handing over command, as the Captain re-entered the control room.

"Crew assembling by mid and stern hatches, Captain," he reported.

"Good. How's our progress?"

"Depth gauges are now reading two hundred feet – and rising slowly."

As if tempting fate, the ship slowed its ascent and hovered in the water. The depth gauges stabilised.

"Reactor power loss!" came a sickening cry from the Reactor Compartment.

"The main turbine has stopped!"

"*How* ..?" Boris Lukin's worst fears had been realised.

"Water's probably short-circuited the main electrical supply," Rem Bukato guessed.

"The automatic bus transfer has tripped." Confirmation of the XO's last assessment came almost immediately from the reactor control station.

"How deep are we?" the Captain enquired.

"One hundred feet."

"Nuclear fission has ceased!" came another desperate high-pitched cry from the reactor room. The main turbo generators began to spool down and fall silent as each one in turn became starved of life-giving steam. The *Cherkassy* was momentarily plunged into darkness until the emergency battery system kicked in and took over. "No power! We'll never make the surface!" Lieutenant Sharif Hamad was well aware that a nuclear submarine required a continuous and dedicated power-source to get itself out of an emergency situation like this. He knew that de-ballasting alone would not be enough for them to re-gain the surface.

"Full rise on both planes," came the Captain's steady response. "As much up-angle as possible."

"Aye, aye, Sir," acknowledged the planesman as he desperately pulled the yoke of the control column back into the pit of his stomach.

"Depth?" roared Tarasov.

"Fifty feet." replied Bukato.

The submarine was stalling. It wallowed and began to sink – bow first.

"Eject ballast from the forward trim tank!" Tarasov responded immediately.

There was no movement from the vessel. "Blow *all* main ballast! Blow safety tanks! Blow auxiliaries!"

Down in Engineering, men worked frantically to try and restore enough steam pressure to at least re-start the main turbine, but their efforts were all in vain.

Tarasov reached out and hung onto a stainless steel ring surrounding the periscope. The submarine began to rise again … slowly. The depth gauge measured forty feet … thirty feet … twenty feet.

"Prepare to abandon ship!" Tarasov yelled down the intercom. "Abandon Engine Room! Abandon Machine and Radio Rooms! Get to the escape hatches!"

Alarm bells and horns reverberated incessantly throughout the *Cherkassy* as men panicked and scrambled from the lower levels. Running feet clattered on steel stairs and gratings as confusion reigned. Fighting broke out under the hatches to freedom… and life. With a final lurch, the crippled submarine broke surface, her huge cylindrical shape coming out of the sea, matt black on top and a dull red on the bottom. The *Cherkassy* bobbed in the cold and forbidding waters, surrounded by white foam and angry bubbles. All escape hatches were released and the ship's company began to spill out like manic ants onto the slippery deck. Life-rafts were hurriedly inflated and slid into the icy sea. Tarasov and his Executive Officer grabbed the submarines classified papers and left the control centre, but could not reach the main escape hatches. Both men turned and made their way back up to the officer's emergency escape capsule located in the submarine's conning tower. Boris Lukin and Sharif Hamad had been luckier. They had managed to make it topsides and were able to scramble into one of the life-rafts.

Another wave of panic and confusion erupted. The submarine began to settle deeper as she wallowed and listed violently to port, throwing the remaining crew from the slippery hull casing and into the icy waters of the Barents Sea. With ruptured tanks and blown hatches, the submarine's hydrodynamic stability had become totally compromised and the vessel began to sink for the very last time.

Tarasov, Bukato and the others had managed to haul themselves up through the escape capsule's lower hatch. The life-giving pod was an oval titanium spheroid, capable of holding up to twenty men in an emergency. Crude wooden benches surrounded the interior, but most of the occupants would have to sit on the deck or stand and lock arms with each other during the emergency ascent. A control panel containing a simple depth gauge and the vital release circuits for the explosive bolts was set into the side of the escape chamber.

Tarasov reached up and actuated a switch marked 'ARM'. He pressed the release button. Nothing happened! No explosive bolts fired! He pressed it repeatedly, but still nothing happened. Precious seconds ticked away until a violent explosion finally blew the capsule free. The men instinctively flung their arms outwards, bracing themselves for the turbulent ride as it raced back to the surface.

The capsule bobbed about on the surface and rocked violently in the undulating swell until the excessive internal pressure blew off its hatch cover, killing one of the seamen. The Captain, his XO and the other survivors scrambled out and slid down into the water.

A deepening cold front had drifted in from the Arctic Circle during the past twenty-four hours, bringing with it a thick covering of cloud and a biting wind. Whitecaps danced like confused spectres on the dark forbidding waters. The icy air was filled with the blood-chilling screams of sailors still trapped on board the foundering submarine. They were soon overwhelmed by the inrush of water cascading through the open hatches and their fading cries mingled with those of their comrades now struggling in the sea... and caught in the vicious suction-pull of the *Cherkassy* as she began to slide back beneath the waves. Valentin Tarasov swam as fast as his strength would allow, but the cold was beginning to sap his energy and the very will to live. The submarine's final plunge began to drag him back as a huge burst of air and foam exploded above it. Tarasov panicked when he heard the great gurgle and began to swim like a demon until overtaken by exhaustion. He rolled over to look back at the boiling surface, with upended life-rafts and debris swirling around in a deadly whirlpool. The sea continued to churn and froth, with a steady underwater rumbling coming from the plummeting sub.

Night came quickly in this part of the world and Tarasov felt the chilling embrace of darkness fast approaching. Finding an empty lifejacket, he looped his arm through the inflated collar and made his way over to one of the deserted life-rafts. After several exhausting attempts, he managed to haul himself out of the water and tumbled inside. The numbing cold was now rapidly giving way to hypothermia and he had just resigned himself to the welcoming arms of the sea, when he saw in the distance, lights heading in his direction. He could hear people calling out from the deck of a fishing boat, as a searchlight finally picked out the bobbing orange canopy. Valentin Tarasov gave a frozen smile, lay back and lost consciousness.

CHAPTER 2

Russia : St Petersburg

Freshening winds swept in from the north. They swirled above the choppy and confused waters of the river *Neva*, heralding the approach of another hard winter. Valentin Tarasov had travelled into the city from his home in the docklands area of *Vasilevsky* Island where he lived inconspicuously in one of the drab and monotonous brick apartment buildings. His journey had taken him towards the imposing Admiralty Headquarters Building. Tarasov was nervous. They had summoned him to what had been euphemistically described as a routine "enquiry" – nothing more than a straightforward investigation into the sinking of the *Cherkassy*. However, he knew what they really wanted: a scapegoat. The navy would never admit to having sent one of its latest and most advanced submarines out on manoeuvres before it was ready. The Chief Petty Officer had been right; she was a death trap – a floating coffin. A description the Admirals certainly wouldn't agree upon.

Tarasov had boarded the shabby trolley-bus at the southern edge of *Vasilevsky*, near to the ocean-terminal of *Morskoy Slavy*. The trolley rattled and bumped from block to block, sending showers of sparks between the dark and gloomy buildings. Passing *Smolensk* Cemetery, it trundled along *Srednij Prospeckt*, where Tarasov decided to disembark in the *Strelka* area, close to the Rostral Columns and the Naval Museum. Being a little early, he decided to walk the rest of the way, but stopped for a moment and placed his elbows on the parapet of the *Dvortsovaya* Bridge and lit a cigarette in cupped hands.

His thoughtful gaze ranged from the Winter Palace and out over the wide expanse of the *Neva* towards the Peter and Paul fortress. This was the Petersburg of Rastrelli, the Bronze Horseman and the Winter Palace ... a sharp contrast to that other working class corner of the city on *Vasilevsky* Island which had been filled with barricades during the 1917 Revolution. It was a clear autumn day with the city looking so peaceful and harmonious, silhouetted against the mid-morning sky. Small thin white clouds scudded across the vast expanse of blue; Tarasov sniffed in deeply. He could smell the sea-air. St Petersburg was truly a naval city. The city of Peter the Great – the founder of the Russian navy. To Tarasov, it was the finest naval city in the world. He had always loved the place, ever since coming to train at the Naval Academy as a young man. However, he was far removed from his birthplace at *Kopeysk*, a dreary community that fed the sprawling city of *Chelyabinsk*. It was just about as remote from the sea as anyone could possibly have imagined. It was love at first sight. He had severed all links with the past – and destiny had dictated that he was never to return to his native home. Valentin Tarasov enjoyed his bachelor status. He was a stocky man of forty-five, and standing six feet four inches, he retained a full shock of blond hair. Tarasov embraced only one love – the ocean. Oh, he had had plenty of women in ports all over the world – and numerous offers of marriage, but his maritime love had always taken precedence. He had forsaken them all for his naval career. Standing at the very heart of his beloved City, Tarasov half turned, as he glanced over his shoulder at the imposing Admiralty Building and wondered just what the cruel hand of fate had in store. Regardless of the consequences, he intended to stand up to them. He was determined to fight.

    Someone else would have to be the scapegoat. Thoughtful, even to the point of being cynical, he nevertheless remained suspicious. In the old days, the solution would have been swift and decisive. He would have been spirited off to Siberia: never to be heard of again. But they couldn't do that now – could they? Anyhow, it wasn't his fault. The *Cherkassy* was simply not ready for sea: and they knew it.

    His natural instincts told him this whole charade was nothing more than a damage limitation exercise to impress the Iranians…just so they could go on selling more of their poorly equipped submarines; whatever the cost. Everyone knew most of the Admirals and Senior

Officers presiding over the enquiry were nothing more than a front for the *Mafiosniki*. It was the world's worst kept secret. They were all on the take, making millions of dollars by selling redundant equipment. His superiors had better take care as to how they intended to apportion the blame. After all, they had no incriminating evidence against him and he was one of the most Senior and respected nuclear submarine commanders in the entire Russian navy. They wouldn't have the audacity! Valentin Tarasov felt confident it would all turn out to be nothing more than a formality.

Tarasov flicked the butt of his cigarette into the swirling blue-grey waters below. He stiffened as he pulled his uniform straight and adjusted his cap. His posture was dignified and with his head held high, he strode boldly towards his destiny across the *Dvortsovaya* Bridge. He wore his number one full dress uniform, complete with white-topped cap, epaulettes and ribbons of commendation spread across his proud chest. His black shoes were highly polished and he wore a crisp snow-white shirt, finished with a starch-stiff collar.

Once across the *Neva*, Valentin Tarasov made his way along the northeast side of the Admiralty. Above him, a thin gilded spire loomed up against the blinding sky as if it were the sword of Damocles, poised and ready to strike him down. All around, young sailors came and went, their eager young faces flushed full of anticipation – just as his had once been so very long ago. They stepped aside, snapping smartly to attention and saluting the Captain as he passed.

Tarasov arrived at the edge of a stark expanse of threadbare grass opening out onto Palace Square. At the centre of the square stood a towering Column surmounted by a cross pinning an angel to the ground by nothing more than its immense weight. The Alexander monument epitomised the same naval establishment whose own great weight was about to descend upon the head of Valentin Tarasov. Across the square lay his destination – the great yellow sweep of the Admiralty Headquarters Building. Above its lofty central arch, Victory silently rose up with her six-horsed chariot, beckoning him forward, into the gloomy labyrinth of passages and corridors. His rhythmic footsteps echoed down the hallway until he arrived at an office designated for the "enquiry."

Upon entering the large sombre room with its vaulted ceiling and shafts of sunlight streaming through the barred windows, Tarasov came smartly to attention in front of a wide table. A panel of high-ranking naval officers were seated on the other side. Enormous paintings of historic sea battles lined the upper walls, complete with full-length portraits of heroic and distinguished admirals, silently gazing down upon the proceedings about to unfold. To the extreme right of his peripheral vision, Tarasov noticed a couple of Government Officials accompanied by some members of the Federal Counter Intelligence Service.

He sensed activity behind his back and heard a small wooden chair being placed ceremoniously a few paces behind him. Tarasov saluted, before being ushered towards the chair and ordered to sit. The panel began by perfunctorily studying a pile of documents spread before them. They glanced up occasionally… and studied Valentin Tarasov. Silence fell upon the assembly when a Vice-Admiral in the centre of the group cleared his throat and noisily pushed back his chair.

The officer fixed his gaze upon Tarasov as he rose to his feet clutching a sheaf of papers.

"Commander Tarasov," he boomed "You know why we're here today?"

"The *Cherkassy* …" Tarasov tried to answer.

"Precisely!" The sharp interruption rang out before the captain could say another word. "To get straight to the point, Commander, we need to know the full circumstances of this tragic loss."

"It is quite obvious what happened." Tarasov stood to face his superior officer. "The submarine was not ready for sea…"

"Not ready!" The Vice-Admiral's face turned purple.

"The work was too hurried. Even my Chief Petty officer remarked…"

"We are not interested in the *opinions* of your Chief Petty Officer." Tarasov was quickly silenced, this time by one of the government officials. "In any case, he's dead and therefore unable to corroborate your statements."

"If, *in your opinion*, the submarine was not seaworthy, then *why* did you take it out, Commander?" This fundamental and penetrating question came from a naval Commodore seated to the left of the Vice-Admiral.

Valentin Tarasov glanced at the officer. "Because I was ordered to!"

A buzz of incredulous whispers and grumbles broke out amongst the panel. Several officers scowled and banged their fists on the table as glares of indignation were flashed towards the Captain.

"Sit down, Commander!" The Vice-Admiral dropped his papers onto the table and momentarily clasped his hands behind his back, before signalling to a junior Lieutenant standing by the door. The man visibly stiffened as he came to attention, saluted, and left the room for a moment, but returned almost immediately with Lieutenant Vladimir Murashov, the *Cherkassy*'s Political Officer. Tarasov was momentarily stunned. He thought the Lieutenant had drowned in the Barents, but here he was, alive and smug as ever. *Zampolit* Murashov was a small, wiry man of about thirty-five with sharp features and cold eyes. His official function aboard the *Cherkassy* was nothing more than to act as a spy for the establishment. On board ship, he'd kept mostly to himself, and his only specific assignment was to sneak around the submarine, looking over people's shoulders. How he'd survived, Tarasov couldn't imagine. But he had: and here he was, standing before the enquiry panel.

"Lieutenant Murashov…" The Vice-Admiral turned and spoke to him in a friendly, almost condescending tone.

"Yes, sir." The smugness disappeared from Murashov's face, leaving an expression of implacable malevolence.

"Please inform the panel what your function was aboard the *Cherkassy*."

"Political Officer, sir."

"And your duties?"

"To observe and report on the efficiency and behaviour of the officers and crew, particularly in view of the foreign guests aboard, sir."

"Report to who, Lieutenant?" enquired one of the other officers.

"My superiors, sir."

"Who are?"

"The Federal Counter Intelligence Service, sir."

He spoke quietly, but beneath the veneer of smiles and politeness, he still exuded a brooding mistrust of all those around him.

"Thank you, Lieutenant." The Vice-Admiral sat down and poured himself a glass of water. He then placed his elbows on the table and peered over laced fingers. "In your opinion … what was the direct cause of the *Cherkassy* disaster?"

"The sinking was caused by a series of judgement errors, sir."

"And who, *in your opinion*, made these judgement errors?"

"Both the Captain and the Executive Officer, sir."

Another buzz of excitement went round the panel. One of the Commodores rose to his feet. "And what was the nature of those errors, Lieutenant?"

"The Captain continued with classified undersea experimental manoeuvres, even though the overall situation on board had become critical, sir."

"And the Executive officer?" queried another member of the panel.

"His job was to advise the Captain when he considered an error of judgement had been made."

"And did he?"

"He did not, sir."

Tarasov was on his feet again as he tried to object, but was ordered to be quiet and remain seated. The Political Officer's mouth went dry as he composed himself, before being allowed to continue with his damning testimony. Murashov cleared his throat and took a deep breath, before attributing further blame for the loss of the *Cherkassy* upon the unprofessional conduct of the Weapons Officer, Fire Officer and Chief Petty Officer. It was exactly what the panel wanted to hear: Human error. They had no doubt their submarine was in perfect working order when it put to sea. The senior officers had been entirely responsible for the disaster – particularly its Captain. Tarasov tried to interrupt on several occasions, but each time was curtly silenced and ordered to remain seated. Towards the end of the proceedings, two members of the special purpose militia were called into the room and ordered to stand either side of Valentin Tarasov. After an hour of incredulous testimony, Vladimir Murashov was excused and allowed to leave the room.

"Commander Tarasov…" The Vice-Admiral gestured for him to stand. The militia men moved closer. "What *exactly* is the condition and status of the *Cherkassy's* nuclear missiles?"

"The missiles are safe." Tarasov's instant reply was sullen and disrespectful.

"In which mode?"

"Standby mode – ready for simulated launch."

"How secure are they?" This next question came from one of the counter-intelligence men.

"They are still in their silos and fully protected. The hatches are sealed and the pre-launch membranes over the inner muzzles are still secure."

"You misunderstand me, Commander." The man smiled malevolently over the top of his half-rimmed spectacles. "I'll re-phrase the question. You were engaged upon a highly classified mission, and more importantly, responsible for some of our latest top secret long-range SS-N-21 Sampson cruise missiles … now could these possibly fall into enemy hands?"

A ripple of derisory laughter spread through the group of officers and government officials assembled behind the table. Tarasov was surprised and slightly caught off-balance by this unusual line of questioning. He was not about to stick his neck in a noose. He remained silent for a moment, considering his answer and waiting for the sniggering to fade away to anticipating silence.

"Well… we were over the continental shelf when the accident happened and she's resting at about six hundred feet – and that's a salvageable depth."

Tarasov paused. He realised he had their attention. Complete silence descended upon the room. "However, she is close to Russian waters and as the *Cherkassy* is designated a warship, she remains the sovereign property of Russia. Technically it would be illegal for anyone to go inside her. Besides, the missiles could not possibly be released without the specific knowledge of someone like my Weapons Officer. Apart from salvaging the complete vessel, the missiles could not be recovered without him."

"Boris Lukin," one of the Commodores nodded sagely as he uttered the remark loudly to his fellow officers. Whispering began again, which Tarasov could not hear, followed by a lot of intense discussion and grunting.

"Besides…" Tarasov decided to take the initiative and interrupt for a change. "The Barents Sea will freeze over soon. Once that happens, nothing can be done until the Spring." Another rumbling burst of nodding and growling ensued.

"May I be permitted to ask a question?" Tarasov interrupted again.

The Vice-Admiral looked up and was clearly irritated by this interruption. He grunted and reluctantly waved his consent. "Did any of our Iranian guests survive?"

"No. Why do you ask?"

"Well, considering we put to sea prematurely, it does seem strange that none survived."

There was an immediate uproar, followed by an explosion of shouting and table-thumping. It took all the Vice-Admiral's authority to restore even a vestige of order to the proceedings.

"Commander Tarasov," he roared, "You will be held in custody until a convenient time can be arranged for your court martial. Take him away!"

The militia stepped forward and grabbed Valentin Tarasov. They quickly overpowered him and hauled him from the room, leaving the Board of Enquiry in a turmoil of accusations and fist-waving. Tarasov was taken under close arrest to *Pavlovskiy* Barracks, just a short distance away along the River *Moyka* on the western side of the Field of Mars. Here he was detained under military guard for a further ten days, whilst arrangements were being made for his court martial back at the Admiralty.

The trial itself was a brisk and predictable affair. A total sham. Tarasov's guilt had already been decided. However, his hopes were momentarily raised when he discovered the actual court martial was presided over by a distinguished Admiral of the Fleet under whom he had served at Sevastapol. Much to Tarasov's dismay, his former Commanding Officer remained aloof and kept his distance.

The *Cherkassy*'s Political Officer was summoned once again and given free rein to expand upon his earlier testimony: despite his protestations, Tarasov had no opportunity to cross-examine. He was well and truly the scapegoat they needed. Despite his past achievements and outstanding record when serving with the former Soviet Union's Black Sea Fleet, they were still determined to sacrifice him upon the altar of international placation. As the proceedings drew to a close, the presiding Admiral decided at the very last moment, on leniency. Instead of a custodial sentence, Commander Tarasov's alternative punishment would be a dishonourable discharge from the navy – with loss of all privileges and pensions. The unwarranted ignominy associated with this final act of humiliation was intolerable. Valentin Tarasov could restrain himself no longer. He leapt to his feet in the court martial chamber.

"Am I supposed to be grateful," he screamed at the assembled officers, "after all I have given to Russia and the Party?"

"Commander Tarasov…"

"My life! I've given you my life!" Tarasov advanced and tried to approach the bench.

"Restrain him!"

Tarasov was grabbed and unceremoniously hauled away from the Admirals as he continued to struggle against his captors.

"How could you treat me, one of your most senior commanders, with such contempt?"

"Commander, you should continue to conduct yourself with the dignity expected of a *senior* Naval Officer."

The Admirals rose and made their way from the room and out through a side door. Tarasov was dragged away, still kicking and screaming, as the MPs hauled him along the corridors of the historic Admiralty building. Groups of startled young sailors stepped aside. They watched in astonishment at the sight of such a senior officer being manhandled down the main flight of stairs. Tarasov's protests from the darkened basement gradually faded as he was thrown headlong through a discreet back entrance and out into one of the Admiralty gardens. It was raining heavily. Tarasov went sprawling into the mud and remained lying on his back, blinking up at the darkening sky. Soft rain washed down over his face as it ran into his eyes and ears. A few sullen passers-by cautiously came over to take a disinterested look, assuming he was one of the City's many derelict tramps.

It seemed like an eternity before he was able to roll over onto his side and painfully pull himself to his feet. Darkness had fallen. The early evening lights of the city cast watery shadows all around. Valentin Tarasov staggered and began to walk aimlessly. He paused to catch his breath and leant against the statue of the Bronze Horseman, before catching a trolley-bus along *Angliyskaya Naberezhnaya*, which took him across the *Leytenanta Shmidta* Bridge and out towards his home on *Vasilevsky* Island.

The trolley-bus rumbled along the cobbled streets of *Srednij Prospekt* and past the Kirov Palace of Culture, where he disembarked near his anonymous apartment block close to the sea terminal at *Morskoy Slavy*.

The whole building was in an advanced state of decay, with pale green paint and plaster peeling from the lofty walls. Little pools of water had collected on the steps and landings and were probably caused by neglect of the roof.

As he trudged up the stone staircase, muffled arguments came from behind closed doors and the pervading odours were of cabbage and dampness. Tarasov fumbled in the gloom as he noisily inserted his key in the lock. Once inside the apartment, he wearily pressed his back against the door of his inner sanctum and let his water-stained cap slip to the floor. He winced with shame and despair as he turned to face the hall mirror. The figure that greeted him was a stranger, muddy and dishevelled. Gone was the once proud warrior who had circumnavigated the globe so many times in defence of the Motherland. He unbuttoned his tunic and hooked a finger behind the knot of his tie as he yanked it loose. His medals had lost their sparkle. Tarasov took a bottle of vodka from the fridge and his Tokarev service pistol from its cabinet. He released and checked the magazine before slamming it back into the butt of the weapon with the palm of his hand. He placed it alongside the vodka bottle on the kitchen table and sat down heavily. He began to drink.

CHAPTER 3

IRELAND : BELFAST

Peter Lawrence was nervous, in fact he was very nervous. He sat well back in the corner of the unmarked Mercedes being driven by his undercover military aide, northwards along the Ormeau Road. Lawrence had never liked Belfast. It was a shady city. You never knew where the bullet would come from. Every time you turned the car's ignition key you took a deep breath and closed your eyes. He didn't like the posturing City Hall, the frowning churches nor the Opera House, and especially not the dark, dangerous bars and clubs. He loathed such a dreadful posting. Anywhere else in the world other than this god-forsaken place would have been far more acceptable. Lawrence was on familiar territory. He had completed several tours of duty during recent years. It was only a couple of years ago when the IRA had declared one of their cease-fires, that the British High Command had withdrawn him from all clandestine dealings with the terrorists and sent him out to Israel. What absolute bliss that posting turned out to be. The warm, bright middle-eastern sun had contrasted pleasantly with the never ending drizzle and dampness of Ireland. The Arab-Israeli conflict was also much easier to handle and come to terms with than all this back-stabbing, corner creeping subterfuge. But it didn't last. Now he was back – and hated it.

From the very earliest tours of duty, a mutual respect and affinity had developed between Peter Lawrence and Eamonn Burke. Lawrence felt confident that he could trust Burke – insofar as you could trust *any* IRA active Service Commander. It was six o'clock on a dreary Godforsaken Sunday morning. The city still slept as the black car turned right into Cromac Street. Lawrence was tall and smartly dressed, in his mid-thirties, stocky and with dark hair cropped short in a military style. He wore a smartly tailored grey pin stripe suit draped over his well-built frame. Peter Lawrence's varied service career had begun in the Royal Navy when he enlisted as an apprentice upon leaving school. He rose rapidly to the rank of lieutenant before being selected for secondment into the SAS. As a younger man, Lawrence had seen active service in the Falklands aboard HMS *Brilliant* – and during that brief conflict with Argentina, he was decorated for bravery in the field, having distinguished himself in some of the heaviest fighting around Port Stanley. When hostilities finally ceased, the SAS had still retained his services as an undercover operative. Peter Lawrence was usually given all the dirty jobs. His particular line of work was always dangerous: just one slip, and the Service would adopt its "deniability mode', leaving him to an uncertain fate with the voracious wolves. That's why he was nervous. But Lawrence and Burke possessed another special bond – the sea. Sailors throughout the world still hold a mutual respect for each other, no matter how different their backgrounds or allegiances.

Foley's Bar was a popular hangout down by the river, on Donegal Quay. The drinking establishment was considered a respectable enough distance from the Falls and Shankhill areas to be designated neutral ground – that is if anywhere could be neutral in this city of blood, bombs and bullets. It was for this very reason that Lawrence had sought out this location in the past. He knew the proprietor was an old associate of Eamonn Burke's and a man that would allow these clandestine meetings during times when the bar was closed to the general public. This would be the only way to come face to face with Burke. Lawrence simply didn't trust any other rendezvous.

The car splashed through the puddles and potholes as it moved cautiously along the waterfront, until it came to a halt close by a small conical building called the Lagan Lookout. Lawrence and his driver remained in the car, studying the front entrance of Foley's Bar which lay about fifty yards away. There was no sign of life. Peter Lawrence caught the driver watching him in the rear-view mirror and nodded as he slid forward and opened the door. He stepped out onto the pavement, paused, then put his head back through the rolled down front passenger window and listened intently to the sharp but subdued crackle of an incoming radio message.

"Stay here," he ordered.

"Yes sir!"

"Don't come in after me, no matter what happens."

The young military aide silently acknowledged, as Lawrence turned and walked slowly away from the car. A light autumn wind blew a curtain of soft drizzle across the quayside. Lawrence turned his collar up and hunched his shoulders for protection, while thrusting his hands deep into the pockets. As he drew closer to Foley's Bar, the outline of a stubbled face appeared at one of the ornate stained glass windows. Instinct told him it would not be prudent to approach the front, and glancing down a narrow alley alongside the building, he noticed a side door. Lawrence huddled in the doorway and heard the click of a bolt being drawn from the inside. When he reached out and pushed the door, it opened readily. He entered and paused in a small foyer, where two large, sinister looking characters prevented him from proceeding any further. Lawrence knew the drill. He turned to face the wall, spread his legs and raised his arms, while one of the IRA men stepped forward and frisked him thoroughly. Once found to be clean, he was escorted through to the main bar. It was a gloomy tavern, smelling of stale beer and smoke. Lawrence blinked as his eyes took a few moments to adjust to the dim light. A movement from one of the more secluded corner booths caught his attention. He slowly crossed the carpeted floor towards the outline of a man seated at one of the tables.

"Lawrence?"

"It's me."

Eamonn Burke stood and offered his hand.

"Good to see you again."

Lawrence firmly shook the big man's hand as they both settled on opposite sides of the table. Eamonn Burke was a swarthy, bearded man of about forty and spoke with a soft southern accent. He smiled a lot of the time. A bottle of Bushmills Irish whisky and two glasses were placed on the table, along with a jug of water and an ashtray. Burke reached over and poured two drinks. Lawrence took some water with his.

"See, I remembered." Burke smiled as he raised his glass in salute.

"*Slainte!*" toasted Lawrence, in the Gaelic.

Both men drained their glasses with one swallow and placed them back on the table. Burke re-filled the glasses, but this time allowed the spirit to settle.

"I was out on the Lough last week." Burke lit up a cigarette and lifted his head to blow a cloud of blue smoke up to the low nicotine stained ceiling over the booth. He slid the pack across the table and offered it to Lawrence, who declined.

"Really?"

"Done a bit o" sailing."

"What size rig?"

"Just a twenty three footer, but it was great sport."

"Last time I went sailing was…" Lawrence looked around as if searching for an appropriate answer, "…oh, about two years ago."

"I'll take you out sometime," Burke offered.

"I'm sure our superiors would love that."

Both men laughed, then paused to take a sip of whisky.

"Don't you have anything to do with the Navy any more?" Burke asked at length.

"Not much," came the brisk response.

"Don't you miss it?"

"What?"

"The sea."

"Of course. Don't you?"

"Oh aye, I do. Might go back to it some day, when all this is over."

"Don't hold your breath, Eamonn."

"Got to end sometime."

"What did you want to see me about?" Lawrence was through with the small talk. He was still feeling nervous and wanted to get out of this place and back on to more familiar territory. Burke took another drink and looked straight at him.

"There's a man in Parkhurst prison…"

"Can't be done!"

"You don't know what I'm going to ask you yet." Burke was clearly annoyed by Lawrence's change of attitude. Having worked with him before, he felt no closer to rationalising the contradictory elements of the man's nature. The SAS man rose from his seat and walked across to the window. He tugged the curtain to one side and could see his black car waiting down the street, with the young driver still sitting patiently behind the wheel.

"You know I can't get men out of mainland prisons, Eamonn."

"This man is different."

"How?"

"He's a priest."

"A terrorist priest!"

"A freedom fighter!" Burke expanded his arms as he raised his voice.

"It all depends on how you view the situation." Lawrence returned to the booth and sat down. "It depends on which side you're on."

"This man is ill. It could be done on compassionate grounds."

"And once he's back here, you'll be able to take care of him?"

"Once he's back here, he won't be your problem anymore."

Lawrence didn't reply. He looked round the bar. The walls were covered with pictures of Republican heroes and flags of obscure meaning. Fading pictures of triumphant Gaelic football and hurling teams decorated an end wall. From the ceiling hung old flintlock rifles, swords, lanterns, *bodhrans*, and many other items of an antique nature.

"*If* I could … and it's a big *if*."

"I'll give you an address." Burke smiled as he cupped his hands to light another cigarette.

"Where?"

"Manchester."

"What will we find at this address?"

"Some arms, explosives."

"How much?"

"Not much … some."

"Bodies?"

"No bodies!" Burke smiled again. "You know there can't be any bodies."

"Its not enough!" Lawrence was just about to rise from his seat, when Burke leaned over and put his hand on the SAS man's shoulder, pushing him back down.

"He's still out there. Stop worrying." He blew smoke in Lawrence's direction. "And of course it's enough. Think of the tabloid headlines. "Bomb Outrage Averted" … "Our Brave Boys" … and all the rest of the rubbish."

Peter Lawrence fell silent again and stared at the window. Burke sat back again, allowing Lawrence his own time to consider the proposition.

"I'll need to speak to someone." Lawrence said at last.

"That's alright. How long?"

"Three days."

"Three days it is then. But don't…"

Eamonn Burke was interrupted in mid-sentence by an insistent knocking on the front door of the bar. He flashed a suspicious look at Peter Lawrence and produced an automatic pistol from inside his overcoat. The two IRA men who first greeted Lawrence, rushed past the booth with guns drawn. They crouched either side of the window and looked out. One of the men crept across to the door and pulled it open, dragging the young military aide inside. The man was flung to the ground, with a pistol placed against his temple, as he was roughly searched.

"Wait!" Lawrence hissed through clenched teeth and raised his hands in a placatory gesture. "He's with me … it's alright!"

Burke grunted and signalled to his men, who dragged the hapless driver across to the booth and threw him at their feet. Burke waved his men away as they faded into the gloom of the bar.

"What the hell do you think you're doing?" Lawrence snapped at the terrified young aide, shakily drawing himself up onto his feet and dusting himself down.

"Sorry sir."

"I told you not to come after me!"

"I was ordered to…"

"Did I not say 'no matter what'?" Lawrence was furious. He felt the rage of the betrayed. Obviously, the young soldier didn't realise just how closely he had come to getting both of them killed.

"I did tell them that sir. But they insisted."

"Who's *they*?"

"London, sir. Urgent radio message. You've got to get back there immediately."

Lawrence stood up and took the aide to a discreet corner, out of Burke's hearing.

"Are you mad?" Lawrence whispered fiercely. "You don't discuss London in a place like this."

"Sorry, sir. I was told to get the message to you immediately."

"For God's sake, man, surely it could have waited until I came out!"

"Sorry sir, but there's a flap on … been some sort of accident with the sinking of a Russian nuclear submarine."

"Well what's that got to do with me?"

"Don't know sir."

"That's all they told me. They said … the signal was bad sir … something about Iran being involved. I think that's what they said sir."

"No more! Not in here. This had better be important, or you'll be driving fucking tractors in the bloody Outer Hebrides! Now get back to the car. I'll join you shortly."

"Yes sir."

The young driver was allowed to leave, while Peter Lawrence returned to sit again at the table with Eamonn Burke.

"What was all that about?" the Irishman enquired.

"Oh, nothing," Lawrence remained dismissive. "He's new, young. A routine message. He over-reacted."

"Lucky for you, *we* didn't."

Lawrence gratefully drained the rest of his whisky in one gulp. Burke attempted to pour another, but Lawrence reached over and put a hand over his glass.

"Well, I suppose we're finished here anyway."

"Listen Eamonn, I've got to get back to London. Rest assured what we discussed will be dealt with. Someone will be in touch."

"Normal channels?"

"Normal channels."

"Three days?"

"No longer."

Both men rose and shook hands. Peter Lawrence made a furtive exit through the side door, glancing up and down the alley before moving across to his car. Eamonn Burke quickly went over to the front window and pulled one of the dusty curtains aside, just in time to see the SAS man climbing into the back seat. The driver gunned the engine and turned the car around, before speeding away down Donegal Quay. Burke was silently joined at the window by one of his men.

"Did you overhear any of that?" Burke enquired without turning round.

"All of it."

"Good man."

CHAPTER 4

Pakistan : Gwadar

T HE BLEAK AND WINDSWEPT NECKLACE of mountains appeared to have been riven and tortured by the claws of some dreadful prehistoric monster. The gently undulating aspect of the valley floor spread out in all directions, rising steeply against the base of several craggy gullies streaking the barren mountainside. It was a desolate place. It had not been disturbed for thousands of years, but now everywhere echoed to the sounds of heavy construction equipment and strange voices. From their vantage point, high up in these tortured mountains surrounding the sandy Makran to the southwest coast of Pakistan, wizened old tribesmen and their herds of goats and sheep looked down in wonderment. Beneath them stretched an international joint-venture project to build a much-needed hydroelectric plant, bustling with feverish activity on the *Dasht Kaur*, some fifty kilometres northwest of Gwadar. The shouts and calls of myriad languages were blown down to the Arabian Sea by the ubiquitous north winds, relentlessly sweeping down over the central Makran Range. Civilisation had barely touched this region and Gwadar's international airport was the only point of entry. Although communications were difficult at the best of times, it was virtually non-existent in the more remote parts. This was a place where the tourists and trekkers definitely would not venture. It was virtually impossible to get official permission to travel through the Makran. The only foreigners present were those directly involved in the development project.

Traditionally, the poorer people from this region of Pakistan, tended to migrate to Oman and Saudi for work. But now they didn't have to.

Labour from as far afield as Iran, India, Turkey, Russia and Armenia had been attracted to the project – not to mention the American and European engineers, who ran the show. It was a smugglers paradise. Anything could be bought for the right price.

Yuri Medvedev toiled away high up on the giant dam with his fellow Russian, Victor Sautov. Medvedev didn't like this hard back-breaking work. His bad leg was beginning to play him up. It ached from having to stand for too long. He and Sautov were used too much more sedentary occupations – as mobile missile technicians back in the Motherland. Before the end of the cold war, they had trained long and hard in their chosen profession and were highly valued by the Russian military establishment. Medvedev didn't like this god-forsaken country either. The place was hot, dry and dusty. Mosquito-borne diseases were rife and, apart from the occasional American food they sometimes managed to acquire, his staple diet of fish and dates left a lot to be desired. This strange environment was all a far cry from his native Moscow and apartment 236 in Building C of Block 6 on *Micurinskij Prospekt* in the *Nikulino* district.

The flat had been allocated as a privilege, following his graduation, with honours, from the Rubin Institute in St Petersburg. Whilst Yuri worked abroad, Helena, and their two children gratefully occupied the small overcrowded apartment. If the family complained too loudly, they would soon be back on the waiting list – and probably spend the next few years sharing a one-bedroom apartment with another family. Their only hope for any improvement of their current lifestyle depended upon Yuri making his fortune in Gwadar. Yuri would often slip into a melancholy mood. He missed his family and the familiar surroundings of his homeland. But nevertheless, they were being paid handsomely with American dollars; and that was the only reason he stayed. However, being a native Karelian, Victor Sautov didn't seem to mind the place. Having been brought up in the vast forested lakeland area of north west Russia, he was used to living in harsh environments. Patience was borne out of experience.

Back home, shopping and the basic subsistence of life remained a constant ordeal. The isolated and dilapidated stores of Karelia's wilderness region were always filled with jostling crowds, strong smells, and puddles of liquid mud near the entrance. The pervading stink within these isolated communities was of stale meat and people who eat too much garlic and wash infrequently. Civilised service was non-existent. Slatternly women from the surrounding villages served everyone with an insolent slowness, and pounced noisily when a customer's demeanour offended. Victor Sautov never complained about the appalling conditions.

Having worked in some of Russia's top secret closed cities, had proven to be a severe handicap when both men first tried to obtain the relevant permission to leave Russia for work on the hydro – electric project. They had been reduced to putting up with low paid menial jobs as labourers and road sweepers, at a time when it seemed as if their engineering expertise would be redundant. Finally, after many months of backbreaking work, coupled with the inevitable borrowing of hard currency from dubious sources, they were able to bribe the right officials and allowed to leave for the duration of the Gwadar project. Now, at last, they had the opportunity to use their fundamental skills and engineering knowledge. Perhaps not in the same old familiar way as before, but at least it was better than cleaning lavatories – and they were certainly earning far more than if they had stayed in Russia. Their ultimate dream was to pay off all their debts – and still have sufficient money left over for a better quality of life. But what would happen when their contracts finished? What were their prospects? Once back within Mother Russia's clutches, it would be virtually impossible to leave the country again. With the rapidly increasing sophistication of Russia's military technology, they were simply not prepared to go back and sacrifice their newly won independence to undergo further extensive retraining…and all for no payment. No, they knew it would be back to the menial work and the scratching for a living – the never ending grind which was Russia today, that is unless you had money – and a lot of money.

Both men knew the construction project was unique. Rainfall was sparse, with long periods of drought being commonplace. The *Dasht Kaur* was not a permanent river and only became a raging torrent following the seasonal heavy rains, which rapidly drained away and silted up the swampland delta. The river's erratic and meandering course was definitely not suitable for a hydroelectric plant. However, most of the local peasants were only too grateful for the opportunity to work and were not concerned with the scheme's far greater technical limitations. By contrast, the two Russians had realised the political implications a long time ago. So did the Iranians. They still kept a watchful eye on developments. For although this was officially designated an international commercial joint venture sponsored by the American Government and the UN, the Iranians were nevertheless more deeply involved in the darker background. They knew that when the project was completed, a more permanent base would have to be established, thus creating a demand for an on-going American presence. All interested parties were acutely aware of the Makran's rugged unguarded border with Iran – and more significantly, its proximity to the strategic Straits of Hormuz. Several feeder airports had already been built, while transport facilities and the whole infrastructure was rapidly being modernised.

Most of the mountainous border region was difficult to cross, which made it a smugglers paradise. Smugglers of all commodities maintained a secret agenda of fear and bribery to ensure their trade in drugs, weapons and contraband went on uninterrupted. The environment was hostile and dangerous to those who ventured into unfamiliar territory – or didn't know what they were doing. Consequently, the project's entire cosmopolitan workforce remained within the project compound, living together in monotonous rows of prefabricated huts, erected by the company on the outskirts of Gwadar. Sanitation was negligible and swarms of angry flies buzzed constantly over heaps of garbage exposed by scavenging dogs. Even though Gwadar boasted an international airport, it didn't have a single hotel of international standards and entertainment was completely non-existent. Most of the limited action happened on site. The Americans thought they were doing everyone a favour by providing the beer and the unimaginative pre-packed food, while the local Pakistani and Iranian pimps provided the women. Fights, stabbings and even shootings were commonplace between the volatile peasant labourers. The Americans and Europeans kept their distance from this unruly rabble – so did the Russians. The only time they fraternised was when they needed to satisfy their natural urges.

It was well into autumn and the climate was beginning to cool. In the past few days the only other living thing which had ventured within the camp was a stray sheep that had wandered by. To relieve the endless monotony of camp life, the cook had shot it and prepared an Arab-style feast. He could have saved his bullets, Medvedev and Sautov reflected. The meat was tough and stringy, with a strong mutton taste. It must have been an old sheep. Yuri Medvedev and Victor Sautov withdrew to their vodka and resumed their umpteenth game of chess – just as they did most nights.

"I don't know which is worse, here or Moscow." Medvedev took a long swig from his bottle. "Victor, is it my imagination, or is the room shrinking?" Victor Sautov sat back and sniffed deeply as he made a show of looking around the spartan hut he shared with Yuri Medvedev. "The room's shrinking. Why do you complain all the time?" Sautov moved his rook to queen three.

"Why do you *not*?"

"There is no point."

"There is!" Medvedev hissed with frustration as he threw his king against the bare wooden wall of the hut. "There has to be more to life than this .. either here or in Moscow!"

"But what can we do, Yuri?"

"I don't know. But we must do something – before we go crazy."

Sautov realised it was their total helplessness that had them climbing the walls. A gentle, but persistent knock on the fly-screen silenced both men. They both turned in unison to face the door. The knocking became more insistent as it rattled the door on its flimsy hinges. This time the door opened slightly. Nasaf Rhullah put his head into the room, a broad toothy grin breaking out from beneath his spiky moustache.

"You boys OK? I heard shouting," he gingerly ventured further into the hut. Rhullah was a thin man, almost emaciated looking. His weather-beaten skin was tanned like leather, and his jet-black hair stood out from his bronzed head like a mop. His nose was big and hooked like a biblical character and his eyes were dark and snapping.

"What do *you* want?" Medvedev grunted with hostility. Having been middle-weight boxing champion for the Russian army his broken nose and missing teeth were evidence of many a hard bout. Yuri Medvedev's fuse was short. He felt nothing but contempt for these oily and unpredictable middle-eastern navvies.

"Nothing. Nothing. What *you* boys want?"

"Nothing from you."

"Vodka. You Russian boys like vodka?"

"We got vodka."

"Hashish? Cocaine? Heroin?"

"We're not addicts!" Victor Sautov rose noisily from his chair and went over to confront Rhullah. Sautov was a short and stocky man with the physique of a body-builder. His close cropped sandy hair and bushy eyebrows overshadowed a huge veined nose and lantern jaw. Nasaf backed away, his grin fading.

"Sorry … sorry. Don't mean offence."

"Get out of here!" Medvedev threw the chess board and its pieces against the door, barely missing Rhullah's head.

"Women?" Nasaf persisted.

"Not tonight!"

"Money?" The word had its desired effect. Nasaf Rhullah broke into an easy grin. He had their attention at last. "Can we talk?" He shrugged his shoulders and raised his hands in a gesture of peace.

"Who *are* you?" Sautov screwed his eyes quizzically as he studied the Arab.

"You know who I am. I am Nasaf Rhullah."

"I mean, who are you *really*?"

"I don't understand?"

"You're not Pakistani, are you?"

"No. I am Iranian."

Both Russians looked at each other in surprise. They had always suspected this persistent little weasel of a man was a Turk or an Armenian – or some other low form of animal life. But Iranian? Victor Sautov felt uneasy.

"I know who *you* are." Rhullah grinned broadly again.

"Oh yes? And just who do you think we are?" Medvedev mocked him.

"You are both Russian missile technicians, no?"

THE CHERKASSY INCIDENT · 53

"No!" Sautov lied.

"Yes … oh yes!" Rhullah drew himself erect and raised his hands in a victory gesture.

"I asked you when you came in … what exactly do you want?" Medvedev came closer to Nasaf, but this time the Iranian did not back away.

"I just want to talk."

"What about?"

"Money! Lots of money!"

The Russians hesitated for a moment and made eye contact with each other. Medvedev circled round and quietly closed the door behind Nasaf Rhullah. The three men moved over to the centre of the room and seated themselves back at the spartan table. Another bottle of harsh vodka was produced from one of the bare cupboards.

"Go on." Medvedev tilted back in his chair as he unscrewed the cap and threw it on the floor. He then leaned forward and slid the bottle in front of Rhullah.

"I have contacts in Tehran."

"Contacts?" Sautov looked uncomfortable. He hunched his shoulders and laced his fingers as he rested his arms on the table.

"High-up contacts. They need men like you."

"Like us? Why?"

"You know about mobile missile launchers." The Russians remained silent. "What will you do when this contract is over? Go back to Russia?" Rhullah gripped the edge of the table with outstretched arms as he sat back and set the bait. Once they bit, he would reel them in.

"That's none of your business!" Sautov remained hostile, but Medvedev quickly reached out and placed a placatory hand on his friend's arm. He wanted to hear what else the Iranian had to say.

"Would you like to work for my superiors?" Nasaf's grin seemed to be permanent. He sat back with arms folded and waited for a response. Neither Russian spoke for a few moments. Then Sautov rose and walked across to the door. He opened it slightly; and peered cautiously up and down the endless rows of huts bathed in ghostly moonlight.

Satisfying himself that they were alone, he closed and locked the door before returning to the table.

"There's something not right about this." scowled Sautov.

"What?" Medvedev was becoming irritated by his friend's continuing reticence.

"Why do they need us? After all, they have their own technicians."

"Let me explain…" Rhullah placed his hands flat on the table. "We need someone who can adapt our existing mobile rocket launchers."

"Adapt them?" Sautov became even more suspicious. "To what?"

"To be capable of firing cruise missiles!"

Sautov jumped to his feet and slammed his balled fist onto the table.

"No!" he shouted emphatically.

"Wait…" Medvedev once again put up a restraining hand. When Sautov had calmed down and resumed his seat, he turned to face Rhullah. "*Nuclear* cruise missiles?"

"Of course not." The Iranian scoffed. "No my friends. Iran has no nuclear capability. Everybody knows that. We have simply bought some surplus cruise missiles – from the Russian government – and we need our existing mobile rocket launchers adapted. That's all. Can you do it?"

"Oh, we can do it alright…"

"But we won't!" snapped Sautov.

"Why not, Victor?"

"I don't trust this man, Yuri."

"Look, my friend… you know as well as I do, that our Government is selling equipment to these people. It's no secret."

"Then why don't they sell them the launchers as well?"

"I can answer that." Rhullah interjected. "It's quite simple. The problems were exacerbated by your Government's continuing grotesque mismanagement, incompetence and lack of central planning when trying to co-ordinate the deliveries. Launchers which are suitable for the desert, were just not available at the same time as we acquired the missiles." he lied.

"Then why did you go ahead and buy the missiles?" Sautov wasn't convinced.

THE CHERKASSY INCIDENT · 55

"Because we wished to conclude the transaction quickly and your Government was desperate for the dollars. Besides, we knew there were men like you already available, who could adapt our existing launchers for us."

"Victor, listen." Medvedev tried to counsel his friend. "They're all making money ... all of them. Why shouldn't we make a little? The generals and politicians are getting richer every day by trading with the highest bidders. They're all in bed with the *Mafiosniki* and don't give a damn about people like us. We gave them our lives – and look at us now. Why should we care, Victor?"

"You are not the only ones with the specific knowledge we require." Rhullah turned the screw. "There are many others."

"He's right, Victor ... if we don't do it, someone else will."

"No! I'm against it." Sautov was adamant.

"Look, they're not nuclear, for God's sake ... they're just like the rockets we have worked on so many times in the past." Medvedev would not give up. "What harm would we be doing?"

Victor Sautov snapped back at him in Russian. Both men moved over to a corner of the room and lapsed into a furious debate in their native tongue, arguing the pros and cons of the proposition. Gradually, Medvedev grew more positive as Sautov began to hesitate, to ponder between replies – and to question his own convictions. Victor Sautov pouted and fell silent, as he contemplated the inevitability of the situation. Medvedev would not give up. He continued to speak more softly as Sautov began to nod his head in acquiescence. Yuri circled his arm across Victor's broad shoulders and hugged his companion, slapping him reassuringly on the back. Yuri Medvedev sighed with relief as he returned to the table and sat astride one of the chairs. His calloused hands gripped the chair back as he weighed up Nasaf Rhullah.

"How much money?"

"More than you have dreamt of, my friend."

"No nuclear warheads?"

"Upon the holy name of the Prophet." The Iranian joined his hands as if in prayer and lowered his eyes in reverence.

"Very well, we will work for you."

Nasaf Rhullah shot excitedly to his feet, grinning from ear to ear. The Iranian rushed round the table, babbling in Islamic and kissing the hands of both Russians. Medvedev threw his head back to take a celebratory drink from the bottle of vodka. He allowed the fiery spirit to trickle down the sides of his mouth, before lowering the bottle with a satisfied gasp and passing it across to his companion. Victor's expression was still troubled.

"What happens now?" Sautov asked quietly.

"Don't worry," Rhullah assured them, "I shall arrange everything."

"You see, Victor," Medvedev confirmed through his drunken haze. "There *is* a way!"

CHAPTER 5

UNITED STATES : COLORADO

Early morning mist hung silently over the lake in ragged pale grey layers. Dawn was breaking. Thin rays of sunlight filtered through the pine trees, warming the still, moist mountain air. Larry Tyson broke the peace and solitude of this false dawn by letting out a loud *"yee-hawww"* as he played a powerful mackinaw on the end of his line. Larry was a big, blonde-haired cowboy, with a huge wide-brimmed stetson pulled well down at the front, to hide the red freckles which covered his face. He became totally engrossed in playing the big fish and completely oblivious to the fact that he was gradually sliding further into the icy alpine waters of the Ruedi Reservoir. As the brightly speckled fish leapt and struggled for freedom, the freezing cold waters lapped around Larry's waist, submerging his Wranglers and the exquisitely decorated cowboy boots of which he was so proud.

"Ross!" Larry called out to his friend Ross Lombardi, who was fishing just a little further down the shore. "Hey Ross, I sure got a big 'un here."

"Easy now, play him, Larry!" came the reply "Play him in!"

Larry Tyson had been brought up on the 'Lazy T' – his family's 2,000-acre cattle ranch alongside the banks of the Madison River near Ennis in Montana's Big Sky country. He had first been put into the saddle at the tender age of four, but by the time he was fifteen he had already won several trophies at local rodeos and county fairs for cutting and wrangling steers. Larry had first met up with Ross Lombardi some five years later when the two men were assigned to the same marine corps outfit during the Gulf War conflict following Saddam Hussein's ill-conceived messianic invasion of Kuwait. Larry and Ross had joined up with a small group of British SAS troops to infiltrate the heavily fortified defences around Baghdad. This joint covert operation had been undertaken to pinpoint strategic Iraqi military installations so that precise co-ordinates could be relayed back to the United Nations Field Headquarters. Here, the incoming cruise missiles digital scene-matching area correlation programmes were updated and fed into the inertial guidance systems, thus ensuring that only key military targets were taken out.

   Both men had travelled up into the Rocky Mountains of Colorado for a well deserved fishing vacation. They were joined a couple of days ago by a few of Larry Tyson's New Mexico friends who had come over from Pueblo. The whole group were staying at Ross Lombardi's log cabin, high up in the timber country which surrounds Aspen. They had successfully fished the mountain reservoir during the past couple of days, catching several good mackinaw and catfish, before moving along to try the Arkansas River's fast- flowing crystal clear waters for rainbow trout and bass. Ever since his earliest childhood in the tough backstreets of New York, Lombardi had fallen in love with this clean, fresh outdoor life. He liked the company of these easy- going cowboys and mountain men.

   Nowadays, Ross Lombardi got away to his secluded mountain retreat at every opportunity. It was all another world; so far removed from the depressing ghetto environment where he learned to be a survivor. It was peaceful. It gave a man time to sort things out. He'd just returned from a particularly rough two month assignment in Columbia, where he'd been working under cover for the CIA. Although he wasn't directly employed by the CIA, the Agency nevertheless called upon him sometimes for the more dangerous and dirty assignments – jobs where they were understandably reluctant to expose their fresh, clean cut college graduates. Lombardi's first encounter with the CIA was some three years after his enlistment in the Marine Corps. It had all started just a few days after his seventeenth birthday, when Ross happened to glance into a shop window and became instantly seduced by the various patriotic posters offering adventure, travel and excitement. He had stood there for a few moments, waiting for his arguments and doubts to fall into line and his heartbeat to stabilise, before drawing himself erect, pushing open the door and striding into the Enlistment Centre in the Lower Bronx. He was convinced it would be a welcome ticket out of the slums. After leaving the marines, the Agency had kept in close contact and used him whenever the going was especially tough. Ross didn't mind being used. He was a single minded resolute man of thirty, with no ties whatsoever. He constantly thirsted for that buzz of adrenalin so familiar to any agent competing against a superior opponent and, besides, the Government still paid him well for his unique services. After all, it was the only way he knew how to keep up the crippling mortgage payments on his cabin – and at the same time maintain the lifestyle to which he had become accustomed. Ross Lombardi was absolutely determined not to go back and work in the monotonous drudgery of a factory or auto-plant like his father. He certainly didn't want to grow old before his time; weighed down by obligations to a wife and family, debts and worry – he'd seen too much of it as a child. So he took all the chances.

"I got him, Ross! I got him!" The big cowboy waded in from the shallows and tried to struggle up the slippery bank, still clutching the precious fish in his arms. "Give me a hand over here will ya, you sonofabitch," he grunted.

Lombardi laughed and shook his head in disbelief as he placed his own fishing pole on the ground and hurried over to assist his friend. Lombardi's long jet-black hair fell forward and swung rhythmically in front of his face as he clumped over in his waders. His tall, lean frame and dark, latin features made him a very striking figure from where he stood high on the reservoir's bank, silhouetted against the early morning sunlight. Scrambling down to the water's edge, he held out a hand for Tyson, but the cowboy was still having trouble with his thirty pound mackinaw. The huge fish certainly hadn't given up its quest for freedom. Larry Tyson lunged forward and made a last desperate grab for the fish as he floundered around in the freezing shallows. However, the wily mackinaw was not beaten. The fish had bitten clean through the line and was now thrashing away for deeper water, just as the cowboy tripped over and disappeared under the surface. When the big wrangler finally surfaced and scrambled to his feet, gasping and spluttering with the intense cold, he reached out to grab his hat, which was gently floating away on the ripples. Lombardi came closer and managed to grab Tyson's outstretched hand, dragging the helpless man up the slippery slope and onto dry land. The voracious predator had regained the darker depths of the lake. Tyson threw his soaking hat on the ground in frustration.

"Goddammit Ross, you should have helped me sooner."

"Don't blame me, Larry. You lost the fish!"

By now, the others had gathered round to see what all the commotion was about. Larry Tyson's face grew redder, obscuring his freckles, as his friends guffawed and burst into uncontrollable laughter.

"Hey Larry, ain't we supposed to be fishin' not swimmin'?"

"Whoa Larry, has it been rainin' down here?"

The big cowboy didn't answer. He just gritted his teeth and strode away towards their Jeep, with muddy water belching out over the tops of his precious boots.

Back at the cabin, the men cleaned up and cooked the rest of the catch, before settling down to drink a few shots of Jack Daniels. Larry Tyson sat alone, huddled in front of a roaring log fire and wrapped in a buffalo robe. He gazed wistfully at the wispy plumes of steam rising from his drying clothes. Four of the men sat around a low coffee table playing a little stud poker, while a couple of others indulged in tests of arm-wrestling. The warm soporific heat of the fireglow, coupled with an endless stream of bourbon, finally took its toll. They all ended up singing. With dignity restored, Larry Tyson moved over to accompany the raucous out-of-tune voices on his harmonica. The New Mexicans vigorously strummed their guitars like some manic out of work marimba band, and soon a full hoedown was in progress. In the middle of all this hootin' and hollerin', Ross Lombardi's telephone rang.

Five hours later, Lombardi had briefly called into the United States Air Force Academy at Colorado Springs, before setting off to drive down Interstate 25. He left at Junction 140A, and drove a few miles further south on Highway 115 towards Fort Carson, before turning off to drive up a long winding approach road to the operations centre of NORAD – the North American Aerospace Defence Command and headquarters to the 721st Support Group at Cheyenne Mountain.

Halfway up the mountain, Lombardi slowed to approach the first guardhouse, complete with a small visitors centre constructed of ribbed concrete blocks nestling beneath a blue crinkle tin roof .The duty sergeant stepped out and carefully examined Ross's credentials. He compared them with the information on his clipboard, before stepping back inside and making a brief telephone call to confirm that Ross Lombardi was on his way up to the main reception area. Lombardi stuck his head out of the car window, wrinkled his nose and looked up at the ominous black thunderclouds rolling off the towering mountain top.

The Command Centre wasn't exactly built *at* Cheyenne Mountain, it would be more accurate to describe it as being built *into* it. The entire complex was hollowed from this granite mountain at the height of the Cold War during the nineteen sixties, with the perceived intention of withstanding a chemical, biological or thermonuclear blast. The facility was a massive co-operative effort by both the United States and Canadian governments. It was an ambitious joint venture to develop and co-ordinate various defence planning strategies, including the collection and classification of data from a world-wide system of satellites, radar and other sensors. This highly classified information was analysed and processed on a range of sophisticated computer systems which were specifically designed to support critical NORAD and US Space Command missions. The Cheyenne Mountain operations centre provided an accurate day-to-day picture of precisely what was in space – and where it was located. It also knew what was happening on the ground – in any part of the world, at any time.

The facility consisted of six main centres buried deep within the complex, with each being manned twenty-four hours a day – three hundred and sixty five days of the year: the Command Centre, Air Defence Operations Centre, Missile Warning Centre, Space Control Centre, Combined Intelligence Watch Centre and the Systems Centre. Ross Lombardi was en route to the CIWC. The very heart of this particular complex served as the United States and Canada's early warning systems in respect of any threats from outer space, intercontinental ballistic missiles or other strategic air activity. It is also capable of detecting early outbreaks of geopolitical unrest which might threaten the North American continent – or other belligerent activities which could possibly destabilise US interests abroad. The Watch continually gather valuable intelligence from every corner of the globe; and assist the other Cheyenne Mountain defence departments to analyse and correlate the vast amounts of data which is necessary to support the decision makers of NORAD and the US Space Command.

When visiting this sinister place, Ross Lombardi always felt as if he were entering the realms of Walt Disney's Fantasia. Having passed through the upper reception complex, Lombardi was still enclosed by two rows of chain-link security fencing surmounted with coils of deadly razor wire. As he approached the lofty arched main entrance cut into the sheer rock wall, complete with the words "Cheyenne Mountain Complex" emblazoned in large white letters around the crown of the arch, Lombardi could hear, in his head, the intimidating rhythmic sound of bassoons pounding out their arrogant defiance. Ross Lombardi knew exactly how the Sorcerer's Apprentice must have felt when attending upon his Master.

Even though Ross Lombardi was well known within the complex, he was nevertheless still subjected to check after check, search after electronic search, before moving through the massive blast door and making his way towards the CIWC block. En route, Lombardi passed the vast network of underground water storage cisterns which were often referred to as the "shooting gallery" by the resident personnel. Several duck decoys were serenely floating about on the surface, with electronic sensors suspended into the depths for monitoring the water quality. There were well over a thousand military and civilian personnel feverishly working away deep inside the mountain. The armed soldiers were easy to spot. They were the ones wearing their berets. The entire complex was self-sustaining. If necessary, it could provide its own power, water, air and food for over a month and remain completely independent of the outside world. Dedicated communications hot lines were connected direct to the Pentagon, the White House, US Strategic Command, the Canadian Government, Military Headquarters and other major military centres strategically located throughout the world.

The main layout of the operations complex consisted of fifteen pre-fabricated buildings, built by the US navy and closely resembling the interior of a ship, eleven of which were three stories tall, and located within a series of tunnels.

Each could function independently, but were nevertheless connected by a series of aerial walkways. The whole structure was mounted on hundreds of huge 1,000 pound steel coil springs intended to provide appropriate shock and impact protection. So unique was this place, that two NCOs were permanently assigned to do nothing else but inspect, tighten and grout the one hundred and fifteen thousand giant anchor bolts which provided the facilities integral strength and stability against the constantly moving rock structure. Three other engineers were also engaged on full-time maintenance of the pneumatic valves which operated the twenty five ton blast doors.

Ross Lombardi was being escorted the rest of the way on foot and couldn't help but feel that he was nothing more than another anchor about to have his nuts tightened. Approaching his final destination, Ross casually glanced up to the tunnel's glistening roof. He gave a wry smile to himself when he noticed several white tarpaulin sheets suspended like giant umbrellas over the central complex – to deflect water penetrating through the rock strata. He marvelled at man's ingenuity with such a low tech solution to one of natures most fundamental problems. Lombardi shook his head in disbelief and wondered what the consequences might be if water found its way into the delicate and sophisticated electronic control systems. Perhaps World War Three could accidentally break out! Lombardi and his escort mounted a short flight of steps as they entered one of the anonymous buildings. They proceeded along a featureless corridor and approached a high-security room in the CIWC block, where he was requested to remain outside an unmarked door. As Lombardi turned his back to the opposite wall, he was silently flanked on either side by two solemn and impassive armed guards who appeared from nowhere. Ross Lombardi continued to study the plain grey walls for about fifteen minutes. Suddenly the door opened and Drew Dalton stepped aside with outstretched arm to invite Lombardi inside the "Battle Cap'. Drew was Ross" CIA contact. Dalton was a thin, easy-going man somewhere in his mid-forties. Despite the relentless advances of early middle age, he had managed to retain a clean-cut freshman look which is usually associated with the more active FBI and CIA field operatives. Dalton had seen a lot of tough action in his time, but now he much preferred the quiet life. His easy and re-assuring air usually managed to subdue any volatile confrontations. Several high-ranking Cheyenne Mountain officers were also present in the cramped room. They were busily pouring over sheaves of printed data spread out on the conference table, along with a man Lombardi recognised immediately as Senator Hefner T Copeland. Drew Dalton took Ross by the arm and introduced him to the others, before offering him one of the vacant bucket seats set around a long oblong table. Lombardi looked around and took in the beige vinyl walls before turning to face a full length glass wall. Through the screen, he could see several military personnel silently going about their awesome duties in the subdued lighting usually associated with an operations room. The whole Command environment was both hermetic and timeless; with no way of telling whether it was night or day in the outside world.

Several personnel were busily seated at flickering control monitors with the various workstations being separated into key sectors along a central console. Above them, and mounted to one side of the forward wall, was a map of the world – divided into its various time zones. Criss-crossing its surface were several thin, overlapping tracks, which Lombardi thought resembled the sine-wave characteristics of an oscilloscope. Creeping along these tracks at various intervals, were a myriad of twinkling lights which indicated the presence of numerous satellites in orbit.

"Sorry to drag you away from your fishin', Ross" Dalton tried to lighten the atmosphere.

"That's OK. Larry was drivin" me crazy anyhow."

"Say, how's the big ox?"

"Same as ever, Drew, keeps gettin' into trouble."

"Gentlemen!" The Senator folded his arms and perched himself on the edge of the table. He wasn't in the mood for any small talk.

"Sorry, Senator," Dalton apologised, "lets get you briefed on what's goin' on Ross."

One of the Generals went on to explain how they were monitoring a sunken Russian nuclear submarine in the Barents Sea. However, this latest turn of events was not unusual in itself – as there were potentially far more dangerous situations brewing within the Third World. On the other hand, the Senator was especially concerned as it was reported that unspecified Iranian personnel were on board when the submarine foundered.

"What were Iranians doin' on board?" Lombardi asked innocently.

"Tehran has already purchased several Kilo-class subs from the Russians. They may be in the market for something more sophisticated," a CIWC officer informed him from the head of the table.

"Christ! The Ayatollahs actually have a submarine fleet?" Lombardi laughed nervously. "I didn't know that."

"Not many people do." the CIWC man assured him.

"So what's the big deal?"

"I'll tell you what the big deal is mister," Senator Copeland jumped to his feet, "Israel has somehow got hold of this information and the hawks in the Knesset are jumpin' up and down. Mossad wants some positive action taken, before they take some of their own. Do you realise how dangerous that situation could become?"

"I'm sure Ross understands the situation, Senator," Dalton intervened.

"I sure as hell hope he does." Copeland turned to the CIWC officers. "Were there any survivors?"

"Some of the Russians made it, sir, including the Captain and the Executive Officer."

"I meant the Iranians, goddamit!" The Senator was growing impatient.

"None that we're aware of, sir."

"Does that mean there may have been, but you just don't know about it?"

"I think we'd know about it, sir."

"You'd better be right!"

"What's the current status?" Drew Dalton tried to use his calming influence once more.

"Well… we got a defence support programme satellite in geo-stationary orbit, right over the sucker. So, if anything moves out there, we'll be the first to know."

"What are the Russians doin' about it?" Lombardi asked.

"They've sent a group up there, to keep an eye on things. They got some Norwegians and Finns with them. Both countries are closest to the site and they're as nervous as hell about nuclear contamination."

"Doesn't the Barents freeze over, at this time of year?" Dalton ventured the question.

"Not strictly true." The CIWC man went over to one of his wall maps. "Sure, parts of the Barents Sea freeze over during the winter, but these other parts are influenced by the Gulf Stream – and the winters in that region are relatively mild."

"So what the hell are we talkin' about?" Senator Copeland expanded his arms in exasperation. Being a rather brusque man, he didn't like wasting time. He simply wanted to get to the point. In appearance, the Senator was flamboyant and outrageous, but with the inimitable style of an old Southern Gentleman, complete with flicked-up long grey hair and whiskers. In another life he could have had something to do with chickens – and a secret recipe. He went to the head of the room, to indicate that he was taking over the meeting.

"The sub went down over the continental shelf, so its no more than six hundred feet down," the CIWC man continued, as he pointed to an area between Murmansk and Bear Island. "The sub is lying about fifty kilometres off the coastal town of Kolskiy Zaliv, on the northern tip of the Kola Peninsula. Although it gets damn cold, the sea never actually freezes over in that area."

"You're telling me that the sub is salvageable?" Copeland concluded.

"For an enterprising outfit, yes sir, it's possible."

"Goddam it!" Copeland pounded the table with his fist. "No wonder the Israelis are doin' back-flips!"

"It may be possible Senator," Drew Dalton intervened again "but highly unlikely."

"Is this the official CIA line?"

"It is Senator."

THE CHERKASSY INCIDENT · 67

"Convince me!" Hefner T Copeland folded his arms. On this rare occasion, he was at least prepared to listen. Dalton sighed and glanced around the room before continuing.

"The Agency has received reliable information that the Russians will attempt a damage limitation exercise some time during the Spring. Even they are convinced it's far too late in the year to mount a full scale salvage operation."

"And, after all, the sub is only just outside of Russian waters, sir. One of the CIWC men joined forces with Dalton in an attempt to keep the Senator on the rails.

"What if the Iranians, or anyone else for that matter, launched an independent expedition to retrieve any incriminating evidence – or worse still, attempted to get hold of the nuclear weapons which were reported to be on board?" This was the big question. The Senator waited.

"Impossible Senator." Drew Dalton kept a straight face, as the CIWC men tried not to laugh.

"Why?" the Senator needed convincing.

"Well .. apart from the time of year, they haven't got the technical know-how. The only man who could conceivably break the security codes and get those missiles out of their silos is the sub's Weapons Officer. And it's unlikely that he survived. The Iranians ain't got anybody with that kind of skill. Anyway, Senator, the accident site has moved to centre-stage. It's got spotlights all over it. Our own defence people here at Cheyenne Mountain are keeping an eye on things via our satellite network – and the Russians on the other hand, have an international team right on top of it." Dalton's words made sense. The Senator began to cool down. "OK, but what am I supposed to tell the Israelis?"

"That's where Ross comes in, Senator." Drew Dalton stood up and moved to join the Senator at the head of the room. The Senator watched him advance and hesitated for a moment, before giving way to the cool CIA man. Hefner T Copeland sat down to light up a large cigar in the no-smoking area. No-one dared to tell him to put the thing out. "The Russians don't want any media publicity about this anymore than we do. And, to tell the truth, that kind of thing does nobody any good. All it will achieve is to get the whole thing front-page attention – and then we'll have swarms of hacks crawling all over the place, trying to dig up this and that. Who knows what could come to light, Senator?"

"I get the point."

"Mister Lombardi is a free-lance, whom the Agency has used many times in the past. His discretion and anonymity are the only prime assets we are able to call upon in this delicate situation. If we're seen to get directly involved, alarm bells will go off all over the place. Ross can go places we can't."

"So what's he gonna do?" Copeland looked up and blew a cloud of blue smoke in Dalton's direction.

"Well… if we can cool Mossad down, the Knesset will cool down as well."

"I'll go along with that." The Senator was beginning to understand and relax.

"Ross still has several good personal contacts within Mossad. We'd like to send him out to Israel – to talk to these people. The Agency is convinced, sir, that he can cool things down without rockin' the boat."

"Then do it!" Senator Copeland rose abruptly and strode to the door. Opening it, he paused, with the cigar firmly clenched between his teeth and gave a withering look at the assembled group. Everyone sprang to their feet. "You keep me posted now… y'hear? I have spent more than twenty years on the Hill and I got the President's ear on this one, so don't foul up!" He slammed the door after him, leaving a cloud of smoke in his wake.

"Phew!" Drew Dalton mockingly wiped his brow and grinned as the tension evaporated. The CIWC men also became visually relaxed. They raised their hands in the air and hit each other's palms in a gesture of united vindication.

"What the hell was that all about?" Lombardi was still a little puzzled.

"Nothin' for you to worry about, Ross." His friend moved over and clapped him on the back. "Just pourin' a little oil on troubled politicians."

"So there isn't a problem?"

"No sweat. Mossad gets jumpy every time they hear a *muezzin* prayer-call."

"What's this all about Israel?"

"Just look upon it as a paid vacation, man." Drew Dalton shuffled and gathered a stack of classified papers together and placed them in his black security briefcase. The Cheyenne Mountain officers had already drifted out of the room. "Arrangements will be made in the usual way." Dalton went to the door and turned. "Oh, I almost forgot, you gotta touch base with a British guy over there … a Peter Lawrence. Ever hear of him?"

"Can't say that I have."

"Well you know how it is … the Agency likes to keep the British Secret Service happy if it can. You scratch my back…" Dalton threw a casual salute and left the room. Ross Lombardi sat back and blew out a long sigh. Talk about things happening quickly – but then, they usually did in his line of business.

CHAPTER 6

Russia : Kola Peninsula

Alexander Volkov leaned over to look out through the smeared and scratched window of the rickety old Russian Air Force twin-engined plane as it lined up its approach for the runway at Murmansk airport. Volkov scanned the bleak horizon, watching the northern sky turn from lapis lazuli to black, with streaks of pulsating yellow light filling the heavens. Although the Aurora Borealis is something rather spectacular to behold in these northern latitudes, Volkov couldn't help but feel this arctic region was still regarded by many as the very edge of civilisation. In fact, 'Murman' was the Saami word for 'edge of the world'. Having argued and shouted through most of the bumpy flight from Moscow, the rest of the party fell quiet and settled down to marvel at the heavenly lights. Volkov was the only environmentalist on the team. The remainder of the company consisted of three nuclear scientists and twenty soldiers. On arrival, this oddly mixed group were due to meet up with some Finnish and Norwegian environmental scientists who should have arrived the previous day. Following several days of intense diplomatic pressure, at the highest possible level, the Scandinavians had been invited along on this mission – by courtesy of a reluctant Kremlin. Since the *Cherkassy's* tragic sinking, all sensitive communications could only be routed through the appropriate diplomatic channels. After all, if they invited these neighbourly people along, it would make it difficult for them to subsequently make any fuss. Everyone was scheduled to meet up in Murmansk, in preparation for the overland journey to Kolskiy Zaliv – an even more remote spot, almost one hundred and seventy five kilometres due north, on the Barents Sea coast.

Darkness had closed in as the plane entered its final circuit and touched down. At this time of year, the nights in this desolate arctic region were interminably long and soon, from November to January, there would be nothing but permanent polar night – fifty days of it. Alexander Volkov thought he would go mad. At the airport, disembarkation and passage through the various formalities had been standard Russian chaos. It involved a long and dazed wait in a crowded room where the spartan standards within the windowless main reception area left much to be desired. Under the gloom of totally inadequate lighting, the cheerless walls betrayed a dinginess that no amount of fresh paint could erase. The floor tiles were cracked, chipped and overlaid with odd bits of threadbare carpet. Deep-seated grime to the whole fabric was beyond the power of any cleaners. The grubby wear-stained desks and cheap vinyl chairs looked like relics from a much earlier age. As the group emerged into the slushy approach road, they were met by a local security escort, who quickly loaded their things onto a battered military bus. With the shabby vehicle's heater not working, it was regarded as an ominous portent of things to come as it took them to the Arctica Hotel.

The Moscow briefings had promised it was a first class hotel with two restaurants and a luxury bar. The reality was far worse than Alexander Volkov could have ever imagined. The buffet restaurant served the same greasy monotonous lukewarm food for breakfast, lunch and dinner – fried fish, sausages, boiled eggs, grated carrots and black bread. The only slightly redeeming feature about the whole place was the noisy bar, stocked with a range of scotch whisky – to which Alexander Volkov was particularly partial. They were surprised to find the Finns and Norwegians were nowhere to be found, especially as they had checked in the day before. That night, Volkov withdrew to his drink at the bar, whereas the soldiers remained at the far end of the room. Alexander Volkov snorted his contempt. He could tell they weren't *real* soldiers. They were more of a hotchpotch of military police, civilian security and the much feared OMON special purpose militia. Their leader was a woman, Captain Lydia Ilyichyova, who by now seemed to have very little control over her men. Half a bottle of scotch later, Volkov took one last draw of his cigarette and stubbed it out in the overflowing ashtray, before slithering off his stool and clumsily making his way up to his room. Standing before the cracked bathroom mirror, he splashed cold water onto his face and shook off the drops. He fumbled for a towel hooked over one of the basin supports as he closed an eye. The wavering image hardened as it squinted back at him. Alexander Volkov was still a young man, but looked much older than his thirty four years. His face was heavily lined and his dark greasy hair receding. Volkov had the haunted look of a man who was thoroughly disillusioned with life – and so he was.

During his university days, he had been filled with all the hope and optimism of innocent youth. Now there was nothing to look forward to. The new Russia had openly embraced all the worst aspects of Western society, but with none of its restraints or controls. They had willingly saluted the flag of democracy, even when they knew that freedom would be a poison to the people. Alexander Volkov had voiced his concerns too often – and in the wrong places. That's why he was here – on the edge of the world. With such tumultuous thoughts racing through his mind, along with images of his wife and three children back in Smolensk, Alexander Volkov slumped onto the firm bed and finally drifted off to sleep – despite the rowdy shouts and cheers drifting up from the bar below. When he awoke in the small hours, total exhaustion had sapped his energy and robbed him of his appetite. He found it hard to maintain interest for the task they were about to undertake. The excessive cold and biting arctic winds shrieking across the landscape had made sleeping virtually impossible.

Next morning, the other environmentalists had finally appeared. Alexander Volkov went down and introduced himself to a couple of bearded Norwegians standing over by the reception desk. In all probability, they were just a couple of amiable fellows, anticipating some kind of grand adventure. They were clearly excited by the prospect of what lie ahead. However, the Finn was something else. This Scandinavian goddess was called Aletta Bjorkman: and she was beautiful. Volkov had never seen anyone quite like her before. Despite her bulky arctic clothes, Aletta's height and stature radiated the demeanour and confidence of a super-model. Her long, shiny blond hair framed the porcelain like features of her nordic face – it was the face of an angel. After a brief discussion about their forthcoming mission, the group shuffled over to join a disgruntled line of guests waiting to partake of the hotel's unpalatable breakfast. Volkov idly stirred his black coffee, unable to eat or take his eyes off Aletta. The soldiers arrived too late to eat – and Lydia Ilychyova took an instant dislike to their Finnish associate, Aletta Bjorkman.

At midday, they were finally assembled and ready to set off for Kolskiy Zaliv. Having loaded their things back onto the bus, they climbed aboard with their new found friends. The group was taken to the central railway station … by the same security escort who had collected them from the airport on the previous day. Travelling by rail was the only way to get to Kolskiy Zaliv at this time of the year. As the train slowly rumbled out of Murmansk, Alexander Volkov's weary bones were grateful for the chance to settle on the seat opposite Aletta Bjorkman. She became totally engrossed in reading a book, in English, by some eminent doctor of molecular biology, while Volkov just stole a glance at her from time to time. All thoughts of his wife and children began to fade. A faraway look came into his eyes, as of someone gazing at a memory of long ago. Their journey across the exposed Kola Peninsula was both tedious and uncomfortable.

The train stopped at every village halt. Outside, the landscape changed dramatically. Cascading rivers tumbled and fell over slippery rocks covered in mottled orange paisley lichen, while scattered snowfields gave way to exposed windswept tundra, blending with the moss and wild flowers trembling in the arctic breeze. This raw environment could only be described as the last wilderness of Europe – spectacular, wild and forlorn. The planned three hour journey became four hours and then six, with the early night rapidly overtaking them. Alexander Volkov passed the time by dozing or drinking from a bottle of scotch he had acquired from the hotel. He was still trying to balance the strange eccentricities of his scientific background with patient diplomacy. From time to time, Aletta Bjorkman glanced coquettishly over the top of her book and smiled at him. The soldiers remained at the far end of the carriage and were as loud as ever, playing cards and fighting amongst themselves. The nuclear scientists, on the other hand, faced the unknown without direct experience or perspective and kept apart from the rest, firmly believing they were the chosen elite – with everyone's true destiny resting in their hands. They knew mistakes were inevitable, grievous mistakes that would cost people their reputations and their careers. The whole atmosphere became charged, as tension within the confined spaces approached crisis point. The Norwegians, on the other hand, tried to remain both neutral and diplomatic, as they wandered up and down the carriages trying to placate the various groups.

Kolskiy Zaliv looked picturesque and quaint from a distance, with its faded blue, yellow and red timber clad houses and barns, perched precariously on the edge of an escarpment which rapidly fell away to the dark forbidding Barents Sea. The entire community consisted of a single main street, criss-crossed with smaller streets and alleyways; dusty in summer, a river of mud churned up by mud-caked military convoys in autumn and rock-hard with frost in winter. On virtually every street corner there were dog-sleighs with teams of howling grubby huskies tethered to chains. This entire closed region was regarded as something of a farce. The western world had long known about these secret military installations from their surveillance satellites traversing overhead. The station building fared no better. Groups of shabbily dressed men and women huddled together on the platform.

On all sides, old women, children, families, lovers and drunks were thrust together in an almost visible atmosphere of garlic, tobacco, damp fabric and ancient sweat. Mothers in knitted headshawls frantically tried to keep tabs on toddlers bundled in immense woolly coats, with scarves tied around their waists. Workmen with stubbly black-jowled faces and missing teeth lined up to receive the train. Here was a stark and vivid sense of interminable struggle, of mankind's constant burden under the yoke of a harsh life that inevitably moulds people into mean shapes. A senior member of the District Soviet dutifully stood by the entrance, ready to receive the party from Murmansk. A mud-splattered yellow bus waited nearby. It would take them to the disused military camp which would be their home on the outskirts of town. Inside the compound's double row of wire fencing stood a long, barn-like wooden structure, raised off the ground on brick piers, with a rusted corrugated iron roof. This building formed the centre-piece and was surrounded by a group of smaller wooden *dachas*, which were to be their base until the following April. After dark, the yapping guard dogs were released and had the run of the twenty five metre strip between the perimeter fences. The scientific group were allocated two to each *dacha*. The Norwegians remained together, as did two of the nuclear scientists, while Volkov was ensconced with the third. The soldiers were billeted in the main long barracks, except for Lydia Ilyichyova, who shared an adjacent *dacha* with Aletta Bjorkman.

Each *dacha* contained two cold, shabby and cheerless rooms with a rudimentary stained lavatory to one side. The primitive plumbing certainly left much to be desired. One room was clearly intended for everyday activities and contained a basic wood burning stove. The austere furnishings consisted of a solitary wooden table and two chairs. The other room was equipped with a single nightstand between a couple of low rough timbered bunk beds, covered with reindeer skins. A miserable and flimsy utility plywood wardrobe was screwed to the far wall. Lace curtains hung lank and grey over grimy windows, with paint flaking from the walls and ceilings. The floors were bare wood and the air musty and dank. Alexander Volkov wearily slung his pack under one of the bunks and sank heavily on the edge. He rested his elbows on his knees and sighed heavily as he put his head in his hands. "Oh my God … what on earth am I doing here?"

Early next morning, a battered army crew bus returned to take the scientists and environmentalists down to Khalovka's small commercial dock area, where the ice-breaking research vessel *Nadezhda* was busily taking on stores and equipment. The ship's superstructure bristled with every conceivable type of radar and radio antenna. Down on the quayside, the underwater TV cameras, deep-towed magnetometers, side-scanning echo sounders, fathometers, geiger counters and a host of other space-age detection devices requested by the scientists, had arrived and were being safely stowed on board. The captain made ready for sea and eased the ship away from the quayside, as they set course for an area some fifty kilometres north of Kolskiy Zaliv, where the nuclear submarine *Cherkassy* had foundered.

The weather was clear and the Barents Sea relatively smooth, with large ice-floes stretching as far as the eye could see. A few off-duty members of the crew and a couple of the environmentalists came up onto the foredeck to peer over the ship's port and starboard quarters. They watched as the thick chunks of ice bumped and swirled in the cold grey waters as it was pushed aside. The blue-green ice floes tinkled like crystal chandeliers when they nudged against each other and bumped along the ship's side, to meet up again in its wake. A flock of Sabine gulls surfed the air currents at the bow of the ship as a pod of seals dipped and surfaced like synchronised swimmers alongside. There was nothing in the immediate search area to indicate that a major disaster had recently taken place. The sea had an eerie calmness about it. When the main engines were stopped, the ship drifted to a standstill, and a sinister silence descended upon the place.

22,300 miles overhead, a U.S.Defence Support Programme satellite gently manoeuvred into geo-synchronous orbit and deployed its eight thousand cell detector array. The satellite's fifteen foot infra-red telescope came into focus as it stared down at the *Nadezhda* and the activities of her crew. Data was duly recorded by the satellite's dual-wavelength processor and beamed back to its masters at Cheyenne Mountain. Both the American and Russian monitoring equipment showed no unusual readings. On the surface, there didn't appear to be any contamination and the air was remarkably fresh and clear. Alexander Volkov and the Norwegians bustled around in the inflatable dinghies taking sea water samples, while Aletta Bjorkman kept apart from the main group and seemed to be more pre-occupied with her own personal agenda. The ship's captain and crew were questioned closely as to whether they had become aware of any unusual catches of fish being recently landed, but everything appeared to be normal. One of the nuclear scientists" first tasks was to secure a large wreck buoy above the submarine, ready to transmit regular signals back to their temporary base. Further samples of water, plankton and marine life were taken at varying depths over a two kilometre radius from the epicentre of the disaster, before the ship returned to Khalovka.

Back at their base camp, Volkov's room-mate barely spoke to him. The third nuclear scientist spent most of his time next door, at his colleagues" *dacha*, returning only to slump into his bunk, after many a late night drinking session. This often left Alexander alone with his thoughts. Discipline was non-existant, and the soldiers had degenerated into little more than a drunken rabble. Volkov at least made an effort to strike up some sort of rapport, but the Norwegians proved to be intellectually overpowering – and Aletta Bjorkman remained unresponsive and totally detached.

On the sixth depressing night, Alexander Volkov once again found himself alone in the small *dacha*. He tried to occupy these endless tedious hours by analysing and cataloguing the daily samples of water and seaweed. Each time he returned to the compound, it was back to tapped phones, constant surveillance and monitored friendships. The terrible and suffocating loneliness of isolation and drink was beginning to take its toll, when Volkov was suddenly shaken from his melancholy reverie by a gentle, but insistent knocking at the door. Alexander Volkov grunted his displeasure at this unwelcome interruption. He half-turned in his chair to face the door and raised a quizzical eyebrow. Peering in anticipation through a cone of yellow light cast by a heavily shaded light bulb over the door, he could see a figure had entered the room. It was Lydia Ilyichyova. Volkov rose and remained transfixed. He gazed at the statuesque woman with a military overcoat loosely draped over her shoulders. Her hair was a thick shining mane of red curls and she was certainly older than he had expected. She had a mature woman's hips and bosom, with heavy make-up emphasising the tiny lines at the corners of her eyes. Her scarlet lipstick seeped into the crevices of her mouth. To her army colleagues she had become known as the "Regimental Mattress." She stood there for a moment, with outstretched arms and a bottle of whisky in one hand, steadily appraising Volkov in a way that made him lower his jaw and feel a deep stirring within his loins. It had been so long, so very long since he had experienced such a sexual awareness.

"Am I intruding?" she asked in a husky voice.

"Ehh .. no, not at all." Volkov was completely surprised by the visit. He had barely spoken to the Captain since they met, over a week ago.

"I noticed you like scotch whisky." She held up the bottle. "Me too." Volkov didn't reply. He just stood there, not really sure what to do. She waited for him to make a move. "Do you have any glasses?" she asked as she glanced around the room.

"Oh, I'm sorry .. please excuse me.." He took a couple of dusty tumblers from a shelf and placed them on the bare wooden table. Ilyichyova came over and removed her coat, draping it over the back of one of the chairs. They sat opposite each other as she reached over and poured the whisky.

"What about your work?" Ilyichyova nodded towards the samples and a pile of dog-eared files which Volkov had been working on.

"Oh… it can wait." Volkov knew there would be more than enough time to arrive at a politically expedient solution before the spring.

"Where is your room-mate?" she enquired.

"He only returns to sleep. But then, you probably know that."

"Its my job to know what goes on in this group."

"What about *your* room-mate?" Volkov was still interested in Bjorkman.

"She reads a lot."

"And your men?"

"What about them?"

"Isn't it also your job to keep them under control?"

"They're riffraff – *svoloch*. They're not regular soldiers."

"Then why are they here?" Volkov already knew the answer to his question.

"This is nothing more than a cosmetic exercise," she scoffed. "As usual, our government is putting on a little show for the West. There is no real threat to the submarine. We will not have to do anything. Let us just call it *soldatskaya smekalka*." She poured more scotch into Volkov's glass. The stove in the centre of the room had been stoked up and was all aglow – as the whisky gradually began to take effect. Lydia Ilyichyova was neither an attractive nor unattractive woman. He could feel her warmth and smell her cheap perfume mingling with the natural musky odour of the sexually aroused female. Alexander Volkov mellowed as he gulped down the welcome spirit and Ilyichyova became more alluring with every glass. If only his wife had been seeing another man it would have made things so much easier. She had always been loyal, but if love had died there was very little he could do about it. How could he go on yearning for those things which were simply out of reach?

When the bottle was drained, he looked up to find the woman had gone. The air remained thick with the haze of cigarette smoke and her cheap perfume. Volkov screwed up his eyes and shook his head. "Where are you?" he called.

"Over here Alexander." He shuffled over to the bedroom where she lay on his bunk, naked, plump and white with huge soft breasts and swelling belly. He blinked and stared at her. Lydia's clothes were strewn across the floor. "Come to Lydia…" she whispered hoarsely, and with outstretched arms, opened her thighs in languid invitation.

CHAPTER 7

Iran : Tehran

Yuri Medvedev's mood had changed during the journey. He remained slumped, deep in thought, taking in the wildly contrasting views from the back seat of the Mercedes. Although the day was warm and beautiful with a soft breeze wafting down from the mountains, Victor Sautov also remained surly and silent as he gazed out of the opposite window. Their journey took them along the main south eastern approach road to Tehran, having taken a detour via the town of Rey, with its many monuments and mosques. They passed through many crowded and colourful streets crammed full of up-to-date shops, where the traffic congestion and noise was comparable to any other large city in the world. The sprawling suburbs gradually gave way to endless rows of impersonal high-rise office blocks gleaming in the midday sun, which made them appear incongruous and ill at ease with the surrounding mosques and minarets. The car finally glided to a halt outside the Universal Hotel situated on Ferdowsi Avenue, close to the Turkish Embassy.

Neither Medvedev nor Sautov had seen Nasaf Rhullah since their initial encounter in Gwadar. However, after much argument and debate the Russians had finally decided to leave the construction complex and take five days" long overdue vacation. As they emerged through the compound's entrance gates, they hefted their bags and scoured the seething mass of humanity for their promised contact. After a few minutes, a swarthy looking courier stepped forward. He glanced nervously up and down the bustling street, before escorting the Russians to some dubious looking characters, who smuggled them across the inhospitable mountainous border between Pakistan and Iran

– near the sleepy town of Pishin. To avoid the inevitable roadblocks placed strategically along the main highway, their Landrover had taken a wide detour out across the rugged and barren countryside towards the town of Bam. Here, they received fresh identity papers and train tickets for the next stage of their journey which took them as far as the holy city of Qom, a hundred and fifty kilometres to the south of Tehran. The sombre Mercedes driver had met them at Qom's central railway station and took them the rest of the way in style. Victor Sautov was surprised the journey had been uneventful. Nobody had challenged them. In fact, it almost seemed as if everyone was over-courteous – as if they knew who the Russians were – and more importantly, why they were here, in Iran. Sautov didn't like it. He wished he'd stayed in Gwadar.

The Russians" temporary accommodation in Tehran wasn't exactly luxurious, but on the other hand it was a palace compared to what they had just come from. There were two single bedrooms, a shower and a large living room. It had been a pleasant surprise to discover the fridge within the ample kitchenette was well stocked with food – including the provision of half a dozen bottles of their favourite vodka. Medvedev examined the supplies and grunted his approval as he unscrewed the cap from one of the bottles and threw it across the floor. Raising the bottle to his mouth, he took one large swallow, before sinking into one of the armchairs.

"This is the life, eh Victor?"

Sautov didn't answer. He thoughtfully rubbed the two day beard which darkened the lower half of his face… and placed a cautionary finger across his lips. He explored every corner of the room, looking for hidden microphones and cameras, before moving over to the window and cautiously peering out through the window into Ferdowsi Avenue.

"What are you looking for?" Medvedev asked impatiently with outspread arms.

"I don't know."

"Oh, come on … this isn't Russia, Victor. Stop being so suspicious."

"It's worse than Russia, Yuri. What are we doing here?"

"We've been through all this…."

"I don't know why I let you talk me into it."

"Money, Victor. The money, you fool!"

Victor Sautov fell silent. Suddenly his stomach rumbled. It reminded him that he hadn't eaten for several hours. He moved over to the kitchenette and took some food from the fridge and began to prepare a snack to be followed by fresh coffee. Meanwhile, Yuri Medvedev still preferred to seek comfort from the vodka.

A soft knock on the door made both men spin round just in time to see an obsequious Nasaf Rhullah entering the room, followed by four other men. Two stone-faced government officials stood either side of Rhullah, as two other senior military officers brought up the rear. Nasaf Rhullah stepped forward and offered a present of Iranian caviar, which the Russians dismissed as being inferior to the stuff produced in their own country. A faraway look came into Medvedev's eyes, as if he were gazing at a memory of long ago. He was getting drunk. Sautov remained impassive and said very little, as he kept his eyes and ears open, trying to read between the lines. The Iranians played on the Russians" desires, their greed and their hate, but mostly on their fears.

"When will we see the launchers?" Medvedev enquired, expansively waving the vodka bottle about.

"Tomorrow, when you're rested," Rhullah assured them.

"We haven't much time…"

"Time enough!"

"These *cruise* missiles…" Medvedev's arrogant and sonorous voice became intimidating.

"What *type* are they?"

"Type?" One of the officers gave a questioning look.

"Yes, *type* … *type*" Medvedev's rising voice mimicked the soldier.

"They are sub-sonic, long-range SS-N-21 Sampson cruise missiles," the other officer confirmed, having received an authoritative nod from one of the government officials whose eyes were close enough together to have confused Picasso.

"Nuclear!" Sautov gasped.

"No, no … not nuclear … I told you." Rhullah gave a nervous grin as he broke out into a cold sweat.

"They are *submarine* missiles!" Sautov wouldn't be appeased.

"They *are* nuclear!"

"But ... I thought they knew..." The other politician looked quizzically at Rhullah.

"Not yet!" he hissed through clenched teeth.

"Oh, who cares?" Medvedev boomed. The room immediately fell silent. Everyone's attention was now focused on the big Russian, weaving about on his feet, as he clutched the precious bottle of vodka to his chest. Medvedev looked round at his bemused audience and bellowed with laughter. He moved over and threw his arm around Sautov's shoulder.

"Who cares, Victor?"

"I do!" Sautov shrugged off the huge arm draped around his neck and walked over to the window. With his back to the company, Sautov's shoulders visibly hunched before thrusting his hands deep into his pockets. He looked down at the bustling street below.

"I'd like to leave."

Rhullah put a finger to his lips and silently ushered the delegation from the room, before moving over to stand behind Sautov.

"I'm sorry." He spoke quietly.

"This has all been a big mistake. Tomorrow you will go back to Pakistan."

"I want to go back now" Sautov's voice remained quiet and controlled, his words concise and his thinking tightly organised. He showed intense concentration and focus of thoughts.

"That's impossible" Rhullah assured him.

"You rest now."

Nasaf Rhullah turned and walked towards the door, whispering something into Yuri Medvedev's ear before leaving. Rhullah briefly turned to look across at Victor Sautov still staring whistfully out of the window, shrugged his shoulders and quietly closed the door as he left. The Russians remained apart and did not speak to each other for a moment. Sautov seemed transfixed and deep in thought as he continued to look out through the grimy net curtains, while Medvedev took another long swig from the bottle.

"Come on, Victor..." he gave an encouraging laugh as he approached his associate.

"No!" Sautov shouted emphatically.

"I knew this was all a terrible mistake, *he* didn't have to tell me … and don't *you* try to talk me round again."

"I'm not trying to," Medvedev shuffled back unsteadily and put his hands in the air as a gesture of appeasement.

"But just remember, we're stuck here until tomorrow, so we might as well make the most of it … and at least have a decent drink in the meantime."

Victor Sautov sighed with resignation. He reached over and took the vodka bottle from Medvedev's outstretched hand.

Later that same evening the Russians were roused from their drunken stupor by the Mercedes driver. He fussed about the suite, gathering up their discarded clothing as he implored them to freshen up. They were expected to join their hosts within the hour for an evening's special entertainment. As Sautov and Medvedev tumbled out onto the crowded pavement, they sniffed the fresh night air and glanced towards the snow capped Elburz Mountains. The distant jagged range gleamed like bone in the moonlight, with early snowfall lingering in the gullies and upon high places above the northern skyline. Down in the city, the short winter season had started, when the night air became cool and refreshing as it wafted in from the desert. They eased their way through the bustling evening traffic towards Ghaem Magham Farahani Avenue, where the driver parked his car down a deserted side street. The chauffeur escorted his charges towards a nondescript building at the end of the road, in front of which was a heavy, panelled door. The driver spoke briefly with the doorman before leaving the bewildered Russians, and retreating into the shadows. He watched as they passed the dinner jacketed security guards to descended a short flight of steps to a lower lobby. Behind a beaded curtain the Russians could hear the erotic sound of middle eastern music from a lavishly decadent room, furnished in rich colours of blood-red and oil-black. The two Russians squinted and wrinkled their noses as a pungent smell of incense wafted around the room. Gradually their eyes became accustomed to the subdued lighting, as they peered through a haze of blue smoke, towards several figures silhouetted at a table to one side of the dance floor. From across the room, two military officers leapt to their feet and approached the half-intoxicated Russians with open arms.

Next morning, Yuri Medvedev was first to wake. He couldn't remember coming back to the hotel, nor undressing and getting into bed. Yet here he was, with his clothes neatly folded, and a pitcher of water standing on the bedside table. Medvedev swung his feet onto the floor and drank straight from the jug. His mouth felt like the underside of a camel's tail. He greedily gulped down the water as an anvil kept beating time inside his head. He vigorously massaged his scalp before tipping the remainder over his head. This last act finally forced him to his feet. He staggered over to the other bedroom and leaned against the doorframe, looking down at Victor Sautov sprawled across the bed. Medvedev kept muttering as he shuffled over to wake his colleague. He sank heavily onto the edge of the bed.

"What happened last night?" Sautov mumbled through his soporific haze.

"I remember the women…"

"Drugs of some sort…" Sautov was beyond caring and leaned forward to spit on the carpeted floor as he cradled his throbbing head in his hands.

"We were drugged!"

"No, Victor … we *took* drugs. There's a difference."

A soft knock on the door brought them back to the reality of their situation. Nasaf Rhullah entered with an even more exaggerated display of humility.

"Good morning, gentlemen," he beamed

"You were suitably entertained last night, I hope?"

"Too suitably," Medvedev groaned.

"Don't worry," smiled the little Iranian, "I have a very special cure for you."

Rhullah busily fused about the room before ushering the two suffering Russians downstairs to the waiting driver. This time, the journey was just a short distance to a private bathhouse. Emerging from an ornately tiled dressing room, the Russian's mouths dropped in unison at the site of so much unexpected opulence adorning the interior. Soft colours, rich dark wood, and delicately decorated lampshades were everywhere. Neat rows of mahogany benches filled the octagonal room and circular mirrors were set at intervals around the faceted walls. Having placed their bare feet upon the richly patterned carpet, they continued to marvel at the frieze of plaster cherubs and nymphs lining the pastel walls. Soothing music drifted through the various chambers, creating a magical feeling of freedom and relaxation. Rhullah explained the ritual of bathing, as in Russia or Turkey, was also considered a great institution in Iran. The group progressed from the hottest part of the steam room to a small, elegant pool richly tiled in a mosaic design of garlands. In niches at either end stood the golden statues of some long forgotten mythological gods, silently gazing down upon the bathers. Medvedev and Sautov lingered as long as they could. The hot water seemed to sweat all the poison out of their systems. The Russians doubts had been truly purged, as the car took them back to the hotel.

"When do we leave?" Sautov casually enquired as they returned to the room.

"Leave?" Rhullah asked with mock innocence.

"Leave for where?"

"For Gwadar, of course!" Sautov's inner reflexes made him suspicious.

"Oh ... nobody is *leaving*." The Iranian grinned, as he emphasised the last word.

"Have you forgotten already?"

"What?"

"Last night. You changed your minds ... and agreed to stay and help us."

"We did not!" Sautov retorted as he came threateningly close to Nasaf. The Iranian backed away before producing some papers from his pocket and flourishing them in the air.

"Here ..."

Sautov reached up and snapped the documents from between his fingers.

"These are copies of the new contracts which you have signed with my government last night, legally binding ... by Islamic law, of course. Do not forget, we still have the death penalty here..." Rhullah gave a nervous, but excited laugh "…usually by stoning. Oh, and by the way there were also signed resignations which have already been despatched to the project leaders at Gwadar."

Nasaf prudently took another cautionary step back while the two Russians avidly read the ominous small print.

"We also have some very interesting and revealing photographs of your entertainment last night." Rhullah spread a stack of stunningly clear photographs across the kitchenette worktop.

"Rather good, don't you think?"

Sautov instinctively raised his fist to strike the Iranian, but Medvedev's hand of restraint was just in time.

"You can't do this!" Sautov yelled.

"Oh, but I'm afraid I can," Nasaf Rhullah gathered his pictures in the silence that followed and drifted casually towards the door, running his fingers lightly across the furniture. His diplomatic mission of fostering enthusiasm for their special project had been a notable failure.

"Transport will arrive to take you to the launcher site in one hour: Be ready!"

The Iranian left, slamming the door behind him.

"What are we going to do?" Sautov asked.

"Whatever they want us to," Medvedev replied philosophically.

"You can't mean that, Yuri."

"I can!" Medvedev finally let go of his colleague.

"Look at the reality of our situation, Victor. We have entered this country illegally, we have signed those documents, they have those compromising photographs … it doesn't matter how."

"These missiles … they must be coming from the *Cherkassy*!"

"Maybe, Victor, just maybe. And do you honestly think they will allow us to leave here, alive, with that knowledge?"

"But we have to inform *someone*" Sautov's voice sounded desperate.

"Who?" Medvedev asked calmly with outstretched hands.

Sautov didn't answer, as the overall futility of their situation began to dawn on him. He sank heavily onto the bed and placed his head in his hands.

"I think I am too old for this kind of operation."

❖ ❖ ❖

Although it was still early winter, the midday sun was warm and invigorating, as they sat back in the open military vehicle taking them in a south-easterly direction away from Tehran. Gone was the friendly Mercedes driver. His replacement wore a distinctive insignia on the shoulder of his combat fatigues, proclaiming he was a member of the special Islamic Revolutionary Guard. The Russians sat squashed in between Nasaf Rhullah, another swarthy soldier reeking of garlic, and two officers from the previous night's entertainment. The whole group travelled in silence. They sped along the tarmac road, crossing several *qanat* irrigation canals, before heading out into the stony *Dasht-e-Kavir* desert, kicking up clouds of dust as they went. The deep brown hue of the stone and sand gave way to a variegated green patchwork of scrub and palms surrounding each oasis dotted along the wayside. Wild asses drinking their fill looked up with disinterest as the travellers passed. Bakhtiari nomads who had drifted down from the Zaqros Mountains, squatted in huddled groups by their low, pyramid shaped black tents near to the military vehicle's destination.

Camouflage netting spread out in all directions, covering the mobile rocket launchers as they nestled like some brooding, malevolent mythical beasts in a shallow *wadi* just beyond the gently undulating sand dunes surrounding the last oasis. They were sinister, obsolete and rusting – with the desert sands drifting into every mechanical part. Victor Sautov spent some time opening up every inspection hatch, fiddling with the controls and climbing all over the vehicles. He slammed a creaking driver's door in disgust, before stepping onto the back of a launcher to inspect the hydraulic hoses and systems designed to operate the launch ramp. The Iranians watched his every move, until he jumped down from the high vehicle and wiped his hands on the seat of his trousers. He shook his head and proclaimed conversion impossible. Nasaf Rhullah rushed forward. His eyes widened with anger as he furiously snapped his automatic pistol from its holster and placed the cold muzzle against Sautov's head. He looked menacingly towards Yuri Medvedev standing by the front of the launcher with the other members of the Iranian escort. Rhullah's complexion became mottled with rage and the veins on his temples and neck began to throb.

"We can do it!" an enigmatic grin creased Medvedev's face as his thoughts shifted mercurially.

"And, of *course*, you will," Rhullah grinned. Medvedev loosely spread his arms to acknowledge the hopelessness of their situation and shrugged his shoulders at Victor Sautov. Striking a deal with the devil was their only option.

"Yes … we will."

Rhullah pressed the gun more firmly, until Sautov closed his terrified eyes and nodded as well.

"Good!" the Iranian quickley re-holstered the weapon.

"Don't worry my friends: the great and glorious Islamic Republic will take care of you."

A short distance away, the Bakhtiari quietly tended to their animals, unaware of the dramatic scene being played out so close to their winter tents.

CHAPTER 8

Russia : St Petersburg

Neon sparks flashed intermittently from a broken sign swinging lazily above the Blue Parakeet Club on the corner of *Nalichnaya Ulitsa*. A light autumn drizzle was falling on the muddy wasteland car park that surrounded the isolated building. The short winter days were beginning to close in. After sunset, the skies had turned opaque lavender, emphasising the city skyline stretching in a low handsome dark-blue silhouette along the waterfront. The cheap rundown facade and Las Vegas style of the club seemed almost incongruous amongst the grey, shabby and forbidding buildings that towered over the neighbourhood. The whole area was flanked by endless rows of decaying factories and municipal depots, pouring out their undiluted effluent into the River Neva. It was a totally depressing area – an area dying of indifference and neglect. The time-worn hotels and clubs were run by local small-time *Mafiozniki*, who kept their beady eyes on the lucrative passenger liners that regularly docked at the Sea Terminal. This was nothing more than a fertile paradise for pimps, prostitutes and drug dealers.

Inside the Blue Parakeet, a raucous floor show was being belted out by six pretty, but well-built girls dancing seductively to a little number entitled "Around the World with you." They set off upon this imaginary journey by wearing snug blue and white striped sailors' jerseys in St Petersburg and gradually dispensing with their clothes as they progressed to warmer regions. One of the girls was an absolute stunner. She had flowing golden hair, voluptuous breasts and big blue eyes: every Georgian seated around the stage had transfixed his own sparkling dark eyes upon this vision of delight.

Over in a secluded corner, Valentin Tarasov sat alone. He had withdrawn to an almost empty bottle of vodka which stood on the table before him. He watched the show through eyes half closed from drink and fatigue. This latest image was a far cry from the sharp career naval officer who had so confidently entered the General headquarters building just four weeks earlier. Gone was the honour and dignity of a man who had been so respected and so proud of his profession; proud of who he was and more importantly, proud of the country he served. Valentin Tarasov no longer cared about these things. He despised the navy, but most of all he despised the very people who had wiped out an otherwise distinguished career. He detested what his country had become. Valentin Tarasov had watched with mounting dismay as Russia rapidly disintegrated during the past few years. Now their military impotence had been revealed for the whole world to see. The Russians were showing everything, talking openly about weapons capability, maintenance problems with ships, engines, personnel, recruitment, food and even down to the supply of toilet paper. The world had almost changed overnight – and yet change was bureaucracy's worst enemy, an expanding crisis to which it had the greatest difficulty in responding. If there were any genuine secrets left, Tarasov had yet to come across them. The low-ceilinged room swam with cigarette smoke and even the waiters looked drunk. Over in one of the booths someone had grabbed the blonde beauty from the floor show, and was trying to kiss her. Tarasov didn't notice. He was completely lost in his own private world – lost in his bitterness and hatred.

As the night wore on, all movement in and out of the club became a blur. Tarasov didn't even notice the tall, powerful, bearded figure of Boris Lukin, his former weapons officer from the *Cherkassy*, enter the premises and approach the bar. The barman looked up.

"Yolki Palki!" Knowing Boris Lukin's reputation from previous visits, the barman cursed his luck that Lukin had decided to come in just now. Lukin gruffley ordered a beer and drank slowly from the bottle, as he turned to survey the scene. Anyone who had worked with Boris Lukin before would have known that within seconds of opening the door he had already carefully evaluated the situation, noted every individual present and correctly assessed from which quarter the first trouble was likely to come – and in what form. Lukin seemed to be looking for someone, as he scanned the room.

"Valentin…" Despite the gloom of the club, Lukin couldn't fail to recognise the shadowy outline of his ex-Captain hunched over his drink. There was no response to his call. Lukin wiped his mouth with the back of his hand, grabbed another bottle from the bar, and crossed the room. He drew up a chair and sat at the table, opposite Valentin Tarasov.

"Captain…" Lukin reached over and placed his hand on Tarasov's arm. The Captain drew in a deep breath and looked up. He tried to make his eyes focus on the face swimming before him.

"Who are you?"

"Don't you recognise me? It's Lukin."

"Lukin? I thought you were dead."

"I'm lucky to be alive … but what happened to *you*?"

Tarasov sat back with his outstretched arms clutching the edge of the table and sighed. He reached up to rub his tired eyes and poured the rest of the vodka into his glass. Lukin called for another bottle.

"They discharged me … the bastards!" Tarasov said vehemently as he spat the very words from his mouth, and shook himself in an effort to clear his head.

"Me too!" Boris Lukin informed him as he stabbed a confirming thumb to his chest.

"That little liar Murashov … he swore things under oath. They *believed* him, Captain."

"They *wanted* to believe him," Tarasov laughed bitterly.

"They *had* to believe him!"

"What do you mean?"

"Don't you see, Boris? They needed a scapegoat – not just one – but several." Tarasov poured unsteadily from the fresh bottle as the two men consoled themselves about the deep injustice which had been inflicted upon them.

"How could the great Russian Naval Hierarchy be seen to make such a big mistake? How could they be openly blamed for an incident which could have turned out to be an even greater catastrophic consequence than Chernobyl?"

"Are you saying, Captain, that..."

"Yes my friend. We were offered up ... just like lambs to the slaughter."

"The bastards!" Lukin uttered through clenched teeth as he pounded the table with his balled fist and made the glasses jump.

"Murashov must have been well briefed – and well taken care of," the Captain asserted.

"But ... how could they do such a thing to us ... and why?"

"Oh come on Boris, don't be so naïve. Absolutely anything is possible in these turbulent days."

"But what is of even greater importance, is the fact that we've lost everything we ever believed in. We were nothing more than convenient acolytes to the system, merely offered for sacrifice upon the altar of expediency ... merely to save the already tarnished reputations of those in authority."

Both men fell silent, as they reflected upon the bitter irony of their unswerving patriotism. They were completely oblivious of a thin, almost emaciated looking man, watching from the shadows. The stranger was of middle-eastern appearance with tanned, leathery skin and a thick mop of jet-black hair.

Several smartly dressed Georgian *Mafiozniki* seated in one of the booths were becoming very loud. The group were all small, dark thick-set young men with wickedly handsome mediterranean faces and impeccable suits that had clearly been made abroad. One, a young man dressed in a smart Italian designer suit, left his sniggering colleagues and came over to the submariner's table and sat down. The sailors stopped talking and turned to look at the uninvited thug. He was barely eighteen.

"Get lost, you sea-tramps!" sneered the young man. The Barman was just in the middle of pouring a round of drinks when he glanced over to the trio. He put down the bottle, gripped the edge of the bar and screwed up his face when he saw the inevitable approaching.

"Easy, boys, I don't want any trouble."

"And who the hell are you?" Lukin wrinkled his nose as he fixed his gaze upon the insolent Georgian.

"None of your business, sailor." The boy snapped in reply as he kicked Boris Lukin's chair from under him.

"Do I take it we've got a problem here?" Lukin enquired as he sprawled across the floor.

"No sailor. You're the one that's got a fucking problem. My friends and I want this table, so push off."

"No. You push off," Valentin Tarasov retorted.

"We were here first."

"Do you know *who* you're talking to?" the boy rounded on the sailor and snarled menacingly.

"Yes, just some piece of shit that's floated up from the sewer!"

By now, several of the boy's gangster friends had sauntered over and surrounded the table. The two sailors were outnumbered four to one. Nasaf Rhullah shrank back into the shadows. Both Valentin Tarasov and Boris Lukin had been in many a dockside brawl, but on this occasion, they were far too drunk and their adversaries were far too young. Lukin, the younger and fitter of the two submariners, was the first to react.

"I can sure do without this," he kept thinking.

"I can *really* do without this. Especially tonight." Encouraged by the apparent ease with which their leader had put the big sailor down, one of the gangsters came over and tried to kick Boris Lukin in the ribs. Lukin saw it coming and turned on his side, allowing the full weight of the kick to land in the heavy folds of his jacket. Boris was starting to get angry and the moment he turned to take the kick, their luck finally ran out. Rolling over on to his back, Lukin surprised everybody by thrusting the heel of his shoe into the gangster's testicles, lifting the man clean off the ground. The man squealed like a stuck pig as he collapsed into a foetal position, clutching his wounded pride. Before the attackers realised what was happening, Boris was back on his feet, smashing the half-empty vodka bottle into the face of the young *Mafiozniki*. Valentin Tarasov staggered forward as he tried to intervene, but both men were quickly overpowered and beaten back to the ground, before being dragged struggling and bleeding, across the dance floor to be thrown out through a side-door and into the dark alley. The *Mafiozniki* thugs followed like lemmings, helping their unfortunate leader hold a scarlet-stained cloth to his torn face. The boy shrugged everyone aside as he drew a flick-knife from the belt of his bloodstained designer suit and faced up to the two sailors.

"Nobody hits me with a bottle," he snarled, with even more blood dripping through his fingers and down onto his Gucci shoes.

"Kill them, Anatoly!" came the unified shout from his friends.

Tarasov and Lukin struggled and tried to get up from the cold wet concrete. Each time they managed to crawl onto their knees, a gang member kicked them back down.

"Kill them, Anatoly!" the cry came again, then it became a vicious chant.

"Kill them! Kill them! Kill them!"

Anatoly cautiously circled the two sailors before approaching Tarasov, who for one frozen moment managed to lock eyes with his attacker.

"That's enough!" The voice had a strong middle-east accent and seemed to come from nowhere. Anatoly looked up frantically to scan the pervading darkness. He could see nothing, but nevertheless withdrew to the perceived safety of his friends.

"Who's there? Come out and you can have some too!"

Three dark shapes emerged from the shadows and faced the *Mafiozniki*, levelling silenced automatic pistols at the startled thugs. Before the gangsters had time to react, a sharp fusillade of bullets made a dull spitting sound as they ripped into the bodies of the young Georgians. Within seconds, every mobster lay dead or dying in the blood-spattered alley. The three assassins lowered their smoking weapons and calmly stood aside, allowing two other men to come forward. Nasaf Rhullah moved over and contemptuously rolled aside one of the corpses with his foot before reaching down to help Valentin Tarasov struggle to his feet. Sharif Hamad, the Iranian Naval Lieutenant who had been a special guest on the *Cherkassy* , went over to assist Boris Lukin.

"Who are you?" Tarasov enquired through the blood and mud which filled his mouth.

"A friend," replied Rhullah.

"Whoever you are," Tarasov held out his hand, "I am very grateful."

They shook warmly and Tarasov even managed a painful smile.

"Captain," Boris Lukin called, "Look!"

Tarasov staggered across to where his companion was being supported by one of the strangers.

"Are you alright, Boris?"

"Yes, *but look who it is*, Captain."

"Sharif? Tarasov peered quizzically at the vaguely familiar face beginning to focus before him, "Sharif Hamad?"

"Yes. It's really me, Captain."

"You escaped too. But this is absolutely incredible. It's fantastic … how?"

"I don't exactly know. But just before the *Cherkassy* went down, I and a few others had managed to make our way topsides. We had just climbed out through the sail access door when a wall of water swept across the deck. My head must have struck the hull and I was thrown unconscious from the submarine just before she sank. All I know is that I eventually woke up on board a Norwegian trawler. They said I'd been out cold for two days."

"But who else survived?" Tarasov was amazed at this unexpected turn of events.

"I don't know for sure. However, they did say there were no other survivors in the immediate area where they eventually fished me out. I had been tangled up in some loose ropes from an overturned life-raft before drifting into unconsciousness. Any longer in the sea and I would also have died," Hamad continued. "When I had recovered, they put me ashore and took me to the Iranian mission in Oslo. The rest was easy."

"But what are you doing *here* in St Petersburg?" Boris Lukin asked with outstretched arms.

At that point, Nasaf Rhullah interrupted.

"I'm sorry to break up this happy reunion gentlemen, but I really think we ought to get away from this place. We have our own transport standing by."

"Why don't you come with us?"

"But… where to?" Boris Lukin was still unsure, but nevertheless he was pleased to meet up with an old friend.

"Certainly somewhere much safer than here."

The two Russians hesitated and briefly looked at each other, before realising they were in no position to refuse such an offer. They quickly followed the Iranians out of the alley and scrambled into the back of a black limousine waiting nearby.

Valentin Tarasov turned and glanced out of the back window, just in time to see the three Iranian killers get into another vehicle, which closely followed them as they headed off in a north-easterly direction along *Maliy Prospekt*, towards the Petrograd Side.

CHAPTER 9

Israel : Jerusalem

A Mossad stretch limousine turned off *Ha-rav Herzog*, and passed by shade-giving yucca and fig trees along *Zalman Shneur* as it made its way to *Yad Vashem*. The driver pulled up on the south side of the memorial area. Benjamin Eshkol climbed out from the front passenger seat and was quickly followed, from the rear of the vehicle, by two other Mossad agents, David Weizman and Ruth Netanya. Eshkol was the most senior of the three. Having completed his National Service as a regular army captain on the West Bank and Golan Heights, his natural skills as an intelligence officer were quickly spotted, and as a consequence, he was seconded to the Israeli Secret Service. He was a tall man, approaching his late fifties, with a shock of greying hair swept back off his face to reveal a glistening bronzed forehead. He had the presence and bearing of a biblical warrior … a man who commanded instant respect. By contrast, his two colleagues were much younger; both in their early twenties. Weizman, a fresh-faced third year fast-lane Mossad professional was always anxious to prove himself, but still lacked adequate hands-on experience in the field. Ruth Netanya was not only beautiful – she was stunning. Ross Lombardi wasn't slow to notice this fact, as he emerged from the opposite side of the car. Netanya wore a neat formal business suit which clung to her voluptuous figure silhouetted against the early morning sun, and her face had the dark classical lines of a modern-day Salome.

   The American had arrived in Tel Aviv the previous night, along with his British counterparts. Although Ross Lombardi had crossed several time zones, the journey from London's Heathrow airport had been even longer and more tiresome for Peter Lawrence and Juliet

Lucas. Their flight had been grounded for several hours due to a technical fault. Upon emerging bleary eyed from the customs hall at Ben Gurion airport, they were met by a Mossad representative who drove them in silence, the sixteen kilometres or so to the Sheraton Tel Aviv Hotel, on *Hayarkon*. Ross Lombardi, Peter Lawrence and Juliet Lucas, a young hand-picked MI6 undercover agent on her fourth assignment, were scheduled to be guests of the Israeli Secret Service. Lawrence had barely spoken to Juliet since leaving London, and last night's atmosphere in the hotel had been a bit frosty, to say the least. Even the attractive international ambience of the Sheraton couldn't lift Lawrence's melancholy mood. The weary trio had just eaten at the Twelve Tribes restaurant when Lawrence suddenly announced he was going to retire early, leaving Juliet to experience any late-night entertainment in the company of a yawning Ross Lombardi.

The Mossad agents had decided to come over and make their first official contact with their British and American guests in the Sheraton's lobby at 06.00 hours that very morning. An early start was essential if they were to avoid the chaotic rush-hour traffic in this city of too many cars and hopelessly narrow streets. Following brief, but formal introductions, the Mossad people had subsequently spoken very little, as the car threaded its way out of the city and along *Arlosoroff* – towards the Holy Land's epicentre: Jerusalem. Now, just as the first probing shafts of sunlight began to herald a new day over Old Jerusalem, they sniffed and savoured the cool morning air as they stretched their travel stiffened limbs. The driver had dropped them off at *Har Hazikaron* which rises to the west of *Mount Herzl*. As he drove away, the group set off at a brisk pace along the *Avenue of the Righteous among the Nations* towards the Historical Museum. They hurried across a broad plaza being swept clean in preparation for the day, towards a building on the far side. The Israelis decided to wait outside. Their guests glanced at each other and hesitated, until they were reverently ushered into the gloomy *Hall of Names* where the names of all known Holocaust victims are inscribed. No one spoke. The party entered the hall in reverential silence and studied endless rows of plaques, each one engraved with the thousands of names, from so many nationalities, and so many cultures. Briefly stepping back into the early morning sunshine, they crossed over to the underground *Children's Memorial*, dedicated to the everlasting memory of the 1½ million young children and babies who were also killed in the Death Camps. Inside, they were surrounded by darkness, except for the myriad tiny pinpoints of light twinkling like stars. Each light representing the fleeting tragic life of a child.

Benjamin Eshkol gently nodded to himself. He thought he had glimpsed these hardened agents hastily wiping tears away as they approached. Perhaps it was caused by nothing more than fine dust and sand, swirling and eddying, as the groundsmen busily swept nearby. He had seen it all before. The whole experience was deeply moving. It had left such a profound and indelible impression, that everyone came away with a greater awareness of their own mortality… and this special place. Grey, like a day without sun, like a life without hope. A grey past – and a doubtful future. It was a truly symbolic site for an international meeting of special agents. Eshkol had deliberately arranged this private early morning visit – long before opening time for the general public. He wanted his guests to know the terrible price paid by his people…. even before the 1948 Proclamation of Independence. He wanted them to gain a much deeper appreciation than mere history. He wanted them to understand the real reasons as to why the Israelis would always defend this rightful heritage with their lives… and the very lives of their children.

Not a word was spoken. Everyone remained deep in thought, wrestling with their inner conscience, as they moved down to the car park and climbed back into the waiting limousine. The driver headed eastwards towards the Old City, along *Derekh Azza* and past the US Consulate. Some thirty minutes later, the party suddenly became engaged in animated discussions over the significance of their visit to *Yad Vashem*, when Ross Lombardi's hypnotic gaze fell upon Ruth Netanya. He was momentarily transfixed. This beautiful young woman displayed her fervent patriotic zeal with pride. A characteristic which deeply impressed the American. Like so many Israelis, Netanya possessed a driving compulsion to ensure the welfare and security of her country. She was resolutely determined to play her part by sharing the burden of responsibility in keeping her country afloat, despite being surrounded by violent seas of hostility on every side. Lombardi admired her commitment, but quickly reminded himself that his own government's objectives and policies did not necessarily line up with those of Israel. The car passed the Taxation Museum and continued along *Mamillah* before entering the Old City through the Jaffa Gate. Upon arrival, they stepped out in *David Street* and stood upon a massive subterranean layer cake of long dead civilisations dating back to Neolithic times: Assyrian to Hellenic to Roman to Byzantine... and in more recent times, the Old City had been taken as one of the prized spoils as a consquence of the Six Day War in 1967.

"Come. It's been a long morning, I think everyone will be ready for lunch," Benjamin Eshkol promised as he shepherded his group together on the pavement.

"Good! I'm famished!" Juliet couldn't believe she'd said that and blushed after such an involuntary exclamation. A brief silence followed, until the tension was broken, when everyone burst out laughing. Even Peter Lawrence couldn't resist a wry smile ... perhaps his young colleague wasn't such bad company after all. Her spontaneous naivety had certainly managed to warm up the atmosphere of this meeting, if nothing else.

Benjamin Eshkol threaded his way through the milling throng of shoppers, tourists and hagglers as he led the agents towards a restaurant renowned as a hangout for government officials. They proceeded to a small private room on the first floor which looked out onto the Church of the Holy Sepulchre. Eshkol stood tall and dignified, as he explained to his captive audience the historical background to this striking edifice of golden stone which dominates the Old City. He went on to confirm it was both the physical and spiritual heart of the Christian Quarter.

The initial coolness between the agents had disappeared since Lucas's impulsive outburst and lunch proved to be a lively affair. The conversation, during several courses of *tres fine* French cuisine, remained on the matter in hand, but a sense of relaxed informality seemed to have been served up with the *sauce bordelaise* as the local wines sparkled in the shafts of sunlight streaming through the window. Benjamin Eshkol smiled, things were at last going as planned.

"Even a mouse with sneakers on couldn't move out there, without us knowing about it," Ross Lombardi gestured with his fork as he spoke through a mouthful of *entrée*.

"You're absolutely certain about that?" David Weizman asked sarcastically, "Because let me assure you Mr Lombardi, we don't intend to just sit back as we did in the Gulf War, when Saddam Hussein was allowed to rain scud missiles down upon us with impunity – and all just as a matter of *political expediency*."

"Trust me!" mumbled Lombardi as he swallowed the *entrée* and wiped his mouth.

Weizman was not convinced.

Benjamin Eshkol carefully placed both elbows on the table, clasped his steepled hands and leaned forward.

"This discussion is merely academic. A loss such as the *Cherkassy* does not remain a secret for very long. Our sources have already ascertained what happened to Captain Tarasov and the rest of the crew. Furthermore, we have received disturbing reports about increased activities by some Russian technicians in Tehran. It can only be a matter of time."

Everyone lapsed into silence, much disturbed by what had just been said.

"Moscow is in absolute chaos," Eshkol continued, "Tarasov and Lukin have failed to turn up for several days. This has made Washington nervous. It has made us all nervous. We are now desperate to ascertain why such important men have disappeared. I know, I know, it could all be terribly amusing – if the stakes were not so high." Eshkol unlocked his hands and turned them palms up for emphasis.

Peter Lawrence was the first to respond as he took a sip of a light Chardonnay. "We understand the Russians have observers over the wreck-site."

"I don't trust the Russians!" Ruth Netanya's abrupt statement focused everyone's attention.

"I never have and I never will," she continued, stern-faced.

No, no … it's not just their own people…" Peter Lawrence desperately tried to assuage her suspicions, "…its a multi-national thing. There are Finns and Norwegians along as well."

"I don't trust them either!" The Mossad woman snapped. Lawrence turned pale and sensed he was moving into dangerous territory. He dabbed his forehead with a handkerchief, even though the air-conditioned restaurant was colder than a morgue.

"Ruth is perhaps being a little extreme," Benjamin Eshkol apologised. She was about to reply when Eshkol silenced her with a glance.

"Her entire family was wiped out in the Holocaust, with the sole exception of her mother, who eventually made it to Israel."

"I'm so sorry," Juliet Lucas reached across to touch the back of Netanya's hand.

"Don't be!" came the abrupt retort, as her hand was immediately withdrawn. Peter Lawrence blanched as an air of coolness once more descended over the group, accompanied by a silence that seemed to last for an age.

"Look, we know the Iranians are desperate to get their hands on a nuclear capability," David Weizman said at length, as he lit up a cigarette and blew smoke into the air. "They've been trying to get the Russians to play ball for a long time."

"So?" Ross Lombardi asked the question without taking his eyes off Netanya.

"So … it's not just us here in Israel, you know. The entire world is at stake."

"The Russians ain't that stupid."

"Then why were there Iranians on that submarine?"

"We've already explained."

No! It's too much of a coincidence. If the Islamic Fundamentalists get hold of those missiles…"

"They can't!"

"How can you be so sure?"

"You don't seem to understand the Fundamentalist organisation. I've already told you."

Voices were becoming raised between Weizman and Lombardi.

"Enough!" Benjamim Eshkol silenced both men with a curt wave of his hand. He continued in a low, calm voice.

"Look… we cannot rule out the possibility of Iran making some sort of a salvage attempt on the nuclear missiles."

"It's too late in the year, even if they had…" Peter Lawrence tried to intervene, but he too was cut short.

"Wait until I finish!" Eshkol gave the Englishman a severe look.

"We must consider the very worst possible scenario. If they *did* try to recover the missiles. What could be done about it? That's all I'm trying to ask."

"OK, OK." Ross Lombardi sat on the edge of his chair.

"Let's say you're right. The Iranians try some far-fetched salvage op. First of all, everyone in the whole goddamn world would know about it. And, secondly, even if they managed to get the missiles back to the Ayatollahs, they don't have anyone who knows what to do with the goddamn things. They'd probably end up blowing themselves from here to goddamn eternity!"

Lombardi slid back into his chair and allowed his attention to drift once more towards Ruth Netanya. She seemed oblivious to his stare, as all three Mossad agents went into a huddle and conversed amongst themselves in Hebrew. Peter Lawrence let out a deep sigh, as he poured another glass of wine for Juliet Lucas, who flashed a coquettish smile his way. He smiled back. Perhaps this wouldn't be such a boring assignment after all.

Benjamin Eshkol took his two companions to one side. They continued to speak in animated tones and gesture wildly with their arms. Their guests looked at each other, shrugged and asked the waiter to bring another bottle of wine. After about fifteen minutes, the Israelis rejoined the group. Ruth Netanya looked as solemn as ever. David Weizman was clearly irritated, but did not speak. Benjamin Eshkol glared around at the others.

"We have agreed to accept your assurances … for now." He called the waiter and gave him a credit card of some sort.

"We will report this to our superiors – but we must insist on being involved closely in all monitoring operations!"

"Well that's OK with the good old U S of A," Lombardi rose to his feet and hitched up his slacks. Peter Lawrence nodded his own approval and reached over to withdraw the chair for Juliet Lucas.

"Come my friends," Eshkol broke into a smile as his card was returned, "... we have much work to do."

CHAPTER 10

Denmark : Esbjerg

Rippling curtains of rain drifted across the harbour and lashed against the dirty opaque windows of the *Jylland* bar, perched on the end of a small pier in the old fishing quarter of Esbjerg. Pungent smells of fish and diesel wafted everywhere, with a light rainbow film of oil floating and swirling on soupy puddles dotted along the quayside. In darkness, it was a forbidding area of the waterfront, where isolated shadowy figures made their way to and from the bar. A solitary black dog wandered aimlessly along the pier and cocked its leg against the tyre of a lorry parked alongside one of the warehouses and claimed its territory. The scrawny mongrel moved on and raised its head to sniff the air as it approached the glowing entrance of the *Jylland*. It began barking, its back legs fixed to the ground and ready for action.

A short stocky figure draped in a reefer coat with turned up collar, peaked cap and sea-boots paused and snarled back at the dog. The figure hunched his shoulders and braced himself in readiness for the hot swirl of cigarette smoke being sucked out of the open door and past him into the cold night air. A babble of many tongues in heated conversation greeted the sailor and the clinking of glasses amid the dimmed lighting and shabby figures confirmed this must be a likely place for a suitable encounter.

Among the rusty, salt-encrusted ships and boats docked that night was the *Norse Warrior*. Her master, Bjorn Ramuldssen, together with the rest of the crew were taking a much overdue run ashore to make up for their spartan time at sea. The *Jylland* was typical of the hard drinking places to be found in this part of the harbour. It was old and built of roughly hewn granite blocks and driftwood, with nets, floats, harpoons, lobster pots and other nautical artefacts adorning the walls and ceiling. Upended lifeboats were cut in half and fixed back-to-back with copper topped tables set before them, to form snug drinking booths. The air was filled with the whiff of oakum and spirit. Bottles smashed against the beer-stained floor, as the crew danced and sang with the local prostitutes. Many of this rag-bag of misfits and outcasts were wanted by the authorities in a variety of countries around the world. Ramuldssen was always casual about papers. He didn't ask too many questions when men signed up to serve on board the *Norse Warrior* – just so long as they obeyed orders and kept their noses out of his business.

It was getting late and most of the sailors had drunk far too much. No-one noticed a gentle rustling of the door curtain behind the bar as a scruffy black mongrel pushed its way through. The dog shook its head and looked around at the noisy groups, before sauntering over to one of the prostitutes sitting on the lap of a drunken sailor. In all this excitement and revelry, the dog sported a huge throbbing erection and mounted the girl's leg with a grip like a limpet. With her top lip wrinkled in disgust, the unfortunate harlot let out a heart-rending shriek and burst into tears. The sailor made a half-hearted drunken swipe as he attempted to brush the randy animal aside, but the prospect of a sudden orgasm only increased the dog's determination to hang on. No amount of shaking would move him. Everyone burst into uncontrollable gales of laughter at this unexpected floor-show. The dog reached his climax, pinned back his ears and slunk away to safety. Several minor fights and arguments were breaking out, mainly concerning the "Ladies of the Night' and who was going to sleep with whom. Judging by the state of the men, it was clear the women wouldn't have a great deal of work to do for their money. Most of the sailors would be nursing sore heads, only to find their pockets had been picked. This suited Ramuldssen; it would force them to return and sign up with him for another trip – at least those who hadn't been murdered or arrested. In any event they could always be replaced.

Bjorn Ramuldssen was a giant of a man, over seven feet tall and weighing in at around three hundred pounds, give or take a pound or two. He scowled from behind a full red beard with his grizzled face and gimlet eyes shaded by a wide-brimmed fedora, from the band of which protruded the multi-coloured tail-feather of a Sumatran parrot. Ramuldssen had been a sailor all his life. He was born amongst the derelict shipyards of Fano Island, and ever since his earliest childhood, he'd sailed his own boat from the silted-up harbour and out into the violent waters of the North Sea. His mother was one of life's endless casualties, a water-front prostitute who had aged rapidly beyond her years. He never knew who his real father was, even though he'd had many "uncles'. They used to capture the young Ramuldssen's imagination by telling wild and fanciful stories of the sea and exotic lands across the far horizon. Ramuldssen's first deep water experiences before the age of sixteen were as a deckhand on a fishing trawler above the Arctic Circle. Following a brief but dubious spell in the Danish Navy, he moved on to acquire his own salvage boat before he reached his thirtieth birthday. Having achieved one of his life-long ambitions, he was now the proud master of the *Norse Warrior* quietly moored alongside the pier. He was prepared to go anywhere and take any risk … as long as the price was right.

Bjorn Ramuldssen ignored all the fighting, singing and dancing as he poured himself another glass of Jamaican rum. He sat in one of the "lifeboat' alcoves at the end of a long bar, from where he could both see the front entrance and a curtained doorway leading to the back of the establishment. Seated either side of him were two Pakistani men dressed in expensive casual wear – and looking extremely uneasy. Sitting opposite the trio and grinning like a Cheshire cat, was Nasaf Rhullah. The Pakistanis and the Iranian sipped at their iced tomato juice spiced with Tabasco.

"Drink up, my friends. Drink up!" boomed Ramuldssen in his thick Norse accent. He raised his grimy, discoloured glass and banged it against the others, almost smashing them to pieces. The Pakistanis winced as they gulped the spicy liquid, but Nasaf Rhullah drank his down in one.

"Mr Ramuldssen…" one of the Pakistanis ventured nervously.

"Call me Captain!" Ramuldssen struck the man a playful blow on the back, which almost sent his teeth sliding across the table.

"Yes... thank you Captain. So, you don't think it's too late in the year for our little operation?"

"No, no ... not too late" Ramuldssen confirmed as he bent forward until his face hovered over their glasses.

"Nevertheless..." Nasaf Rhullah dropped his voice as he joined the huddled canopy, "we would like to get under way as soon as possible."

"We start tomorrow if you like," Ramuldssen grunted, "or, at least as soon as this miserable crew of sea-dogs sobers up!"

"That won't be necessary," Rhullah sat back and lit up a cigarette as he reached over and poured the last of the rum into Ramuldssen's glass.

"We can wait until you're properly equipped. But, what if there *is* ice?"

"The *Norse Warrior* can cope with even the thickest floes," Ramuldssen boasted. "She is a good vessel. A strong vessel. It will be alright, I know the area well."

"There might be..." the other Pakistani hesitated as he looked towards Nasaf Rhullah, "trouble. Other people are also after the gold."

"We can take care of ourselves," grinned Ramuldssen as he waved his great hand for another bottle to be brought to the table. "We have always been more than a match for many a modern day pirate."

"And your crew?" Rhullah looked doubtfully round the bar.

"Yes, look at them. They may be drunk now, but when they sober up they will be snapping like hungry wolves."

"Ah, but how can we be sure you will be able to successfully complete this mission?"

"The *Norse Warrior* may not be the prettiest ship afloat, but she has certainly become well known for her regular salvage trade in these waters." Bjorn Ramuldssen gave a knowing wink and tapped the side of his nose with his index finger.

"It really sounds as if you're our man." Nasaf Rhullah beamed whilst his extended hand was vigorously shaken by the Norse giant. Ramuldssen released his grip and again clapped the Pakistanis on their backs before proceeding to pour more rum into his filthy glass.

"Drink! Drink up my Paka friends. I like you Pakas very much, you give me plenty work..."

Behind the wooden booth, a sailor in a reefer coat, peaked cap and sea-boots who hailed from the town of Carrickfergus in Northern Ireland, pressed his ear against the boarding. The sailor heard, in his unfocussed brain, Ramuldssen talking to his "Paka" friends and the Irishman's interest was immediately aroused.

The group went back into a huddle as Bjorn Ramuldssen spread a chart and other papers across the table. He began to trace the intended course for the *Norse Warrior*, out of Esbjerg and up the Norwegian coast as far as the North Cape. From there they would head eastwards into the Barents Sea, rounding the Northern Peninsula, but taking care to keep outside of Russian waters until they came to the salvage site off Kolskiy Zaliv.

"Why is this gold so hot?" Ramuldssen stroked his chin.

"Because it belongs to Russia," the first Pakistani confidently informed him.

"It is in international waters?"

"Yes. It was aboard a German submarine which was sunk during the Second World War."

"But the gold was definitely Russian?" Ramuldssen queried again.

"Plundered by the Germans."

"And the Russians want it back?"

"Of course!"

"Then why don't *they* salvage it for themselves?" Ramuldssen slammed a huge balled fist upon the table, making each of them reach out to steady his glass. The Pakistanis were the slowest to react, and cursed in their own tongue as liquor and tomato juice spilled off the table and onto their expensive clothes. The Irish sailor stirred behind the booth.

"Because they don't know exactly where it is," the second Pakistani laughed nervously as he wiped the deep red stain spreading across his trousers and tried to defuse the situation.

"And I presume you do?"

"Otherwise…" Nasaf Rhullah permitted himself a sly grin as he interjected, "we wouldn't be here, talking to you, would we?"

The Iranian liked an audience that didn't question the substance of his theories, nor apply pressure when he was formulating his strategies.

"No ... no you would not," Ramuldssen gave a stifled chuckle to himself as he began to carefully skim over the sheets again.

"Very well, my friends. In that case we must come back via the west coast of Ireland before we continue on down to our destination in North Africa."

"But *why* such a long way round?"

"Because the North Sea and English Channel are crowded ... and constantly patrolled. If we were challenged, and anyone should come after us, we would not be able to shake them off. Too many customs vessels and too many police, you understand?"

"Yes, I see."

"The other route will take a bit longer, perhaps a few extra days, but we will be standing well out into the international waters of the Atlantic."

Rum was liberally sloshed into Ramuldssen's smeary glass, as the men embarked upon their umpteenth toast to continued success with their salvage mission. Meanwhile, behind the upended lifeboat, the little Irish sailor staggered to his feet and made his way unsteadily towards the public telephone and closed the door behind him. As he fumbled to insert more coins, his unsteady finger had just finished tracing the many digits of the number, when he heard a familiar voice on the other end of the line.

"Is that you, Sean?"

"It is," came the faint reply

"Who's this?"

"It's Michael ... listen. Listen very carefully..."

CHAPTER 11

Iran : Gulf of Oman

T HE RUSSIANS LISTENED TO THE STONES CRUNCHING noisily under the heavy tyres and kept peering through the dirty windscreen of the armoured car as it approached the cluster of tents. They noticed a solitary red and white pennant fluttering at the centre of the encampment from the top of a black *Hamadan* tent. The dry Makran air tasted of salt and shafts of sunlight glanced off the shimmering desert. Valentin Tarasov and Boris Lukin descended from the dust-encrusted vehicle which had just brought them all the way from Zahedan, capital of Baluchistan, and stretched their tired legs. Their tortuous journey to this hilly south-eastern area of Iran which borders Pakistan had been a difficult challenge. It was remote, uninhabited and inhospitable, consisting of wild desert terrain, which gradually gave way to the sweeping foothills of the Makran.

A scattering of small towns gleamed like polished ivory in this hostile landscape. It formed an endless stretch of dried and broken earth, with clouds of sand and dust eddying throughout the encampment. To one side of the tent, several of Sharif Hamad's countrymen knelt on prayer mats, as they faced towards the Holy City of Mecca. Each man bowed his head in supplication as they offered the second of their five daily devotions. Hamad turned his weathered face toward the skies. It was a wise face, burnished by the blistering heat and the genetic years of nomadic life. His mind was focused on the mission, his destiny and his faith.

Ever since his earliest childhood the Koran had impressed upon him the coming of Judgement Day – the final fulfilment. Hamad reflected upon those who lived according to the holy words and as such will be joined by all the faithful in Paradise. The Russians were glad of the rest and waited in the shade of the armoured car. They were not far from the coast and only about sixty kilometres from the border. A hint of brine hovered in the cool desert air, reassuring the Russian sailors, before they ducked to enter the command tent through a flap being held open by a smiling Sharif Hamad. Inside, brightly coloured carpets lay strewn across the sandy floor and a simple meal of kebabs and rice was spread before them. The militiamen remained on guard, taking up their positions outside the tent. Tarasov and Lukin had been flown into Shiraz from St Petersburg, with brief stopovers at Samara and Ashkhabad. Their hosts had behaved impeccably, giving them anything they desired – and some things they didn't.

The Russians were then flown in a small twin-engined plane to an unmarked desert runway near Zahedan, where they were met by the armoured vehicle assigned to bring them to this clandestine rendezvous in the desert hills. Their constant companions during this final stage of the journey had been a couple of heavily armed Hamas militiamen accompanied by Sharif Hamad, who acted as interpreter and attended to their every need. Seated on rough camelskin cushions inside the tent were several turbaned men, who were introduced to the Russians as "Government Officials'. Seated beside them, and shoving handfuls of rice into his mouth, was Rem Bukato. He smiled over the edge of the bowl. He seemed to be expecting the arrival of his fellow officers from the *Cherkassy*. Valentin Tarasov and Boris Lukin were stunned to see Bukato. They stood, open-mouthed, before rushing across to embrace their colleague as he put down the bowl and rose to his feet.

"Bukato!" Valentin Tarasov kissed his Executive Officer on both cheeks and held him at arms length. "You survived?"

"Only just!" Bukato pointed to a deep scar across his forehead.

"They dismissed you too?"

"Everyone who survived."

"The bastards! Those men were good sailors. Loyal to the Motherland."

"But what are *you* doing *here*?" Boris Lukin enquired, embracing the young man less eagerly than his Captain.

"The same as you, my friend," came the smiling reply.
"Oh really… and what might that be?"
"Please gentlemen…" Sharif Hamad interrupted and beckoned for them to be seated. One of the turbaned officials rose to his feet and spoke directly to the Russians in *Farsi*.
"He says we intend to recover the nuclear missiles from your sunken submarine," Sharif Hamad interpreted.
"I knew it!" Tarasov clapped his hands together as if vindicated in some way.
"Shhh!" Sharif Hamad hissed. "Do not interrupt!"
The official continued speaking, allowing polite interjections for interpretation by Hamad.
"The missiles will be taken from the *Cherkassy*… and transferred to an Iranian submarine."
Boris Lukin laughed out loud at such a wild proposition, but was immediately silenced by a frowning Sharif Hamad.
"Our submarine will be specially adapted to carry the missiles," he continued, "They will be transported by sea to a safe destination and from there to Libya."
"And just where *is* this safe destination?" Valentin ventured to ask, without invitation. He did not need the services of Sharif Hamad to interpret the reply.
"*Irlande!*" The official continued with his lengthy dialogue, while Hamad translated for the Russians, confirming the final stage of this audacious operation would be to fly the missiles from Libya to Iran. The official concluded his address and sat cross-legged on one of the cushions. He gestured with open arms, in a manner which seemed to invite questions. All three Russians began to babble at once. Sharif Hamad raised his hands for silence before allowing Valentin Tarasov to go first.
"It's impossible! The area is being constantly monitored by Russian and American surveillance … not to mention many others. You'll be spotted before you even get anywhere near to the Barents Sea."
The turbaned official again rose to his feet and explained the part to be played by Bjorn Ramuldssen's decoy salvage vessel. The Russians considered this latest statement to be equally preposterous.

"And just how do you propose to remove the missiles from the *Cherkassy* and transfer them to your vessel ... that is assuming you are not blown out of the water?" Boris Lukin smirked.

"We were hoping you would be able to tell us that" Hamad retorted, his face set in a mask of deadly seriousness. Lukin laughed and threw his hands into the air. He rose to his feet and ran his fingers through his tousled hair as he paced round the large tent.

"The firing mechanisms are still armed!" he shouted.

"Then we will disarm them, but with your help of course," Sharif replied calmly and coldly.

"It's winter up there. Have you any idea how cold it gets?" Rem Bukato enquired.

"No idea whatsoever," came the blunt reply.

"The missiles will still be sealed in their fibreglass canisters. However, they could be released ... possibly by using flotation bags." Boris Lukin was musing, almost persuading himself whilst stroking his chin in the process.

"Good!" Sharif Hamad smiled, "Then that is how we will do it."

" But what about the cold?" Rem Bukato repeated loudly.

"We will use our own divers."

"Maybe. But I am still the most important person who will have to get back on board the *Cherkassy*!" Boris Lukin exclaimed as he stabbed his thumb into his puffed out chest to emphasise the point. "I am the only one who knows *all* the procedures."

"Of course you will." Hamad's smile returned. The turbaned officials gave a benign smile and rose to their feet, jabbering away in *Farsi* and kissing the confused Lukin.

"Wait!" Valentin Tarasov shouted, bringing the premature celebrations to an abrupt halt. The Iranians stood still, looking curiously towards him.

"Do you really understand just how sophisticated the SS-N-21 is ... and more importantly, how it operates?" Tarasov had their attention.

"Let me tell you. During the first thirty seconds of flight, the missile runs through a series of internal checks and arming sequences. If the slightest failure is detected on any of the computer logic circuits it would cause the weapon to shut down. However, if everything is validated, the computer software initiates the next command – to light the end of the solid rocket motor. The missile will then fly along its chosen trajectory for a further eight seconds before the rocket motor finally cuts out. When the missile peaks, it hurtles back earthwards, with the solid rocket motor being blown off by twelve explosive bolts as it descends to 700 metres. At this altitude, the underside intake diffuser is deployed to ram air into the axial compressor. As the compressor's speed builds up, kerosene jet fuel is pressurised into the fuel lines.

This is then mixed with hot air entering through the combustion chamber where it is ignited. These hot gasses are then forced through the turbine to keep the compressor rotating during the flight. The supersonic velocity created by these exhaust gasses thrust the missile into its next phase. Small fins and horizontal wings become extended amidships to pull the missile out into level flight. Hopefully, just in time. If all has gone well, the missile will continue towards its target at 800 kilometres per hour; following the natural terrain at an altitude of only 12 metres. Apart from all these overwhelming technical difficulties, and don't forget the cold, there are still other complex security procedures necessary for the actual launch of cruise missiles and nuclear weapons."

"Do you…and your Executive Officer know these procedures Captain?" Sharif asked.

"Of course, but…"

"Good. Then it's alright." Sharif Hamad smiled once more and turned again to his superiors.

"No its not alright!" Tarasov shouted, "You still don't seem to fully understand. It's just not that simple. We have no way of knowing the extent of radiation contamination. Anyone who boards the wreck without proper protection could be going to certain death!"

"We will provide whatever protection is necessary, Captain."

"The sophisticated surveillance technology trained on the site will not be fooled by some rust-bucket Danish salvage ship."

"That is a chance we are prepared to take."

"Well, it's a chance I am *not* prepared to take!" Valentin Tarasov looked towards the other Russians. They all nodded in agreement. The turbaned officials didn't need translations to understand this latest outburst and frowned quizzically at Sharif Hamad, mopping his brow and looking nervously towards the tent-flap.

"Gentlemen, gentlemen…" he pleaded. "Look, why not at least come and see our submarine? We would certainly appreciate your professional opinions."

The Russians looked from one to another and then towards the tent-flap. They were fairly sure what would happen if they refused.

"Please gentlemen. What have you got to lose?"

That was precisely what they didn't know. At length, Valentin Tarasov shrugged his shoulders.

"Why not?" His tone was resigned.

"Why not indeed?" Sharif repeated. Beaming smiles re-appeared on the faces of the officials as they stepped outside the tent for their return trip to the coastal town of Humendan.

❖ ❖ ❖

Several huge 100 ton travelling cranes towered over the flat and monotonous coastal skyline. Horizontal shot-blasting machines turned in the steel shops. The slipways buzzed with the frenzied activities of the shipyard workers. They looked completely lost against the broad backdrop of the graving dock. Work was being carried out on several vessels. Away in the distance, the aft superstructure of a giant oil-tanker stood shrouded in scaffolding in one of the dry docks. Progressing alongside, was the re-fitting of two recently acquired outdated frigates and the re-painting of a cargo ship which operated under a dubious flag of convenience.

This place was so big the Russians were amazed it wasn't on any maps – at least not on any official ones.

They had been indulged with the limited comforts of Humendan the previous night. The submariners had been impressed with their hosts generous hospitality. After the almost casual and indifferent manner in which they had been treated in Russia , it was certainly a pleasant change to discover there were others in the world who still appreciated their talents and abilities.

Sharif Hamad's driver took them along the precarious edge of the dockside, dodging between the cranes and forklift trucks, derricks and giant carriers. The Russians sat in silence. They began to feel different. This was no primitive makeshift yard from the last century, as they expected. This was a fully equipped, ultra-modern dock, with all the latest technological equipment. Miles of gantries and scaffolding rose alongside the unfinished ships silhouetted against the sky and the deafening staccato noise of riveting, welding and cutting reverberated in the still morning air. Pungent fumes from oxy-acetylene and molten iron wafted everywhere and filled their nostrils. The frenetic shouts and calls of the hundreds of workers made an indecipherable sound. Their vehicle came to a halt at a security gate close to the supertanker that they had spotted earlier.

Armed guards were everywhere. Once security clearance had been completed, they were allowed to proceed towards the tanker, passing jumbled piles of twisted metal and builders debris, recently dusted with fine sand that had drifted in from the desert. The car became dwarfed like some child's toy as it pulled up alongside an access gantry rising from the dock and up the sheer black side of the *Konari* towards her main deck towering above. Everyone climbed out. The Russians sauntered over to the edge of the dock and peered down into the dark abyss. The huge bulk of the ship was squatting on support blocks arranged transversally across the sunken floor of the dry dock. Intermittent torrents of water shot straight out from holes in her sides and fell in lazy arcs towards the darkened void below. Shadowy workmen scurried about and sent streams of sparks flying, as their grinders worked back and forth across the hull plating. Above the general bedlam and dockyard cacophony, Sharif Hamad motioned for them to follow him as he began to ascend the gantry.

Towards the aft section of the supertanker, everyone entered the hallowed realms of officer territory through an oval opening that had been left when the door had been swung back against the superstructure. After a brief introduction to Captain Ramsar and his officers, the bemused Russians were ushered through to the lower decks where they were escorted along a narrow corridor humming with machinery some two decks below. As the party approached a low sealed doorway formed into one of the transverse bulkheads, two armed guards appeared from the shadows on either side. Sharif Hamad stared impassively forward as one of the guards carefully compared his likeness with the solemn photograph imprinted on his ID card, before allowing the party to pass.

The group stepped over the high threshold and into a twilight zone where they stood on a high- level steel lattice catwalk, running the full length of what had been the ship's main central oil storage tank.

"YOLKI PALKI!" exclaimed Rem Bukato.

The others leaned on the handrail and looked down in wonderment as Boris Lukin sucked at the fetid air that had built up within the huge chamber and let out a long low whistle.

Once their eyes had become accustomed to the subdued lighting, they began to make out the distinct humpbacked outline of a Russian Delta III nuclear ballistic submarine perched in the lower hold of the tanker, like some ominous black trophy on display. Tarasov knew that all Deltas were actually enlarged versions of the Yankee class, but modified to carry bigger missiles with an even greater range. The double hull of the submarine measured 524.9 feet in length with a beam of 39.4 feet and a free-draft of 28.5 feet. She displaced 13,250 tons submerged and was capable of travelling at 24 knots. Power was supplied by two pressurised water-cooled reactors and two geared steam turbines designed to deliver 50,000 shaft horsepower to the twin five bladed propellers. More than enough power to light up the whole of Tehran. Tarasov knew the vessels well.

They were super-smooth in the water and, despite the additional equipment now being fitted, they were still considered stealthy enough to evade even the most modern detection devices. Experience had taught Tarasov that previous Western attempts at detection from water, land *and* the air had almost always failed. This class of submarine had proved to be an excellent and reliable surveillance tool during the heightened years of the Cold War. They were considered to be extremely reliable. Of the fourteen Delta class submarines built, not one had ever been lost in operation since entering service in 1976. This was impressive indeed! The Delta III carried a full crew of one hundred and thirty, with two rows of eight missiles set vertically abaft the sail. She was fitted out with the very latest sophisticated active/passive attack and search sonar, plus facilities to quickly deploy passive linear arrays.

"I see you are suitably impressed," remarked Hamad as he leant back against the sweating side of the tanker and folded his arms.

"But … how?" replied Tarasov with an incredulous sweep of his arm.

"We had the tanker modified by our Korean friends in Hungnam. They fitted clam-shell doors to the bow and reinforced the midship section to form a separate command centre for our submarine. When the works were completed, the tanker underwent her sea trials to the east of Vladivostok where we met up with some of our friends from the Russian Pacific Fleet and took the Delta on board. Come, let us go down and see how the work is progressing. Who knows … you may even see some of your old comrades!"

The men paused briefly to watch a huge crane lowering a periscope into position within the conning tower. Sharif Hamad exuded his usual confidence. But what Tarasov feared most was the possibility of events spinning out of control. With the Iranians having acquired such an awesome capability it not only troubled Tarasov, it intruded upon all his hopes and violated his ambitions. His only hope of salvation for the time being was to comply with their wishes.

Hamad reached over and grabbed a hardhat, indicating for the Russians to follow his example, before proceeding past another sentry and crossing a narrow gangplank stretching out onto the cluttered deck of the Holy Islamic submarine *Zarand*. They continued towards the forward hatch, a circular hole penetrating the surface of the deck, and descended a long vertical steel ladder into the main control room. All three Russian submariners felt an electrifying surge of adrenalin as they stepped on board. It was like being in the company of an old familiar friend.

They felt alive, useful, fulfilled. This was where they belonged. They were home!

The submarine's Captain approached and saluted.

"Sir, I invite you to inspect the ship."

Hamad visibly stiffened and wearily returned the salute.

"No, Captain. I do not have time for an official tour. I merely need to show our Russian friends how work is progressing. And besides, I know this boat intimately. I will assume that it is combat ready. Dismissed."

Captain Gabrik was clearly taken aback. He blinked to clear his thoughts before slowly lowering his salute, followed by a self-conscious nod of acknowledgement. Declining a ship's tour with the Captain was an insult. The Captain wondered just who these Russians were and what was the significance of the forthcoming mission.

The Russians were allowed to roam freely all over the submarine, from the Captain's state room to the modified rear torpedo room – and from the "people tank' to the sonar room. The aft torpedo room bulkhead had been specially strengthened and fitted with air-locks to form a compression chamber. Two separate access ducts linked the improvised chamber back to the last pair of missile silos. They would be used to deploy the salvage divers into the Barents Sea once they had arrived at their destination. Thirty crew-members specifically assigned for diving duties would have to live within this cramped chamber. They would start breathing helium before being subjected to a gradual increase in pressure over a period of several days, as they approached the wreck of the *Cherkassy*. At first glance, the inside of the submarine appeared to be in a state of utter chaos.

Military and civilian technicians worked feverishly alongside each other on the numerous pieces of electronic equipment. Instrument panels lining the walls were covered with hundreds of green, yellow and red lights blinking on and off like Christmas decorations. The compartment buzzed with energised circuits. Several panels had been pulled out from their cabinets. Wires were looped and left dangling everywhere. Tarasov was particularly interested in the new radar, sonar and decoy equipment being fitted, whereas Boris Lukin went over to inspect the special facilities which had been constructed for receiving and storing the missiles to be received from the *Cherkassy*. Rem Bukato checked over the reactors and turbines surrounded by spotless compressors and valves. Several signs displayed the ominous nuclear symbol that warned of radiation. The control centres were as good as anything he'd seen before. For the first time, they began to think that maybe -just maybe, this mission could be successful after all.

Later, back within the comfortable and civilised surroundings of the Humendan hotel, the Russians discussed the forthcoming mission. They had been very impressed with the supertanker's preparations and were now in two minds whether to just play along with the Iranians – or to actually go through with this insane venture as originally agreed. Sharif Hamad gave them just one more night, during which the previous hospitalities were repeated. Next day, they were collected early and driven out to the nomadic tent in the desert. The Hamas guards stood motionless either side of the entrance. The turbaned officials waited inside, seated on camel skin cushions. This time, their spokesman did not stand up, but addressed them briefly from his seated position.

"Have you decided?" Sharif Hamad interpreted.

"Well…" Tarasov began to reply.

"Ah! I presume you still want to talk about money, don't you?" Hamad seemed to be prompting. He smiled and turned to speak to the seated officials, before turning back to address the Russians.

"We will pay each of you two hundred thousand American dollars."

There was a stunned silence. The Iranians looked puzzled.

"Come now gentlemen. Remember how badly you were treated by your own Government. You will be able to go back there as kings … or remain here if you prefer. On the other hand, you can go wherever you wish in the world. We will provide all the necessary paperwork and identification documents."

"The money…" Boris Lukin spoke hoarsely, "how would it be paid?"

"Twenty five per cent now, to be paid into an account of your own choice – or in cash if you prefer. The remainder upon completion of the mission."

The three sailors huddled together and spoke quietly to each other in Russian, while the Iranians looked on and awaited their answer. After a few moments of intense debate, Valentin Tarasov finally walked across and shook Sharif Hamad firmly by the hand. The turbaned officials gave a sigh of relief and rose to their feet, gibbering away and kissing everyone present. Outside the tent, the heavily armed Hamas guards said nothing. It was one of those moments that decides lives. They simply watched the distant horizon and replaced the safety catches on their automatic rifles.

Sharif Hamad realised they still had to achieve a decisive victory. This was only part of the game. One wrong move could consign them all to eternal darkness. They were on the brink of making the world sit up and take notice.

CHAPTER 12

United States : Washington

Washington had always seemed so artificial to Ross Lombardi. The abundance of Monuments and ministries smacked of Federal Government. No other American city was so full of itself, so swaggering and formal, with broad straight avenues and endless piles of marble architecture deferring more to the temples of ancient Greece and Rome. There didn't seem to be anything tangible he could easily identify with other cities and certainly nothing which resembled his own humble background. No skyscrapers like New York, no factories like Cleveland... and no baseball team like Chicago. The capital had no all-night liquor stores and no Italian grocery shops where ordinary people could gather to talk and complain; at least none up front for the tourists to see. There didn't even seem to be any kids in this city. Lombardi was sure there had to be – but where were they?

Ross Lombardi was driving his Chrysler LHS in from Washington Airport, past the Pentagon and across the Potomac River. He rounded the Lincoln Memorial and headed eastwards along Constitution Avenue. The Ellipse rolled past on his left, with the Washington Monument and its joggers slipping away to the right. He knew the vision he saw through the tinted windows was only the "official' city. There was also another side to Washington – the Washington of the shadows. Places like "chocolate city' and "shantytown' where the poor and homeless still lived and died in abject poverty.

Ross turned north on 15th Street. This took him up past the Treasury Building on the east side of the White House and then on past McPherson Square to Vermont Avenue. He tussled with a host of unanswerable questions invading his innermost thoughts. He remembered why he was here and grimaced at the prospect of another boring meeting with the Israelis. On this tedious drive in from the airport, he found himself questioning the merits of the whole operation. The only consolation was that Ruth Netanya would be there. His memory kept drifting back to their last encounter when she had played the ice-cool, hard-nosed professional that she undoubtedly was. But perhaps on this occasion he might just thaw the ice-maiden a little.

His ultimate destination was off the beaten track, at some obscure and unofficial meeting-house out along Rhode Island Avenue, towards the Mount Rainier area. Out here the landscape changed dramatically. The inner city kitsch gave way to row upon row of solid middle-class houses with manicured lawns and the obligatory two cars in every garage, facing onto grassy squares. Away in the distance, the pasturelands and tobacco country of Maryland beckoned.

Lombardi brought the Chrysler to a halt in the leafy driveway of a nondescript suburban bungalow. Several unmarked cars were parked discretely amongst the shrubbery and it seemed as if he was the last to arrive. A couple of clean-cut FBI agents checked his ID at the door. They seemed to be recruiting them younger every year, Lombardi thought. These guys looked no more than eighteen. More to the point, where did the FBI keep finding such lightweights?

Was there some secret recruiting ground for college kids, rich in all the privileges and advantages which are underwritten by strong paternal connections and a well-bred background, but totally lacking in all the fundamentals of street credibility? Or was there some university campus just concentrating on the importance of sartorial elegance? One of them escorted him into a large rectangular lounge area. Lombardi noticed the slightly opaque glass and knew it would be bullet-proof. To the casual observer the house appeared to be normal; but in reality the reinforced panels of brickwork could withstand armour piercing shells or even a sizeable bomb. Coffee and soft drinks were set out on a glass table and Lombardi helped himself to a mineral water before joining the main group. The three Mossad agents he had met in Tel Aviv were present, along with some other Israeli government types whom he hadn't seen before. Lombardi looked around at the assembly as Drew Dalton made the introductions, flanked by several medium-weights from the White House and the Pentagon. The solemnity of their meeting was due partly to the gravity of the situation, but more likely from their improvising of several complex international scenarios. Lombardi tried to ease the tension and smiled as he squeezed Ruth Netanya's hand. She looked into his eyes with an expression of surprise and awakening interest. Although most of the group knew each other from their meeting in Israel, Lombardi and the Mossad agents nevertheless still went through the motions for the sake of the new team members.

"OK everyone…" Drew Dalton began, after the introductions.

"I guess you all know this is an informal progress meeting, requested by the Israeli Internal Security Services."

"Does that mean we can go by first names?" Ross joked, as he flashed a smile in Ruth's direction. She lowered her eyes coyly and began to shuffle the papers resting on her lap. The ice-maiden seemed to be thawing a little.

"Now Ross…" Drew retorted, "…let's keep things just a little professional, OK?"

"OK, just a thought." Lombardi shrugged and sat back in his chair.

"Agent Eshkol is concerned about the Iranian situation, despite assurances that everything seems quiet in that area … for the moment at least." Dalton motioned one of the White House aides to his feet.

"It's our reading of the situation that Iran is moving closer to Western values every day. The power of the hard-liners is decreasing and recent election results have brought several liberal figures into some of the top positions of power." The man sat down and one of his companions took the floor.

"The ordinary Iranian in the street is fed up with all the dogma," the second aide continued. "The post-revolution religious zeal is waning. They want more freedom and more money. Behind the scenes, there are signs that the Iranians want financial reform. They want to do business, not make war."

"And they know if they make war on Israel," a Pentagon officer chipped in, "they make war on the United States."

"There, that's sorted," Ross stood up, "let's all go get a sandwich!"

"Not so fast..." Benjamin Eshkol gave a look of thunder as he rose from his chair and began to circle the room. "I'm glad to see that Mr Lombardi thinks this is all a big joke, or worse than that, a waste of time. Listen, I've got better things to do, you've also got better things to do. So let's all just save some time. You were called here to make sure our respective governments do not suffer a high profile humiliation of yet another foreign relations fiasco. Do you understand?"

"You betcha!" Lombardi beamed, "But there's still some great fishing up the Colorado River right now. Be glad to take you along." Ruth tried to hide a smile at his irreverent attitude towards her boss.

"The situation in the Middle East may be relaxed as far as the United States is concerned..." Eshkol decided to ignore Lombardi's last remark, "but don't forget, you are many thousands of miles away from the problem, we are not!"

Drew Dalton shuffled and squared the intelligence documents on the table, and went over to Eshkol standing by the window. What had seemed like a straightforward situation just a little while ago was now getting very sensitive.

"Just precisely what *is* your problem, agent Eshkol?" Drew Dalton tried to be as polite as possible while holding a restraining hand to Ross Lombardi.

"The *Cherkassy!*" was the abrupt reply.

"The what?" Dalton looked round the room for enlightenment.

"The Russian nuclear submarine that sank in the Barents Sea." Eshkol reminded him.

"Oh, not that again..." Lombardi raised his arms in mock despair.

"No, not that *again*, Mr Lombardi. The problem is *still* there. It never went away."

"I thought we explained..."

Pandemonium broke out in the room as everybody began to speak at once. David Weizman and Ruth Netanya added their own misgivings to those of their senior agent. The Israeli officials went on to endorse their government's concern, whilst at the same time agreeing with Mossad's assessment of the situation. The Americans appealed for balance and calm, while going back over the familiar ground of international surveillance and monitoring, especially in connection with the Kola Peninsula expedition and the repeated assurances given by the Russians who confirmed the *Cherkassy's* Iranian contingent had gone to a watery grave.

"It's not enough!" Benjamin Eshkol wearily shook his head and brought the squabbling to an abrupt halt by pounding his fist on the circular meeting table.

"Well, what more can we do?" Drew Dalton asked in a resigned tone.

"Listen…" Eshkol composed himself, "our agents in the field are reporting unusual Iranian activity in certain areas."

"Which areas?" Ross became curious.

"Pakistan, for one!" David Weizman stood beside Eshkol.

"Two Russian missile technicians have recently disappeared from an international joint venture project to build a new hydro-electric plant."

"What the hell were Russian missile technicians doing on such a scheme?"

"I would have thought a man of Mr Lombardi's calibre would be aware that redundant Russian scientists will work anywhere." Ruth Netanya's voice was mocking, almost inviting him to retaliate.

"Of course I knew that!" Lombardi decided to shut up, for the moment.

"But what's the significance?" one of the Pentagon officers queried.

"Russian scientists are notorious for getting lost when they're abroad."

"We've been keeping an eye on the site for some time" Weizman continued, "especially because of the number of Iranians involved. These Russians were observed crossing the Iranian border with a man called Nasaf Rhullah."

"And who is this Nasaf Rhullah?"

"He is a senior commander with Hamas and known for his close connections with Hezbollah.

"The room fell into an electrified silence. The Israelis finally had everyone's attention.

"Another equally serious matter has arisen in Denmark," Benjamin Eshkol continued after a suitable pause. "A Danish salvage ship called the *Norse Warrior* is docked in the North Sea port of Esbjerg."

He waited for queries from the Americans. None came. This time they listened in silence.

"The same Nasaf Rhullah has been observed in the company of the ship's captain, a man called Bjorn Ramuldssen."

The room now erupted with urgent voices and animated gestures. The unfolding of events now assumed the nature of a runaway train. Shock followed surprise as the unimaginable was overtaken by even more unexpected revelations. Drew Dalton wanted to know why the Pentagon wasn't up to date on this. They blamed the White House, who blamed the FBI agents, who in turn blamed the CIA. The Israelis spoke excitedly to each other in Hebrew. Drew shot a glance at Ross, who was now gnawing a fingernail. A good sign; Lombardi only did that when his mind was completely focused on matters operational rather than strategic. Dalton instructed Ross to get back in touch with Peter Lawrence, his counterpart in London, and find out what the hell was going on. In the middle of all the commotion, Benjamin Eshkol moved over and poured himself a cup of coffee before settling back quietly in his chair. One miscalculation and the ensuing international crisis would plunge them all into personal disgrace.

"OK, OK…" Drew Dalton finally raised his hands in the air to subdue the excitement. He spoke directly to Eshkol. "We'll get onto this immediately. When are you due back in Tel Aviv?"

"Tomorrow."

"You'll have to postpone it for a day. I need you to come up to the White House with me."

"I'd still like to do a little preliminary investigating of my own," Ross interrupted, "especially before I get back to Peter Lawrence in England."

"What kind of investigating?" Drew Dalton gave a quizzical look.

"You know how it is. I need to discuss the whole situation with one of these Mossad agents a little more thoroughly … if that's OK?"

Dalton looked towards Eshkol, who sighed heavily and shrugged in a couldn't-care-less fashion.

"It will have to be agent Netanya. If I'm to go to the White House, I'll need agent Weizman with me."

"Agent Netanya, is that OK?" Dalton asked as he gathered up his papers with the manicured hands of one whose sole communion with nature mostly took place on golf courses.

"Perfect." Lombardi replied with a satisfied smile.

❖ ❖ ❖

That night, Ross drove Ruth downtown along New York Avenue. The city lights glittered in the dark of the evening as the restaurants and clubs began to fill up.

"You hungry?" he enquired.

"Yes."

"Like Italian food?"

"Is it kosher?" she laughed.

"Of course!"

"Then I'd love to try it."

He took her along Pennsylvania Avenue to the *Trattoria al Sole* on 20th Street and later to a jazz club near Washington Circle where they drank beer and dry martinis until the early hours.

"Didn't you say you wanted to do some investigating?" she reminded him over the rim of her glass.

"Did I?"

"You did."

"Then that's what I'm doing" he grinned.

"Ask me some questions then."

"OK … are you married?"

"No."

"Engaged?"

"Not yet."

"In love?"

"Only with my country."

"That's good. There, I'm through for now."

"For now?"

"There may be more later."

They rode the elevator up to the fourth floor of the Four Seasons Hotel on Pennsylvania Avenue. Ruth giggled like an excited schoolgirl on a first date and put a finger to her lips as she opened the door of her room. Inside, they couldn't wait any longer. Lombardi held her tightly, kissing her lips and neck and shoulders. Ruth gasped gently as she broke away, pouted her lips and made her way to the bathroom. Ross shrugged his shoulders, opened the mini-bar and prepared fresh drinks. He nodded with approval as he surveyed the softly lit room and listened to the muffled sounds of traffic bustling along Pennsylvania Avenue. He went over to the window and stared at the star-studded sky. Turning away from the window, he paused to look at the king-sized bed, before slipping off his clothes and settling on the comforter. He reached out and placed his drink on the nightstand.

The bathroom door opened and Ruth appeared in a gossamer light negligee. Her slim body, tanned from the middle-eastern sun, and slightly muscular from military training, was beautifully outlined in the lighted doorway.

"I see that you've made yourself at home," she purred with a provocative smile as she came over and sat on the edge of the bed.

Ross propped himself on his elbow and extended his other arm. Ruth folded herself into his arms and nuzzled his chest. Her dark hair fell around her shoulders as she kissed him lightly on the lips.

"Ross" she whispered, "you and I are risk takers. For us, each tomorrow is a precious gift." Ross slipped the negligee off her shoulders. "Don't deny your feelings," she gasped as his fingers lightly caressed each new area of her body. "Let's enjoy the moment ... because we can't predict the future."

Across Pennsylvania Avenue, a dark figure remained huddled in one of the doorways, hidden by an awning which shaded an exclusive menswear shop. The figure had been watching the two lovers silhouetted against the window on the fourth floor of the Four Seasons Hotel.

The light went out abruptly. The shadowy dark figure struck a match against the wall and cupped it in his hands as he lit up a cigarette. Smoke billowed out from the doorway and evaporated into the cold, early-morning air.

CHAPTER 13

ENGLAND : LONDON

Rules is reputed to be the oldest restaurant in London. Situated at the very heart of Covent Garden's theatre-land, it has always been a favourite haunt for writers such as Charles Dickens, William Makepeace Thackeray, John Galsworthy, H.G. Wells and Graham Greene. Throughout its long history it has proved a haven for endless literary talent and even the occasional Royal. The Prince of Wales' favourite spot for wining and dining the beautiful Lillie Langtry is discretely situated on the first floor. Beneath their signed portraits, Peter Lawrence sat opposite Juliet Lucas and noticed how delicately she approached her food. He reached over and poured her a second glass of *Valserrano Crianza* before approaching his hors d'ouvre. Neither agent spoke for what seemed a long time. In fact, the main course of rump steak with new potatoes and buttered broccoli had arrived before the first word was uttered.

"This whole situation is becoming critical," Lucas spoke without looking up, then took a sip of wine.

"What situation?" Lawrence appeared surprised by this sudden statement.

"Isn't that why we're here?" Her voice and eyes were questioning.

"Yes ... of course it is. Why else?"

"The Iranians are positively up to something," Lucas mused, going back to her food.

"Oh, *that* situation ..." Lawrence spoke under his breath.

"I do happen to be considered something of an expert on Islamic *and* Middle Eastern matters. I did get a First at Oxford," she assured him.

"Yes, I know. That's why you've been assigned to this case." Lawrence almost yawned with indifference.

"You don't seem to be taking it very seriously, Peter."

"Listen, Juliet..." Lawrence leaned across the table and lowered his voice. "If you don't mind me saying so ... this assignment is a complete waste of time. But at the moment it's much easier and much safer than being blown to kingdom come in some godforsaken backwater – so let's go along with it for as long as it lasts, OK?"

"My God!" Juliet's face reddened with suppressed temper. "If you think it's such a non-starter, then perhaps you could please explain to me why Iranians were on board the *Cherkassy*?"

"I don't know ... maybe it was a fishing party?"

"Don't be such a fool, Lawrence!"

"Don't call me a fool..."

"Then don't behave like one!"

"I'm sorry. I don't mean to be facetious." Peter didn't want to antagonise her. "But. don't you see, the Israelis are being paranoid *as usual*; and Whitehall is just going through the motions ... *as usual*."

"What makes you so sure?"

"God, you *are* naive Juliet ... to humour the Americans of course! Once you've had a bit more experience in the field, you'll be able to figure these things out for yourself."

"Don't be so patronising!" She snapped and began to cut her meat violently. "Iran desperately wants a nuclear capacity. The Russians..."

"The Russians won't sell nukes to Iran."

"Maybe not, but they've certainly given Iran a perfect opportunity to steal some sunken missiles right from under their noses."

"How?"

"I've already said ... why were the Iranians on board the *Cherkassy*? I wouldn't be surprised if the sinking was deliberate: not an accident. They obviously know the vessel – and the Russian officers who sailed her, but perhaps more importantly, they know the exact position where she's lying."

"All the Iranians on board were drowned."

"How can you be so sure?"

Peter Lawrence sat back and rolled his eyes in despair. The evening was definitely not going as planned. The dinner invitation was on the pretext of discussing their assignment, but with the *real* purpose of getting her into bed. Now the silly mare actually insisted on arguing about the bloody Iranians! He had to do something to mitigate the situation. They finished the rest of the meal in silence, and Juliet declined the offer of a brandy to finish things off.

"I'd like to go home – now – if you don't mind" she said coldly.

"What? Already?"

"Yes, please."

"Very well…" Having exhausted all his powers of persuasion Lawrence resigned himself to failure on this occasion.

The black taxicab drove them north-westwards across the West End before turning due west along Oxford Street. Juliet had a small flat in Clarendon Place, just across Roman Road at the top end of Hyde Park. Lawrence told the cab driver to wait while he walked her to the door.

"Listen, I'm sorry…" He tried a last reconciliation.

"No! You listen, Peter…" she interrupted. "I've got to convince you that this is quite serious."

"Perhaps I *was* just a little patronising…"

"Look, you're a good agent, Peter. I've always admired you. I wasn't just assigned to this because of my Middle Eastern knowledge…"

"No?"

"No. I actually *asked* to be assigned. I even begged… just for an opportunity to work with *you*."

"I didn't know…" He was slightly taken aback by this revelation and looked away from her eyes. "I'm not really…"

"Look, we can't stand here in the cold arguing all night. Would you like to come in for coffee?"

"The taxi?"

"Tell him to go!" Without waiting for a reply, she unlocked the door and disappeared inside the flat. Lawrence remained motionless for a moment, then hurriedly paid the cab driver and followed her inside. The flat was warm and inviting. Lucas had already removed her coat and was busily making coffee in the small, but well-equipped kitchen. Peter Lawrence stood in front of the mock coal-effect gas fire and warmed his hands. She had switched on the CD player and the haunting strains of Claude Debussy's *Clair de Lune* softly filled the room. Juliet returned with two cups of steaming coffee and invited him to remove his coat and sit down.

"Listen, Juliet…" He leaned across and looked into her eyes. "We've gotten off to a bit of a bad start, you and I."

"You could say that" she purred and lightly ran a slender finger around the rim of her cup.

"At least, shall we try again?" he offered.

"Oh why not?" She giggled mischievously and put down her coffee cup. Juliet went over and turned off the lights. All that remained was a flickering glow from the fire. Peter sat back contentedly and watched as Juliet kicked off her shoes and unzipped her dress. The garment fell to the red carpet at her feet and she stood before him in nothing but a diaphanous basque. He studied her body for a moment without moving. The mellow firelight played across the swell of her breasts and the soft contours of her stomach and thighs. She looked so very young – untouched and virgin-like in the glowing embers. Her entire body glistened with an ethereal luminescence. Not a word was spoken. She assisted him with his jacket and shirt. Soon they both lay naked on the scatter rug in front of the fire. Despite Juliet's innocence, her hands were expert. Peter was ready to risk everything – just for this one exquisite moment. He groaned as her sensuous lips lightly wandered up and down his tingling body. He gently rolled Juliet onto her back, caressing and kissing her breasts and the mound of her stomach. Moving down, he sensed the musky odour of the sexually aroused female as she parted her glistening legs to accommodate his tongue. Her breath came in increasingly rapid gasps. She moaned and writhed. Just at the point when Peter wanted to go inside her and bring everything to an earth-shattering climax, the mobile phone rang in his overcoat pocket draped over a chair back across the other side of the room.

"Christ Almighty!" He cursed. Juliet just sighed. He felt her body relax when the moment had passed.

"For goodness sake answer it!" she whispered.

"No!" He waited a moment. The ringing stopped and they resumed where they had left off. Five minutes later, the muffled sounds of his mobile began to ring again.

"Oh for god's sake *answer* the bloody thing!" she screamed through clenched teeth.

Cursing profusely, Lawrence stumbled across the room and tore the intruding phone from its hiding place. The firelight played over the soft sweat of his naked body and glistened over muscles tensed like steel springs.

"Who is this?" he roared into the receiver.

"Jeremy Sinclair" came the restrained reply. "Sorry Peter, did I interrupt something?"

"You could say that!"

"I'm sorry old man, but you've got to get your arse down here straight away."

"Down where?"

"Horseguards, of course. You know the office … *and* the drill."

"*Straight* away?" Lawrence looked across at Juliet, now propped up on one elbow and pouting like a spoilt child.

"Afraid so, old boy."

The receiver at the other end clicked as Jeremy Sinclair rang off. Peter Lawrence remained motionless for a moment, before returning to the naked woman sprawled in front of the fire.

"Who was it? What's wrong?" she asked.

"Business!"

"Something I should know about?"

"No. At least, not yet."

"I simply can't believe," she murmured, "that you have to leave so suddenly in the middle of the night."

He glanced at his wristwatch and squinted at the face. "Unfortunately, I don't have much choice."

Juliet held him tighter. "I could hold you all night."

Peter gently caressed her back. "I certainly don't wish to report for duty… especially with you lying here."

Juliet knew that Peter's work was dangerous, but she had secretly hoped that he would not be exposed to any unnecessary risks so soon. She looked searchingly into Peter's eyes. "When will I see you again?"

He brushed her cheek with his lips "I don't know."

Juliet nuzzled closer "I love you, Peter: I'm always worried about you and what you are doing."

"Hey, I didn't know you cared so much and besides, what I'm doing now is a hell of a lot safer than being shot at every other day."

A long silence followed. Peter roused himself and slipped his arm around Juliet's waist. "I've got to go." He quickly began to dress. "Listen, I'll call you…"

She made no reply as he grabbed his overcoat and hurried out into the cold late October night.

❖ ❖ ❖

The black cab dropped him at the southern end of Whitehall. Peter decided to take in the cool night air, as he walked the rest of the way to his secret rendezvous in Horseguards Avenue. The recessed entrance to the building was inconspicuous. He pressed the entry-phone at the side of the highly glossed black door and greeted the security guard. The early-morning dampness made him shiver. An MI6 officer clutching a sheaf of papers briskly stepped forward to escort Peter to his meeting on the third floor. Jeremy Sinclair was a slightly built Oxbridge man of about thirty-five, with straight blond hair severely swept back and a wide mouth, which immediately creased into a smile as Lawrence approached.

"Peter, old chap … hope I didn't disturb something too important?"

"I can get back to it, Jeremy," he sighed.

"Glad to hear it, old boy."

Sinclair was regarded as an important man in the Defence Department. He reported directly to the Minister of Defence and held quite a lot of personable connections at Westminster. Despite this, he was an amiable character who quickly distinguished himself by displaying an uncanny ability to analyse a mountain of apparently unrelated data and draw accurate conclusions. His rise through the ranks of the secret service had been a textbook example of how to balance his connections with patient diplomacy. Peter Lawrence liked him. Suddenly, a side door burst open to reveal Adrian Dyson striding into the room. He proceeded to a desk in the centre, and motioned for the other two agents to be seated. Lawrence and Sinclair sat in silence whilst Dyson flipped through the dossier which lay before him. Dyson was Peter Lawrence's immediate superior. Conservative by nature, Adrian Dyson had become a full colonel within MI6 during the cold – war period. Of average stature, he still looked sartorially elegant at this ungodly hour, dressed in his dark grey Savile Row pin-stripe suit from Gieves and Hawkes, complete with billowing silk handkerchief from the top pocket and highly polished black brogues from Lobb. An avid squash player, Dyson nevertheless still had to work hard to maintain a trim physique for a man approaching early middle-age. His greying hair and moustache were the only clues to his real age. The son of a wealthy stock-broker from Sevenoaks, Dyson had started his military career by attending Sandhurst Military Academy followed by a brief spell at the Royal Military College of Science in Shrivenham. This was followed by two years as an intelligence officer for the SAS where he became hooked on the intrigue of research within the intelligence community.

"I've had Washington on the line!" he declared without further ado. "Bloody Iranians are up to something."

"Really, sir?" Sinclair ventured to comment.

"Of course *really*! I've just said so, haven't I? Lawrence …"

"Yes sir?"

"Their man is coming back … whats-his-name?"

"Ross Lombardi, sir."

"That's the chap. He's got the details. Stick with him Lawrence, get to the bottom of this."

"Yes sir."

"And quickly, Lawrence. Quickly!"

"Of course, sir."

Adrian Dyson dropped the dossier back on to the desk and rose from his chair. He was just about to leave the room as rapidly as he had entered, then halted in his tracks, as if he'd remembered something.

THE CHERKASSY INCIDENT · 139

"Oh, and by the way ... you're going back to Belfast."

"*Belfast!*" Lawrence protested. "But you've just pulled me out sir."

"Well you're going back again!" Dyson was the type of man who would always march towards the sound of gunfire and didn't like his decisions being questioned, by anyone.

"But how can I give this Iranian assignment my full attention if I'm back in Ireland?"

Lawrence wasn't exactly happy and was even prepared to risk the wrath of his superior.

"Belfast *is* the Iranian assignment, Lawrence" Dyson snapped angrily.

"How so, sir?"

"Your contact over there ... his name escapes me ... you know who I mean."

"Eamonn Burke, sir."

"That's him, that's the fellow, he's got some info on this business."

"What info, sir."

"If I knew that, I wouldn't have to send you back over there, now would I?"

"No sir."

"Won't talk to anyone else but you, Lawrence. So back you go. Oh, and take that Lombardi chap with you."

Adrian Dyson breezed out of the meeting-room, slamming the door loudly in his wake.

Peter Lawrence looked questioningly at Jeremy Sinclair, who merely shrugged his shoulders to indicate he knew nothing about the assignment.

"When is Ross Lombardi arriving?" Lawrence enquired.

"Tomorrow morning."

"When do we leave for Belfast?"

"Tomorrow evening."

"Oh that's just great!"

When Peter reached the main entrance and stepped out onto Horseguards Avenue, dawn was just breaking. He paused and whistled tunelessly, as he looked over to a spectacular orange glow rising above the 'London Eye' and the office buildings on the eastern side of the

River Thames. The pale light filtered into the dark blue sky. This radiant sunrise heralded the beginning of a day that Peter Lawrence would never forget. He thought of Juliet Lucas and her beautiful young body and wondered when, if ever, he would see it again.

CHAPTER 14

IRELAND : BELFAST

Two plain-clothed operatives from 14 Intelligence Unit had been early in picking up the visiting agents from Belfast Airport in one of their unmarked Ford Scorpios, and now dropped them outside O'Connell's Bar in the Divis Street area. Peter Lawrence was following Eamonn Burke's instructions to the letter... apart from one important aspect: Ross Lombardi. Both men felt exposed and vulnerable as they glanced uneasily up and down the street, waiting amid the devastation, slogans and wall-murals. A decidedly hostile atmosphere hung in the air as several local inhabitants on the other side of the street formed into a huddle and began eyeing up the strangers. Nothing in his previous experience could have prepared Ross Lombardi for the growing unease he now felt on the windswept streets of Belfast. Peter Lawrence, on the other hand, knew only too well what *could* happen. With each passing car their heartbeats increased, half expecting a loyalist hit-squad to pull up and open fire. The terrible scars of bitterness and conflict were all around: rioting and vehicle hijackings were a common feature of everyday life. The latest round of Peace talks had produced yet another fragile cease-fire, which seemed to be holding. However, a true and lasting peace in Northern Ireland had always proved to be elusive.

Across the dismal street, the huddled group became more animated and their voices grew louder. Lawrence detected this change of mood and noticed that most of the men were aged between seventeen and thirty. The vast majority were far too young – and couldn't possibly have known the IRA's real reasons for the earlier struggles. They belonged to a new generation, shaped by conflict and bitterness. From the very first day the barricades went up, the Provisionals had easily won their hearts and minds with carefully orchestrated seditious propaganda. Fingers were now being pointed at the two strangers, and the occupants of O'Connells Bar began to peer out through the rain spattered windows to see what all the commotion was about. Lawrence anxiously looked up and down the street. He was sure this was the right place… but there was still no sign of Eamonn Burke. The ugly mob had finally gathered up their courage and began to advance menacingly across the road. Lombardi's hand instinctively slid into his overcoat.

"What the hell do you think you're doing?" Peter Lawrence hissed.

"Now I know how Custer must have felt at Little Big Horn," Lombardi answered without taking his eyes off the group.

"Don't tell me you've got a gun?" Lawrence asked incredulously.

"Sure … ain't you?"

"Jesus Christ!" Lawrence began to walk away, tugging Lombardi by the arm. The group quickened their pace and began to follow, joined by others from the bar. Suddenly, a black Mercedes screeched around the corner and skidded to a halt by the kerbside. A large bearded man emerged from the passenger side and moved round to stand on the pavement, between the retreating pair and the advancing mob. The men came to a ragged halt and grinned sheepishly at each other, shuffling their feet and saluting in the general direction of the large man. They briefly muttered amongst themselves before hurrying back to the warmth and safety of the Bar.

"In the back!" ordered the bearded man with a jerk of his thumb.

The British and American agents quickly scrambled into the vehicle as it revved up noisily and sped away up Castle Street. Lawrence gave Lombardi a gentle nudge with his elbow as he noticed the driver watching them in the rear-view mirror, but nobody spoke as the car travelled eastwards over Queens Bridge, before turning north along Lagan Weir to disappear into the City's Docklands area. They looked out at the drifting curtains of rain as the car finally came to a halt outside a deserted warehouse north of the ferry terminal on Donegal Quay. The large bearded man stepped out and opened the car's rear door for Lombardi and Lawrence. Both he and the driver fell

THE CHERKASSY INCIDENT · 143

in behind the two agents as all four approached the warehouse. Two more men appeared at the door and indicated for Lawrence and Lombardi to spread-eagle themselves against the wall. The body search revealed Ross Lombardi's colt automatic. A fist slammed into his kidneys. Lombardi gasped with pain and slumped to the floor, curling into a foetal position. His back felt as if he'd been hit by a runaway truck. One of the escorts crouched beside Lombardi and yanked his hair until his head snapped backwards.

"My friend rarely leaves any bruises, but he just might beat the fucking livin' daylights outa ya." To impress his point the man gave an excruciatingly painful kick to the groin. "But on the other hand we could perhaps become great buddies … that is, if you co-operate and never try to pull a stunt like that again." Lawrence came over and dragged Lombardi to his feet as they were roughly shoved inside the warehouse.

From their position of cold isolation, the world around closed in rapidly and became a place of uncertainty. They began to understand the terror and helplessness others had suffered, knowing that death may be their only escape. The big man stepped forward and led them across the vast open space of the warehouse. He pushed back a creaking door which opened onto a large room. At first sight, the room appeared to be empty, but as Lombardi and Lawrence's eyes became accustomed to the gloom, they noticed six masked men in military fatigues with automatic rifles held across their chests, standing beneath a large tricolour pinned to the far wall. In front of them, the dark shape of a man was seated at a wooden table and Peter Lawrence sensed it was Eamonn Burke. The ragged sound of their footsteps echoed inside the empty room as the pair approached across the expanse of floor.

"Who's he?" Burke asked without raising his head from a sheaf of documents he was studying.

"Ross Lombardi" Lawrence answered. "He's American."

"And what's he doing here?" Burke's tone became hostile.

"He's involved" Lawrence confirmed.

"In *what*?"

"This submarine thing…"

"I said only *you*!" Burke shouted, as he sprang from his chair and stabbed a defiant finger at Peter Lawrence.

"I know, I know, but this is something different from our normal line of business. He's an indispensable factor in this matter. It's essential for him to hear your information at first hand."

Burke didn't answer for what seemed to be an age. He looked hard at Lawrence, then across to a dishevelled Lombardi, then back to Lawrence again.

"All right ... sit down" he said finally.

Peter Lawrence let out a small sigh of relief and sat down at the table. He gestured for Ross Lombardi to do the same. Their escort seemed to have melted away into the background somewhere, even though there was nothing in the building to hide them. A bottle of Powers Gold Label Irish whisky stood on the table, along with two small glasses. Burke filled the glasses and pushed one over to each of the men.

"What about you?" Lawrence asked.

Without answering, Burke raised the bottle and took a long swig. He wiped his mouth with his sleeve and replaced the bottle on the table.

"Well Peter..." Burke began, "what with all this talk of peace and negotiation and toleration the likes of me and you will soon be redundant, eh?"

"As far as Ireland is concerned" replied Lawrence "I certainly hope so."

"That's all right for you, Peter" Burke continued. "You've got business all over the place ... like this submarine thing. But what about me? I'm a soldier, a fighter, not a politician. What will I do?"

"You've still got the Loyalist gangs to contend with up here."

"Chicken feed, Peter," Burke spat on the floor. "Without the backing of the British Army they're nothing. There'll be no deals with the Brits until we hold all the aces. If they think it can be contained here, they're in for a rude awakening. Time is still on our side."

"Last time we met, you talked about going back to the sea."

"I don't know, Peter. I don't know."

"What about your information?" Ross Lombardi ventured as he butted into the small talk. Eamonn Burke gave him a long, hard look before replying in a loud voice.

"There's nobody talking to you, mister American. Just remember, you weren't invited to this party and if it wasn't for Peter here, you'd be dead by now. *You* don't ask questions. You just sit there with your mouth shut ... and listen!"

"It's OK Eamonn," Lawrence answered quickly, "he didn't mean anything. He doesn't know."

Burke raised his hand for quiet. He again filled both glasses and took another slug from the bottle.

"Now Peter," he said at length, ignoring Lombardi, "let's get down to business. I've had a message."

"Who from?" Lawrence asked.

"Let's just say, it originated in Denmark, a place called Esbjerg."

Lombardi was about to intervene again, at the mention of those names. Peter Lawrence kicked him violently underneath the table. The American gave out a small groan, but otherwise kept quiet. "It came from a source which is normally very unreliable ... in other words, a go-boy who's constantly drunk."

"Then, what's the significance?"

"Let me finish, Peter. This message was relayed to me via a series of different sources. Each of those sources in turn had a great laugh at the message and only passed it on so they could share the joke with someone else."

"But *you* don't think it's funny?"

"No, Peter, I do not."

"Why not?"

"Remember the last time we met?" Burke asked.

"Yes, I do."

"And we were rudely interrupted by your driver, who took you to one side for a few private words?"

"That's correct."

"Well, those few private words were ... overheard, Peter."

"They were?"

"Aye they were. Although it didn't mean very much at the time, two particular phrases from that conversation stuck in my mind."

"Which phrases?"

"'Russian submarine' and 'Barents Sea'. Now this garbled message from Denmark went on about paratroopers invading the west coast of Ireland and other such horseshit … but those two phrases repeated themselves again. 'Russian submarine' and 'Barents Sea'. Isn't that some coincidence? But there was another word mentioned, which finally made my mind up to contact you."

"Oh really? And what word would that be, Eamonn?"

"Iran."

There was an electrified silence in the warehouse. Both Ross Lombardi and Peter Lawrence downed their whisky and Burke again refilled their glasses.

"We'll need to see the full transcript of the message, Eamonn." Lawrence requested.

"Just what the hell is going on, Peter?" Burke asked quietly as he hunched over the bottle.

"I'm afraid that's classified."

"I've still got that contact on the inside…" Burke reminded them. "He could be very valuable."

"You said he was unreliable."

"Sometimes he is, but not on this occasion."

"I think this man could *actually* help us." Ross Lombardi couldn't keep quiet any longer. This time, Eamonn Burke allowed him to speak.

"To our superiors, Ross, this man is an enemy of democracy."

"Listen," Burke interrupted, "I may be this and I may be that, but I do *not* want to see fundamentalist Islam ruling Northern Ireland, never mind the rest of the world. Now, perhaps you think I'm just a thick Irishman, but I can put two and two together and I already have a fair idea…"

"Tell him!" Lombardi hissed.

Peter Lawrence hesitated, then gave Burke a brief outline of the situation.

"So, tell me, just how can you guarantee this so called source?" Lawrence asked when he'd finished.

"By joining him on the salvage ship." Burke raised his hands, as if the answer were elementary.

"What? You, personally?"

"Why not? After all, I *am* an experienced sailor and I know my man can get me aboard. Me and you already have established communication channels…"

"But what if you're discovered?" Ross Lombardi ventured "Why would you risk everything and stick your neck out like this?"

"I'm bored here. It's not like it used to be!"

"Is that really the only reason?" Peter Lawrence enquired.

"Look. You're a smart man, Peter. I'll let you figure it out for yourself." Burke took another long swig from the bottle of whisky.

"I don't know if I could swing it with my superiors…" Lawrence said thoughtfully.

"I'll swing it with your superiors," Lombardi assured him.

"And just how the hell will you do that, mister clever American?" Burke asked sarcastically.

"Rather, *my* superiors will swing it with *his* superiors," came the sardonic reply.

"And who might they be?"

"They don't come any higher, mister Burke."

The rest of the Irish was drained by the three men. Communication details were confirmed and handshakes were exchanged.

"The past's forgotten," Eamonn declared as he patted Peter on the shoulder. "Now, the only thing that's really important is where we're going."

Lombardi and Lawrence were dropped back outside O'Connell's Bar in the Divis Street area. Their return escort waited nearby and the damp, cold Belfast night was beginning to close in. They drove in silence, northwestwards along the Shankill Road, towards the airport and away from the tired deserted streets of this optimistic city.

CHAPTER 15

UNITED STATES : COLORADO

Senator Hefner T. Copeland shook his head in disbelief as he paced up and down the war room like a caged animal. He had just returned from a sensitive political lunch in Colorado Springs where he had been discussing the never-ending problems of nuclear proliferation with one of his Senate colleagues. Upon arriving at the battle cap he had been bursting with a sense of righteous triumph, but having just studied the bunch of flimsies which had been handed to him from the chattering line printer over in the corner he now radiated the profound insecurities of a newly graduated attorney.

Around him, a group of senior CIA Officers and Cheyenne Mountain people whispered to each other and made animated gestures of disbelief. The National Security Advisor turned to the Duty Officer and said "Any further traffic from Washington?"

"No sir. But we're expecting another advisory within the hour." Drew Dalton took a sharp intake of breath and rubbed his forehead, while Ross Lombardi eased back into one of the swivelling bucket seats, and sipped his coffee. It was Peter Lawrence's first visit to the Cheyenne Mountain Operations Centre and the sheer scale of the place deep in the heart of this granite mountain had filled him with a sense of awe. He'd been an undercover agent for a long time and thought he'd seen everything there was to see – but this surpassed everything. It was the ultimate in sophisticated data collection and surveillance. He was convinced there was certainly nothing in Britain, or anywhere else in the world for that matter, which could be compared to it. He'd flown to Washington with Lombardi just a couple of days ago, after first sorting things out in London regarding the Eamonn Burke connection.

Adrian Dyson hadn't been exactly happy about using a known IRA gunman on a delicate international assignment like this, but after several telephone calls to Washington, the green light was finally given by Whitehall. Now everyone was embroiled in a heated discussion deep inside the Cheyenne Mountain Operations Centre. They needed as much technical and physical backup as they could muster, before flying on to Israel for a further link up with the Mossad agents.

"Jesus," Copeland hissed, "this is some half-baked maverick sideshow!"

"Possibly. But it's still got the full backing of Washington… and London," Lombardi confirmed.

"Unofficially!" Copeland was quick to point out as he spun round. "I am even more concerned since this whole operation could prove deeply offensive to an ally of the United States and one with whom we enjoy a most special relationship."

"Maybe, Senator, but we're still gonna need backup!"

"This guy Burke," the Senator waved his hand with an irritated flourish, "he's a goddam IRA killer, for Christ's sake!"

"We're well aware of that: but he's still the only one who's got the right contacts we need to pull this off!"

"What's the CIA line on this?" Copeland's eyes narrowed as he focussed on Drew Dalton.

"Well, we're with *you* this time, Senator." Dalton fixed his return gaze upon the Senator, afraid to meet Lombardi's eyes. "We can't get involved officially."

"I'm not asking you to get involved *officially!*" Lombardi was beginning to get angry.

"I just need some sensible backup – even *unofficial* backup will do."

"What exactly do you need, Ross?" Dalton finally turned to his undercover agent. At least he knew how to respect authority, which was more than could be said of his subordinate.

"Money, men, information…"

"Money you got! Also, we'll give you all the information we can from here. Can't help you with the manpower."

"Why not, for Christ's sake?"

"Listen Ross, this thing's so sensitive it could go off in our faces. You, Lawrence and Burke … you guys are beyond the pale. Look, we're not even sure there's a problem."

"You've got the Mossad reports, and ours. What else d'you need?"

"These reports are speculative. Nothing's conclusive Ross. It could all be a wild goose chase."

"If it gets tight and we ain't got the manpower, Drew … we're dead! You know that."

"Sorry, can't help you Ross!"

"Then I'm out of it!" Lombardi stood up and made to leave.

"No you're not!" Dalton stated emphatically as he tried, one last time, to impress upon Lombardi the gravity of the situation.

"Is that an order?" Lombardi enquired sarcastically.

"You got it, fella! Goddam it Ross, if I have to, I will personally make you account for every cent on every line of your missions budget. And then I will personally retire you from the services of Uncle Sam if necessary."

Ross Lombardi spun round.

"Let's get outta here!" he shouted across to Peter Lawrence. "This place is beginning to close in and make me very mad!" Lombardi flung the door open and stormed out of the war room. Lawrence grabbed the arms of his chair but hesitated for a moment, and looked questioningly towards Drew Dalton. Dalton nodded and impatiently motioned for him to follow Lombardi. Peter Lawrence quickly gathered up his papers and hurried after the agent, scurrying along as he tried to keep up with Lombardi, striding through Cheyenne Mountain's complex maze of corridors.

"Hey! Watch it fella!"

"Who the hell is that guy?"

"Somebody call security."

The sound of angry voices followed in the wake of the two agents as they left a trail of scattered paperwork and shaken personnel behind them. Lombardi and Lawrence climbed aboard a blue military shuttle bus about to depart for the half-mile ride down the main access tunnel towards the reception complex at the entrance. When they finally emerged from Security, they strode across to the upper car park.

Lombardi didn't say a word. He jumped into his electric blue Thunderbird and gunned the engine. Lawrence had barely closed the door when the vehicle leapt forward and sped away down the mountain towards Fort Carson, away from the simmering wrath they had just left behind in the "Hall of the Mountain King."

Lombardi drove north along Highway 24, skirting Skyway and Manitou Springs. It was getting cold this late in the year and to Lawrence the snow-clad mountains seemed so close that he could almost reach out and touch them. The rocky Colorado countryside rushed past the speeding car. He was amazed to see a bizarre red sandstone rock formation thrusting angrily skywards in the Garden of the Gods away to his right. Eagles swooped and soared in the steel-blue sky above this primeval landscape – the restless souls of long departed braves watching over their ancestral homelands. Lawrence briefly contemplated upon the origins of this fourteen hundred acre geological phenomenon. He quickly came to the conclusion that it formed a sharp contrast with the cold grey granite of Cheyenne Mountain, forged on the anvil of creation more than one hundred million years ago.

Other landmarks flashed past as Lombardi angrily pressed the gas pedal to the floor – places like the Cave of Winds and Ghost Town, which Lawrence would have liked to have seen at first hand. But Lombardi was in no mood to stop for a guided tour. Just outside Green Mountain Falls, their innermost thoughts were rudely interrupted by a wailing siren. Lombardi grimaced as he checked in the rear view mirror and saw a flashing blue light fast approaching. He cursed his luck and slowed down, to pull off the road. The Highway Patrol officer kicked down the stand and parked his motorcycle about ten metres behind the Thunderbird.

"Oh my god…" muttered Lawrence as he slid down in his seat and covered his face with his hand when he noticed the officer flip the restraining strap off his large, holstered handgun. As the window rolled down on the driver's side, he just hoped Ross Lombardi would keep his big mouth shut. A late autumn sun glinted on the approaching officers buckles and badges. The sky and surrounding world were reflected in the wrap-around shades which hid his inquisitive eyes beneath the visor of his gleaming white helmet. A fine layer of powdery dust had settled across the toe-caps of his highly polished boots. Officer Kaminski, for that was the name etched upon the badge above the breast pocket of his immaculately pressed blue uniform, wasted no time in letting them know that he was the big Kahuna that went with the territory.

"OK guys, where's the fire?" Kaminski asked sarcastically.

"Were we speeding officer?" Lombardi played the innocent.

"Hundred and nine … I'd say that was speeding, mister."

"Sorry officer, but we're on official Government business." Lombardi nonchalantly took out his badge and Identity Papers and offered them to the patrolman. The Officer studied them carefully and glanced at the two occupants before handing them back.

"OK," he said at length "I'll let it go this time. But just because you got Government connections don't mean you can go a hundred and nine on my roads."

"Thank you officer."

"You go easy now mister." He pointed a crooked finger at Lombardi. "If I catch you speeding again, you'll get a ticket – regardless of your connections."

"Don't worry, you won't catch me again." Peter Lawrence puffed out his cheeks and exhaled slowly as Ross Lombardi rolled up the window and proceeded with the serenity of a priest on his way to Holy Communion.

They turned off the main highway at Woodland Park and followed the contours that hugged the South Platte River along narrow winding mountain roads, until they came to Trout Creek Pass, near Buena Vista in the Pike National Forest area. Lombardi brought the car to an abrupt halt in a shower of gravel outside a timber-clad roadhouse called Silverado Sally's. Over the doorway a gaudy neon sculpture of a cowgirl shooting a six-gun flashed its brash message to the world. Darkness was falling and so were the first light flakes of autumn snow. Peter Lawrence turned his collar up against the sharp wind and followed Ross Lombardi into the dimly-lit interior of the bar. The regular patronage of Silverado Sally's consisted mainly of cowboy types and mountain men, with six or seven of them sitting on bar stools drinking Budweiser, Coors or Rolling Rock as they watched the latest ball game on the overhead TV.

They didn't even glance at the strangers. There were half a dozen pool tables over to one side – and three of them were occupied. Ross Lombardi looked around, while Peter Lawrence rubbed his eyes and tried to acclimatise to the gloom. Lombardi grabbed a beer, pulled the ring tab, and walked across to the pool tables on the darkened side of the room. A giant of a man with blonde hair and a freckled face was playing eight-ball pool against another black bearded colossus. Just as the blonde man was about to take his shot, Lombardi's ethereal hand penetrated the bright pyramid of light falling across the table and picked up the cue ball.

"Hey!" the men roared in unison. Peter Lawrence withdrew to his beer and wished he'd brought a gum-shield. Ross Lombardi had probably just started World War Three ... and he was on the losing side. It took the big men a critical moment to focus on the shadowy figure of Lombardi, standing back in the gloom beyond the table-lights.

"Ross, you old rattlesnake!" Larry Tyson roared as he threw down his cue and went round to embrace his friend with a bear-hug that took Lombardi's feet off the floor.

"Larry, you big ox! Hi Jake..." Lombardi greeted both men, "Hey Peter, come on over and meet some friends of mine."

"Hello ..." Peter Lawrence felt the bones of his fingers crack under the pressure of Larry Tyson's handshake.

"Hi Pete, say what's a limey like you doin' up here in this wilderness?"

"I don't exactly know." Lawrence managed a wry smile. "Just tagging along with Ross." Lawrence's London accent seemed oddly exotic in a bar dominated by the descendants of early pioneers and the great grandsons of the Confederacy.

"You here to do some fishin', Ross?" Jake enquired in a raising tone of disbelief.

"More serious business than that, Jake."

"What's more serious than fishin'?" Larry Tyson roared.

"Politics!" Lombardi snapped.

"In that case it's best I get us some beer." Jake called for a pitcher of Rolling Rock and four glasses, as they went over and settled in one of the booths. The men waited until the barman had gone before continuing with their conversation. Lombardi drew them into a huddle and gave the big men an overview of the situation. He explained they were going to need some reliable manpower … just in case things got too physical.

"How many guys do you need?" Tyson asked.

"About a dozen." Lombardi replied.

"Qualifications?"

"Ex-military if possible. They need to be able to handle weapons … and themselves."

"What sort of terrain?" Jake enquired as he became more interested.

"Desert maybe, at first" Lombardi confirmed "Also some marine action, if things get out of hand."

"That's some tall order, Ross." Larry Tyson swept his Stetson aside and scratched thoughtfully at his shock of blonde hair.

"I know, Larry. If you can't do it, I'll understand."

"What about weapons?" Jake came closer.

"No problem. My people will lay on all the equipment we need. Any running extras will be supplied by the Israelis."

"And cash?"

"No problem either."

"Limits?" Tyson enquired "Guys of this calibre are gonna cost a lot of dough."

"No limits." Lombardi assured him. "Money and equipment ain't a problem … it's the right calibre of manpower we need. That's more important. That's why I'm here, talking to you guys. The people I need for this type of operation have to be the best: and they've got to be able to keep their mouths shut."

Larry Tyson grunted and poured out the beer. They all drank without speaking for a few moments. Tyson placed his palms down on the table and rose to his feet.

"Let me make a call, Ross." He crossed the room to a phone booth and went inside, closing the folding door behind him. The others sat back and watched as he spoke to someone for about five minutes. They couldn't hear what was being said but they knew some hard bargaining was going on. Tyson's expression changed at several stages during the conversation and once he even punched the glass door of the booth so

THE CHERKASSY INCIDENT · 155

hard it almost smashed. Gradually, his countenance softened and he nodded a few times before hanging up. Back at the table, Larry Tyson stood with both hands thrust deep into his pockets and his hairy throat poking through his open-necked shirt as he looked down with narrowed eyes at Ross Lombardi.

"Cost you sixty thousand up front," he stated with the confidence of a man who felt he had the upper hand.

"OK." Lombardi didn't bat an eyelid.

"That's just for starters. Another sixty grand before we set out – all expenses paid – and sixty grand for every man on his return."

"Sounds fair," Lombardi demurred "You'll vouch for these guys, Larry?"

"Sure will!"

"Then it's a deal!" They all shook hands. Lombardi turned and beckoned to the barman. "Another pitcher over here … and a bottle of Jack Daniels."

CHAPTER 16

ISRAEL : HAIFA

THEY CLIMBED DOWN FROM THE SMALL PLANE that had brought them in from Tel Aviv. Ross Lombardi wondered just what the hell he was doing here. He still wasn't convinced there was anything to all this Russian submarine stuff. OK, so he'd heard all the reasoned arguments, coupled with some garbled message from a drunken Irish sailor – but it still didn't add up to a hill-o'-beans. Right now, he'd rather be back home in the States, especially as the skiing season was about to start, or better still, fishing for winter bream in the snow-covered Rocky Mountains. Drinking bourbon by a roaring log fire also had its attractions. However, he'd well and truly committed himself and his Colorado friends to the mission: and there was certainly no backing out. He hefted his bags and followed in the wake of his two English colleagues as they crossed the hot tarmac ramp of the small airport outside Haifa. They sauntered over to a small terminal building, where Benjamin Eshkol was impatiently waiting to rush them through the usual formalities. He ushered them to a Mercedes which had been parked in a restricted area. A police officer stood nearby – contemplating whether to give him a ticket. None of the Western agents knew where they were heading, but guessed this would probably be used as nothing more than another convenient platform for a paranoid and hysterical Eshkol.

No-one said very much. Peter Lawrence just sighed and resigned himself to the inevitable. He was happy enough to play along with this assignment for the time being. Besides, there was always the prospect of unfinished business with Juliet Lucas, who now sat beside him on the back seat of the Mossad car. He reflected upon their last meeting...

and wondered if their embryonic relationship would go any further. He certainly hoped so. Or would it merely end before it had even begun ... just like all his other relationships.

Lucas was the only one of the three visitors who actually took the assignment seriously. She was well aware that a personal relationship with Lawrence could totally compromise her professional situation. Nevertheless, it had happened and, provided it was handled carefully and didn't get out of hand, it might even be turned to advantage at a later stage.

Instead of taking the *Ophir* highway into the city, Benjamin Eshkol drove inland towards Nazareth, with the busy road threading its way through the dry and dusty *Jezreel* valley. He finally brought the car to a halt at *Qirat Tivon*, the sacred location of the ancient city of *Beit She'arim*. The Israeli got out and beckoned enthusiastically for the others to follow.

"Not *another* tour" groaned Lombardi as he slid wearily from the car. The Mossad agent ignored this last remark and forged ahead, stopping only when he reached the top of a small hill. From this vantage point, it was possible to see most of the valley. Eshkol flung his arms into the air.

"This, my friends, is the Promised Land..."

Lombardi rolled his eyes and Peter Lawrence sighed loudly.

"This has been occupied by my people since palaeolithic times," Eshkol continued, undaunted. "It has survived the Romans, the Crusades and the Ottoman conquest. This is the land of God! This is the House of Gates, the seat of the *Sanhedrin*, the Supreme Court of Jewish Law! Here Rabbi Yehudah Hanassi set down the *Mishnah*. Here, the Necropolis and the very catacombs beneath our feet house the tombs of my forefathers. I will allow no Arab nor Gentile to trespass over this land again!"

"OK. So now we've seen it. Can we at least get back to Haifa?" a weary Ross Lombardi asked in a semi-pleading tone.

"It is extremely important that you understand what this is all about," Eshkol retorted as he came down and approached the group.

"Yes, we know," Peter Lawrence agreed as he quietly stifled a yawn.

"Oh, but I don't think you do!" The veins on Eshkol's temple stood out as he shouted with another expansive sweep of his arm. He wouldn't be distracted from his grand exposé of oppression and tyranny. Eshkol rolled up his sleeve to reveal what at first appeared to be a small blue smudge. He thrust his forearm towards them. Although faded with age, they could still make out the number 687353.

"Yes, my friends, I was there. I was only five years old. My mother hid me from the guards at Auschwitz and when the camp was finally liberated, we were left to wander across Europe. We eventually travelled down to southern France and ended up at the port of Sate in the summer of 1947. Here we boarded a ship, the *Exodus*, and set sail for freedom and a new life. Haifa was our first sight of the Promised Land. Imagine our horror and disbelief when we remained anchored offshore and were not allowed to land. Everything was so tantalisingly close – and yet so far" A distant expression came across his face. "And do you know who actually stopped us from landing, Mr Lawrence?" He choked back the words. "The British!" Peter Lawrence felt uncomfortable. "My mother managed to grab me and jumped overboard in the confusion which followed as your sailors systematically opened fire on the passengers. Yes my friend, defenceless civilians. We barely made it to the shore, but our people on the beach quickly took us into hiding." Lawrence was clearly embarrassed. Eshkol had made his point. In his more mellow moments he would be the first to admit he had a streak of arrogance, but maintained it was only a selfless arrogance conceived from an overwhelming sense of duty and service for the State of Israel. Tears filled Eshkol's eyes as he turned away and quietly rolled down his sleeve before leading them back to the car.

To Benjamin Eshkol, everything was either right or wrong. There was no in-between, no grey areas, no room for compromise.

Eshkol was a proud man who had always longed to be a man of action. He wanted to fight. He wanted to kill for his country. He didn't wait to be called up for his obligatory two years of military service. No, he volunteered at the first opportunity. Despite his fervent patriotism, he nevertheless still felt absolutely devastated at being rejected as a result of some lingering physical deficiencies and an asthmatic condition caused by his childhood experiences. Despite a look of utter dejection, one of the officers on the selection panel had spotted other qualities in the young Eshkol. He was quietly ushered into a side room of the recruiting offices... and into the mysterious world of the Secret Service. It turned out to be a good strategic career move, and one which led him to becoming the very eyes and ears of the State. A true Hawk.

Eshkol paused by the car and took a few puffs from his nebuliser. "You know that Nasaf Rhullah's name is on the crew list of the *Norse Warrior*?"

"Your people already told us that in Washington," Ross Lombardi confirmed.

"If it was up to me, we wouldn't hesitate. We would send some of our air force to the North Sea and blow Captain Ramuldssen and his entire crew out of the water."

"There are such organisations as NATO and the UN for sorting that kind of thing out," Peter Lawrence pointed out.

"Oh yes? And where were they in '82 … or in '78 and '73?" Benjamin Eshkol laughed derisively.

"Look, it's getting late. Can we at least get back to Haifa," Lombardi insisted. "What d'you say?"

Lawrence looked across to the American. Both men shrugged their shoulders. On the other hand, Juliet Lucas had become completely captivated by Eshkol's passion and patriotism, hanging on to his every word. After more ranting and fist-shaking in the general direction of the Syrian border, the Israeli was finally persuaded back into the car. Each agent stared out of opposite windows and remained deep in thought, as the group retraced their tracks along Moria Boulevard and through the Haifa suburbs.

This was Israel's third city. It dominated the northern part of the country both politically and commercially. There is an old Jewish saying, "In Jerusalem they pray, in Tel Aviv they play, but in Haifa they work!" This was, indeed, a working city and one so proud of its tolerance and pragmatism. But it was also an attractive place, sweeping up towards Mount Carmel, away from the bustling port. The higher up you climbed, the more exclusive the residential areas became. The view from the car was outstanding. A cooling breeze blew in through the open windows as they proceeded up Hanassi Boulevard, past Gan Haem Park and turned west along Yefe Nof towards the coast. Benjamin Eshkol had become quiet and brooding. He didn't like the modern Haifa – it held too much of a liberal reputation for his liking. Druze, Muslim and Christian Arabs were tolerated and even local busses were allowed to run on the Sabbath. Eshkol was convinced they were all Arab spies. He always preferred to do business in Tel Aviv, but on this occasion the politicians had decided this would be a better place to meet their western counterparts. It was not so conspicuous – and didn't have so many prying eyes.

The car continued down the steep winding gradients towards the western sun and their final destination; the three-star Hotel Carmelia on Herzliya Street, where the agents had been booked into separate, but adjoining rooms. They collected their luggage from the trunk of the car and went up to their rooms to freshen up. Benjamin Eshkol agreed to meet everyone down in the lobby at seven thirty.

He arrived on time and took them to a safe Mossad house just off Derekh Ha-Yam. David Weizman and Ruth Netanya joined them in a large room overlooking the City. Polite greetings were exchanged. Ross Lombardi lingered with Netanya's hand just a little too long. He tried to look into her eyes, but she turned away, resuming her original professional coolness.

"OK," David Weizman began, "We're here to take a logical look at the situation and to co-ordinate our strategies. Let's try and see if we can make some sense out of what we already know."

"No two-bit salvage bucket can bring up those missiles, that's for sure," Lombardi swept his jacket aside with a flourish and thrust his hands deep into his trouser pockets. He strolled over to the picture window and looked down at the funicular rail cars clawing their way up from the twinkling lights of the harbour below, before rejoining the others seated around the coffee table.

"Maybe…" Weizman mused as he rolled out a large map of the Middle Eastern region on to the table. "We know the Russian submarine *Cherkassy* went down in more than six hundred feet of water just north of Kolskiy Zaliv." He waited for agreement. Everyone nodded. "We have already established that Iranian naval personnel were on board – but what we don't know is why the Iranians subsequently abducted some Russian missile scientists – and also why they are crewing up a salvage ship?"

"Which is actually incapable of raising a rusty bicycle from the bottom of the River Thames," Peter Lawrence scoffed with a wagging finger to emphasise the point.

"We're missing something…" Weizman mused as he stroked his chin and studied the map. "There's something else … another vital piece of the jigsaw."

"But what?" Juliet Lucas enquired naively.

"If we knew *that*, we'd be in total control of the situation." Weizman's brows were knit in furious concentration as he again shuffled through the pile of documents and photographs.

"I don't like all this uncertainty!" Benjamin Eshkol retorted. "We must have more verifiable information!"

"Perhaps there *is* something else…" Peter Lawrence slowly raised his hand, as ideas began to form in his mind, sparking and colliding as they pitched and tumbled through his head.

"What?" Eshkol and Weizman snapped in unison.

"Well … my people in London have an undercover contact on the *Norse Warrior*. A definite connection has already been established between the salvage ship and the Barents Sea."

"And just who is this contact?" Eshkol asked impatiently. He was a man who had developed a penetrating grasp of tactics and a clear understanding of covert operations. He just wanted to get straight to the point.

"An Irishman. We've been communicating with for some time – and he's reliable."

"That's enough for me!" Eshkol growled as he slapped his hands down upon his knees. "We must destroy the ship immediately."

"No!" Ruth Netanya insisted "Don't you see … if everybody is correct, the *Norse Warrior* is just a decoy. There has to be another ship. Destroying the salvage vessel will not compromise their mission. We must find this other ship – and fast."

"By God she's right!" Ross Lombardi slid forward in his seat to study the chart and pile of documents more closely. "We've been sold a dummy!"

"You must go to Pakistan immediately," Benjamin Eshkol went over to a side desk and rapidly punched out a series of digits on the secure telephone.

"And just exactly who did you have in mind?" Lombardi asked hesitantly.

"Why *you*, Mr Lombardi … and Mr Lawrence. Find out all you can about these Russian missile scientists. Somebody must know where they are."

"When you say immediately…" Peter Lawrence queried as he shot a glance at Lombardi.

"Oh I mean tomorrow … or at least no later than the day after. Just as soon as it can be arranged." Eshkol waved impatiently, cleared his throat and spoke urgently in Hebrew into the receiver.

"What happens if we actually locate them?"

"We'll send in a task force," Eshkol slammed the receiver down on to its cradle and returned to the table.

"*Into Iran?*" Juliet Lucas gasped in amazement. She was enthralled. This was what she wanted. Things were really moving and more importantly, she was right in the thick of it.

"We certainly have the means, Miss Lucas," Eshkol assured her. "Even if it means going into Tehran itself, believe me, we will do it!"

"And your man will continue to monitor activities on the *Norse Warrior?*" David Weizman enquired of Peter Lawrence.

"Of course."

"Good. Then my team will continue our own investigations. We must find that other ship … and also the whereabouts of the original Russian crew from the *Cherkassy*." Eshkol replied.

"Not many survived; as far as we know" Lombardi confirmed.

"The Captain, Executive Officer and Weapons Officer were amongst those we know for sure who made it," David Weizman said.

"You are absolutely certain about that?" Lombardi asked with a hint of cynicism.

"As sure as we can be. We know they subsequently took the full rap for the Russian Government after the accident. They were dismissed from the service."

"But more to the point – *where are they now?*" Eshkol queried. "We must find them!"

The meeting broke up, with agreements to take the mission a stage further and compare reports in due course.

❖ ❖ ❖

Later that same evening, Peter Lawrence and Juliet Lucas decided to go down to the port area of the city to see some of the local colour. Lawrence would rather have stayed back at the hotel, but Lucas had insisted on seeing some Haifa night-life. They were settling down to a quiet drink in the back of one of the local bars which had outdoor tables spilling onto the pavement, when Lawrence noticed Ross Lombardi entering with Ruth Netanya. Both men pretended they hadn't seen each other and quickly looked away. The women, however, waved and insisted they make up a foursome. The night moved on, with generous quantities of Scotch being consumed by the men and liberal pernods appearing in front of the women. Conversation centred around their private likes and dislikes; and they actually managed to get to know each other just a little better.

Soon it was way past midnight and time to return to the hotel. The couples decided to take separate taxis and Juliet Lucas naturally assumed this was nothing more than a standard procedure for security reasons.

Juliet collected her key from the hotel's front desk and joined Peter waiting in the hallway at the top of the stairs.

"Do you remember "Clair de Lune?" she turned and asked him seductively outside her door.

"How could I ever forget," he answered softly.

"Shall we see if the hotel has it?"

"Do you think we should?" His lips were already brushing hers.

"Oh, I do" she purred.

"And what if they haven't?"

"I'm sure we can find a suitable alternative" Juliet gently broke away and smiled sensuously as she pushed the door open. Her coat slipped from her shoulders and she kicked her shoes away across the floor.

CHAPTER 17

IRAN : GULF OF OMAN

Captain Ahmed Ramsar could feel the ship tremble with power from the massive engines ten decks below. He glanced at the chart and then peered into the radar hood before picking up his binoculars and stepping out on to the starboard bridge wing of the supertanker *Konari*. The quarter mile of decking which lay before him, festooned with a labyrinth of pipes, valves and catwalks pitched gently in the swell as they navigated through the busy shipping lanes within the Straits of Hormuz. Ramsar, deep in thought, tugged at his stubby black goatee, his jaw resolutely clenched, which made him appear aggressive or intensively determined. He raised his binoculars to scan the horizon. Away to starboard, three destroyers of the Coalition Forces cruised back and forth, towing sonar array systems. He smiled. Somewhere ahead, they would have detected the two kilo-class diesel/electric submarines which had left harbour just ahead of the *Konari* and were now headed out into the Indian Ocean for routine exercises. Ramsar had recently been seconded from the Iranian Navy and was currently charged with the safe transfer of his very special cargo to its ultimate destination. As the *Konari* rounded Muscat, they set course due south, intending to pass down the eastern coast of Madagascar before rounding the Cape of Good Hope and breaking out into the South Atlantic. Meanwhile, cocooned deep within the supertanker's modified hull, feverish work continued on the recently acquired Russian Delta 3 submarine, *Zarand*, in preparation for her designated covert mission.

Sailing up the west coast of Africa a dull red glow away to the east announced another breaking dawn, as the *Konari* hove to off the palm fringed coast of the Islamic Republic of Mauritania. This country had long held sympathies with Iran and after eighteen days at sea the port of Nouakchott provided a welcome opportunity for a much needed run ashore. The Russians disembarked with Sharif Hamad and after some frenetic haggling with one of the local merchants, the Iranian had managed to procure a jeep. Everyone climbed aboard and took a ride out into the desert. The hot dryness of the air upon their faces was a welcome change from the humidity and stuffiness on board ship. Hamad brought the jeep to a halt beside a small oasis tucked into a secluded wadi several miles inland. A wizened group of nomadic herdsmen had just struck camp and were in the process of gathering their scrawny flock of sheep and goats together. The Bedouins paid little attention to these strange visitors and headed out into the desert with barely a backward glance. In this wilderness it paid to be discreet. It was approaching noon and the tantalising glint of water proved irresistible to the Russians, in the centre of this green island, surrounded by a sea of yellow sand. They stripped off their sweaty clothes and rushed headlong into the pool, laughing and splashing like excited children. Sharif Hamad checked their supplies for the day and looked on from the jeep. At least he would allow them this small pleasure. God only knew what few pleasures remained of their shallow and transient lives. Despite Hamad's mood swings, he was certainly not inhuman. He was not a man without feelings for his fellow creatures and much regretted his superiors" decision to eliminate these Russian friends… once the mission had been completed. He had easily become disillusioned after arguing and pleading with all levels of the military and political establishment in Tehran.

    These Russian officers could be so useful. They could settle down and lead productive lives within the Republic – passing on their valuable expertise to others. But no, his pleas had fallen on to deaf ears. Once again, the fundamentalists had triumphed over the liberals. Sharif Hamad had always been a progressive man. He believed in live and let live – but unswerving loyalty to his country came before all else. He would carry out his orders without hesitation. He would sacrifice the Russians – and himself if necessary, to the divine will of Allah.

    "Sharif. Come and join us" Rem Bukato spluttered.

"I'm fine where I am" The Iranian laughed and waved dismissively at the antics of the men in the water.

"Coward!" Boris Lukin cupped his hands and bellowed like a water buffalo. But Hamad would not be enticed. He began to unload the jeep. After their refreshing swim, the Russians carefully hung their clothes over the bushes to dry in the hot noonday sun. Hamad took a tarpaulin from the jeep and spread it on the ground beneath the palm trees where they all sat down to eat. The food they had acquired from the merchant in Nouakchott was a strange mixture of Arab, French and Chinese specialities with a strong aroma of spices. The men ate greedily, washing it down with copious quantities of the local red wine – straight from the bottle. They were subsequently roused from their alcoholic siesta by a call from an impatient Sharif Hamad, sitting with his feet upon the dashboard of the jeep, smoking a cigarette.

"Get dressed … it's time to go," he told them.

"How long have we slept?" Valentin Tarasov asked, raising himself on one elbow and trying to focus on his watch. He looked back towards Sharif Hamad, where the sun flared behind the man's head as he moved ever so slightly, causing Tarasov to squint. The sun shot like rays from somewhere behind the Iranian. Tarasov noticed the man's Adam's apple bobbing above his open-neck shirt, and the veins standing out on his forehead as the jet-black eyes bore down into his own.

"Too long." Hamad flicked his half-finished cigarette into the sand.

The Russians silently gathered up their things and climbed back into the jeep for the bumpy return journey along the dirt road to Nouakchott. Hamad was anxious not to stay too long in one place. Even though he was convinced they had shaken off all Western surveillance, he still didn't want to run the risk of a satellite scan re-establishing their position. Once the Russians re-boarded the *Konari*, they set a course for the Northern Atlantic.

Night had fallen and it was becoming difficult to discern where sky and sea actually met as Captain Ramsar scanned the pitch-black horizon. Forty eight uneventful hours had passed since leaving Nouakchott and out there, invisible to the naked eye, but not to his radar, would be a number of inquisitive vessels trying to make sense of the *Konari's* latest manoeuvres seven hundred and fifty miles south west of Madeira. The giant ship had slowed down during the past hour, but maintained just enough steerage-way as she was brought round to face the long undulating swell.

"What is the latest weather forecast?"

"It will hold for the time being – but a cold front is forecast by dawn tomorrow," replied the navigator.

"Very well." Ramsar resumed pacing up and down the darkened bridge. So far they had been lucky, but the deteriorating weather several hundred miles to the west was beginning to threaten their mission.

"Maintain this course and speed."

"Aye, aye, sir."

The Captain glanced at the ship's glowing instruments on the rear wall of the gloomy bridge. He turned his back on the first officer, picked up the telephone and dialled the Chief Engineer in charge of below-deck operations.

"How soon can we launch the submarine?"

There was a brief pause. "Flooding of the dock is progressing. We will be ready within the hour" came the reply.

Valentin Tarasov still had reservations. A burning conflict of doubt still raged within him. Was it right to put his own personal interests above the safety of the entire world, or was he merely seeking revenge upon the Russian Authorities who had treated him so badly? He didn't know the answers, but studied the hull plating of the submarine as if it would yield up clues or inspiration.

Rem Bukato's hand gently fell upon his shoulder and stirred Tarasov from his private thoughts.

"We must get aboard now, Captain."

Tarasov wearily shook his head and murmured, "I think I am getting too old for this kind of operation."

"Nonsense. A commander without fear or doubt when about to embark upon such an important mission is a fool."

Tarasov grunted his acknowledgement and stood back when he noticed a strange group of men approaching. They wore Hamas headgear, but were somehow different from the other Arabs. "Who are these men?" he enquired.

"They are *felo de se* … martyrs," Sharif Hamad informed him. It is considered a blessing for them to die for Allah."

"But why are they coming with us?"

"Just a precaution," Sharif Hamad followed the suicide squad across the gangplank and boarded the submarine. Valentin Tarasov frowned deeply, shrugged his shoulders and followed the others on board.

Ten decks above, Captain Ahmed Ramsar decided to take advantage of a narrow window of opportunity when he knew the heavens would be free of American spy satellites. He ordered the huge clam-shell doors to the bow of the supertanker to be opened. When the *Zarand* finally shed the last of her umbilicals she was released from captivity. Ramsar ordered the *Konari* to go slow astern. The submarine's sinister black bow gradually emerged from the eerie green glow cast by the tanker's cavernous interior – and headed out into the gentle Atlantic swell. Half a nautical mile of total darkness separated the two vessels, before Ramsar gave orders for the clam-shell doors to be re-closed, allowing the *Konari* to resume her normal maritime activities.

Captain Valentin Tarasov completed his walk-through of the submarine. Space on board the *Zarand* was at a premium. The extra anti-detection equipment crammed alongside the salvage gear took up a lot of the room. A hand picked and highly dedicated Iranian crew of ninety was well below the usual full complement, but this deficiency was adequately supplemented by the three Russians and the suicide squad which made up a further twelve. The Hamas death squad did very little – except dismantle and clean their weapons and generally get in everybody's way. Sharif Hamad moved amongst the crew and tried to keep the peace between the various groups and be as accommodating as possible; but nothing he did seemed to satisfy them. It soon became clear these men held some strange mordacious influence over the Iranian seamen. Three were quartered in a long wide space designed for weapon storage at the bow of the vessel, whilst the remaining nine stayed in the modified torpedo room. They roamed at will throughout the submarine, glaring menacingly at anyone who dared to challenge their authority. Most of the Iranian crew were berthed in cramped quarters at the forward end of the boat. They avoided contact with the Hamas killers as much as possible. On the whole, both parties kept their distance. It was as if the fanatics were regarded as some form of super-beings. Valentin Tarasov shared a small cabin with his Russian colleagues, and each of them took it in turns to man the Control Centre.

"Captain …" Tarasov was woken urgently by Boris Lukin.

"What is it?"

"The Executive Officer needs you in the Control Centre."

"What time is it?" Tarasov yawned and looked at his watch.

"16.00 hours Captain."

"What's wrong? Why does Bukato need me at this hour?"

"He has a problem in the Control Centre." Lukin turned and left the room without further explanation. Tarasov grumbled to himself as he slid out of his bunk and got dressed. He ran a comb through his tousled hair before splashing some cold water onto his face from the tiny stainless-steel basin tucked alongside a fold-down desk. He quickly dried himself off and tossed the towel over the back of a chair before stepping through to Control. Valentin Tarasov felt several pairs of eyes lock onto him as he entered. Rem Bukato stood on the periscope platform shouting in Russian at two members of the Hamas death squad. The killers ignored the Russian's vitriolic onslaught and continued to move around the sailors seated at their control positions, examining the equipment with child-like interest – picking things up, looking at them from all angles and putting them back down again.

"You men…" Tarasov roared. "What are you doing up here?" The pair of Hamas fanatics casually turned and looked at him quizzically.

"They don't respond Captain," Bukato said in an exasperated tone. "I've ordered them to leave, but they take no notice."

Tarasov stepped forward and drew his automatic pistol, levelling the weapon at the head of one of the men.

"Perhaps they'll understand this!" he hissed.

The Iranian glared at the Captain, beads of perspiration standing out on his forehead and anger flooding across his eyes. He smiled malevolently in the direction of his companion who quickly responded by drawing his gun and pointing it at Tarasov. Rem Bukato stepped to one side, snatched his Tokarev automatic from its holster, and aimed it at the second man. It became a dangerous stand-off. Nobody moved for what seemed like an eternity. Sharif Hamad suddenly appeared in the Control Room and elbowed his way past a knot of confused sailors, followed by Boris Lukin. He moved over to speak quietly in Arabic to the Hamas killers. They didn't respond at first, so he tried again. Although the Russians couldn't understand his words, they could certainly understand his meaning. He had made it clear that if they shot Captain Tarasov and the XO, the mission would be over. The electrifying tension began to ease as they lowered their weapons, and the sailors grudgingly stepped aside to allow the killers to leave the Control Centre. Rem Bukato, shook his head and breathed a huge sigh of relief as he re-holstered his pistol.

"What exactly did you say to them?" Tarasov asked.

"I told them we were all on the same side," Sharif Hamad replied casually.

"I won't have them unaccompanied in the Control Centre," Tarasov growled. "I don't care where else they go, but I will not have them in here without my permission ... understand?"

"I will speak to them Captain" Hamad promised.

"Just make sure it doesn't happen again." Tarasov fixed his gaze before handing control back to Rem Bukato and striding angrily back to his quarters.

Valentin Tarasov pulled himself back into his coffin-like bunk and tried to get back to sleep, but it was impossible. He wondered just what Sharif Hamad had really said to the killers. Had he told them they would get their chance later on? Could the Iranians be trusted? Would they keep their side of the bargain, or would they simply execute the Russians when they had achieved what they wanted? How on earth did he get himself into this bizarre situation? Was he really so drunk that he couldn't see all the implications? Questions and doubts flooded his mind. How he wished to be back in St Petersburg, back in his beloved city. Tarasov longed for a return to those times before the *Cherkassy* accident – to a time when he was happy, settled and at the peak of his naval career. How did all this madness start? He was still awake and staring at the overhead curvature of the hull. He listened to a low rhythmic humming coming from the ventilation system, when it was time to relieve Rem Bukato in the Control Centre.

Two days later, the *Zarand* came up to periscope depth just fifty miles off Clare Island near to the west coast of Ireland. A flash coded message was sent out to the *Norse Warrior*, still anchored in the North Sea port of Esbjerg. The message informed Captain Bjorn Ramuldssen to get under way in readiness for his journey to the Barents Sea. It was important that both vessels synchronised their voyages to ensure they would be able to rendezvous at the final destination. Once the message had been transmitted and acknowledged, the *Zarand* re-submerged and proceeded in a northerly direction towards Iceland. Tarasov ordered the boat to be rigged for silent running. He knew the ocean bed within the narrow corridor between Iceland and the Faroe Islands would be bristling with several rows of sonar buoys laid by the Americans. The *Zarand* continued in a north-easterly direction towards the Norwegian Sea, gliding silently through the icy dark waters, her computer systems tuned to the bewildering sounds of the ocean. Since the dawn of time, ice had formed above the Arctic Circle and with the onset of global warming there was always the risk of encountering a rogue iceberg in these more southerly latitudes. As a precaution, speed was reduced to ten knots and Tarasov ordered the submarine to be rigged for deep submergence down to 650 feet. He barely noticed the steady down angles and level-offs at one hundred-foot intervals as the hull stabilised, groaned and popped from the immense sea pressure. He looked around at two of the Hamas martyrs who had quietly gathered in the control room. He noticed their nervousness. Their uneasy sweat-soaked faces instinctively turned upwards towards the curved roof, as if desperately trying to see the cold surface more than a tenth of a mile above. Tarasov was in his element. Perhaps they were not super-human after all. The time was rapidly approaching when they would confront their destiny. The cold lifeless hull of the *Cherkassy* awaited them in the freezing waters of the Barents Sea. Only God knew what the outcome would be – but was God on their side? The Iranians obviously believed he was, but Tarasov wasn't so sure.

Part of the ever elusive answer to Tarasov's doubts and fears hovered in geosynchronous orbit 22,300 miles overhead. A Strategic Defence Satellite had silently moved into position and deployed its infra-red telescope as it stared down upon the *Norse Warrior*. In microseconds, an endless stream of data began finding its way back to Cheyenne Mountain. There, after further encryption by the vast bank of supercomputers, it was electronically sorted and despatched by secure fibre-optic cables to several classified "need to know" recipients in different time zones around the world.

CHAPTER 18

Esbjerg : The Norwegian Sea

The *Norse Warrior* looked deserted from across the oil smeared glassy waters of the harbour. Nodding gently at her moorings, her flags were limp and her decks were bare, except for a few fifty-gallon steel barrels lashed behind the wheelhouse. Large coils of steel wire and chains lay between the clutter of drums and winches of a powerful capstan unit in the broad expanse of her afterdeck. The white paint of her superstructure was streaked with rust and neglect. A tall, two-legged structure known as an A-frame, had been braced out over the stern. Upon closer inspection, a lone figure could be seen creeping along the deck. The figure took up a crouched position beneath one of the stairways leading up to the bridge. With his back pressed against the superstructure, Eamonn Burke inched towards one of the radio room's open portholes. Inside, Bjorn Ramuldssen and Nasaf Rhullah were hunched over a chart, busily discussing the latest deciphered signal. Burke backed away from the porthole and withdrew silently towards the afterdeck. He paused and briefly glanced around the ship and surrounding quayside, before stepping over the threshold of a watertight doorway and making his way down to the engine room.

Below decks, Burke had hidden a small radio transmitter behind one of the salvage boat's main oil tanks which supplied the huge diesel engines. He squeezed past a chugging bilge pump so that he could reach between the tank and the side of the hull. His groping hand fell upon the rucksack containing his transmitter: clutching it to his chest, he crawled through a small hatchway leading to the forward hold and into the cable locker. Once inside the cramped space, he wriggled over a stinking pile of ropes and opened up the bag to unwind a length of thin copper wire. His heart was thumping. He quickly inserted a jack plug into the back of the transmitter and draped the rest of the aerial from several points beneath the overhead deck. His anxiety began to rise and beads of perspiration speckled his brow. He took one last look towards the hatchway to make sure that he was alone... before transmitting his message to London – "Orders to sail arrived 07.00 hours – from somewhere to the west of Ireland – out."

Despite having transmitted on a couple of previous occasions, Burke nevertheless couldn't help feeling that his luck was about to run out. All was chaos aboard the *Norse Warrior* with drunken sailors assembling in the ship's galley. Normally this area would have been cleared by now, but today it was filled with a grumbling crew of cutthroats and thugs, speculating about their future. A strange mixture of expressions materialised on their weather-beaten faces, ranging from the curious to the downright hostile as Ramuldssen and Rhullah entered. Both men stood with their backs to the closed servery and began to address the men. However, they couldn't divulge too much information, especially as the whole purpose of the operation was classified. Eamonn Burke had been able to sign on a couple of days earlier following a suitable introduction from one of his Irish associates. Bjorn Ramuldssen certainly didn't ask any questions or hesitate when hiring him. The Captain had become increasingly philosophical. He generally lost one or two of his crew every time they had a run ashore, either through fights or arrests. Burke's friends back in Belfast just couldn't understand why he was prepared to go on risking his life – especially for the British Government. But to Burke, it wasn't as simple as that. It was the same dichotomy throughout the entire world: when people felt threatened, they were always happy to have the soldier in front of them.

Yet, when that threat receded, the soldier invariably became nothing more than an outcast and an embarrassment. Besides, this thing had much deeper implications, and one's that reached far beyond his little corner of the world. This was still an international problem and it could affect everybody. At 09.00 hours the *Norse Warrior* cast off and sailed out of Esbjerg. Once clear of the harbour mouth, she made turns for eighteen knots and began to pitch rhythmically into the advancing swell as she crossed the mouth of the Skagerrak, before rounding the craggy southern tip of Norway, just off Stavanger.

When they crossed the Arctic Circle at dawn on the third day, the barometer suddenly dropped as a low-pressure front rushed in from the north. Winds gusting up to a force seven made the icy seas toss about in a wild confusion of whitecaps. The massive prow of the *Norse Warrior* plunged into the eight-foot swells of the quartering seas. Water cascaded over the foredeck and slammed into the wheelhouse and the rotary wipers struggled to spin away the water to maintain a clear view. Bjorn Ramuldssen gently eased back the vessel's speed to ten knots and posted lookouts until they had passed through the worst of the weather. Every plunge into the advancing swell brought them ever closer to their destiny with the Iranian submarine *Zarand*. Progress was being synchronised by coded signals being passed between the two vessels at frequent intervals. Tension on board the *Zarand* had risen during the past few days. Morale was at an all-time low. The situation between the Hamas Death Squad and the rest of the crew remained fragile. The submarine had barely managed to hold station below the ocean's thermal layer and was now lying a little over a hundred miles north-west of the salvage vessel. The *Norse Warrior's* radio operator sat bolt upright and suddenly pressed one earpiece tighter.

He rapidly scribbled down a series of notes onto his clipboard.

"Captain, the *Zarand* will be moving into position for our rendezvous off the island of Langoy at 08.30 tomorrow."

"Acknowledge. Message received and understood," grunted Ramuldssen as Nasaf Rhullah came up and joined him in the doorway of the radio shack.

Meanwhile, Eamonn Burke remained hidden in the ship's lee and braced himself against the starboard topsides as he gazed out at the myriad of twinkling lights from the small coastal towns dotted along the passing Norwegian fjords.

It was about 04.30 hours on the fourth day when they were suddenly hailed out of the darkness by a Norwegian voice over the radio. The seaman on watch alerted Ramuldssen over the intercom, which made the Captain scramble out of his bunk to make his way up to the bridge.

"Who are they?" Nasaf Rhullah was quickly at the Captain's side.
"Norwegian coastguard," Ramuldssen answered.
"What do they want?" Rhullah was alarmed.
"They want to know our destination and our business," the Captain growled.
"This is Captain Ramuldssen of the *Norse Warrior*. We are on a return passage, through international waters, to the island of Bjornoya to complete our contract to dismantle the whaling station."

Tension mounted. Hissing static bounced around the wheelhouse before giving way to a series of clicks.

"How long do you propose staying on Bjornoya?"

Ramuldssen hesitated. He clutched the microphone closer to his mouth and winked through a wreath of whiskers at the petrified Rhullah before taking a deep breath and pressing the transmit button. "We plan to stay for two or maybe three weeks, finish dismantling the station before winter sets in and return in the spring to collect all the scrap metal."

Ramuldssen and the *Norse Warrior* had become a familiar sight in these northern latitudes during the past eighteen months. The coastguards knew he had a legitimate contract on Bjornoya. They had checked. He had been boarded before, but not on every occasion. He was just gambling that his luck would hold on this dark and inhospitable morning. He hoped the coastguard was feeling tired and fatigued at the end of a cold and boring patrol and would be only too anxious to make the port of Bodo by daybreak.

"Our mission will have to be aborted if they come aboard," hissed the desperate Iranian as he anxiously looked around at everyone gathered in the wheelhouse. Ramuldssen nonchalantly raised his bushy eyebrows and shrugged his huge shoulders as they awaited a response from the coastguard. The whaling station had been established more than one hundred years ago on the island of Bjornoya at the height of the whaling boom. It had been located on this inhospitable island for two very good reasons: to process the whale carcasses and their valuable by-products as quickly as possible before putrefaction set in but, perhaps more importantly, to ensure the awful stench didn't reach the mainland. The station flourished for nearly forty years, but declined rapidly between the two world wars until it was finally abandoned to the elements in 1936.

Some six months had elapsed since Ramuldssen first secured his dubious contract to dismantle and salvage the whaling station on behalf of the Pakistani registered *Nasirabad Marine Salvage Corporation*. This third generation family business had been responsible for breaking-up and salvaging much of the world's ageing maritime fleet along the beaches of the Makran Coast of Pakistan. Here, their chosen method of operation was to drive their latest acquisitions hard upon the beach and then devour them like swarms of manic environmental locusts. The long sweeping bays of this shoreline were littered with an endless expanse of exposed and rusting steel ribs thrusting upwards from the remains of what had once been proud ships. The current Chairman of the Company enjoyed strutting about the beach like some regal potentate with a large sycophantic group of followers in tow. When he was about to declare the final resting place for his latest prize, he would go down and stand at the water's edge in his long flowing white robes. He would then point to it, waiting out at sea, with his stick held at the end of an outstretched arm – as if he were Moses about to part the Red Sea for the Children of Israel. This was scrap dealing on a Biblical scale. When first approaching the Chairman to undertake the dismantling of the worthless whaling station, it had been so easy for Nasaf Rhullah to ply this man with endless compliments and appeal to his overwhelming sense of vanity. It proved to be a perfect cover for Iran's more sinister mission.

Everyone jumped as a strong Norwegian voice boomed from the radio. "Captain Ramuldssen, our latest weather report predicts this storm should abate by midday. The outlook for the next forty-eight hours also indicates winds reducing and conditions moderating with occasional fog. We wish you good luck and a safe voyage."

"Do you think they actually *believed* us?" Nasaf Rhullah asked as Bjorn Ramuldssen gave the order for full power and set a north-easterly course.

"Who knows?" The Captain shrugged. Perhaps this time they had been lucky.

Eamonn Burke was working out on the bridge wing and remained within earshot of the two men as he busily checked one of the life-raft lashings.

"I think this whole mission could be far more difficult than I first thought," Bjorn Ramuldssen remarked scornfully.

"What do you mean?" Nasaf Rhullah asked defensively when the others had left the bridge.

"It means we should renegotiate the terms, *that's* what I mean."

The Captain pushed back his greasy cap and smiled menacingly.

"We can't do that. It's impossible. You have already agreed with the Pakistani charterers…"

"Pakistani charterers? Don't make me laugh, my friend. I know what's going on."

"Oh, and what exactly do you know?"

"Look… let's level with each other and get a few things straight. We're after Russian nuclear weapons." He gave a knowing tap to the side of his nose. "Those so-called "charterers" are not the one's out here having to risk *their* lives and *their* vessel." Ramuldssen waited in silence for Rhullah to think of a suitable answer.

"Well… what exactly do you want?" the Iranian asked at length.

"More money, of course!" Ramuldssen laughed.

"How much more?"

"Double!"

"Listen, you're wrong…" Nasaf Rhullah decided it was time to explain.

"We're going to have the whole world down on us like a ton of bricks. The Americans, the Russians, the British, the Israelis … everybody!"

"What? Don't give me any more of your lies … and don't treat me like a fool!" Ramuldssen was becoming angry.

"You *are* a fool if you think this rust bucket could actually salvage Russian nuclear weapons," Rhullah replied, with a smug expression.

"Then what exactly *are* we after?" A confused Ramuldssen turned to look the Iranian straight in the eye.

"Nothing!"

"Nothing?" Ramuldssen queried in a moderating tone.

"Precisely. We are nothing more than a decoy, my friend. The *real* salvage work will take place beneath the surface. The object of our mission is merely to draw attention away from our submarine … and the real purpose of her operation." Rhullah knew he had regained the advantage.

"We'll still be blown out of the water!" Ramuldssen exclaimed.

"Why? We are doing nothing wrong. After all, there is plenty of legitimate salvage work to be had in the Barents Sea – and the Russians are constantly dumping all sorts of stuff out there."

"That may be true, but they still won't believe us." Ramuldssen threw his hands in the air.

"Of course they won't believe us," Rhullah agreed. "That's the whole point. But they still can't prove anything unless we make a wrong move."

"And you are still pretty confident we won't make a wrong move?"

"Now you're beginning to get the whole picture, Captain." Rhullah lit up a cigarette in his cupped hands and took a deep draw before flicking the match through the open door of the wheelhouse. "The *Zarand* will be in and out before they realise what's happening. 'Money for old rope' as you say."

"I don't know about that. It's still a big risk," Ramuldssen mused.

"The deal is a fair one, Captain. I can promise you no more money."

Ramuldssen stroked his beard thoughtfully and realised his options were now very limited. He broke into a broad grin and burst out laughing. It was a bellowing laughter which echoed across the sea and rebounded off the Kjolen mountains.

Eamonn Burke quietly slipped away along the heaving deck of the *Norse Warrior*. The ship had altered course and was now heading north-westward to skirt round Rost and Vestvagoya as well as to lose any inquisitive coastguard vessels that might still have second thoughts and decide to follow. Back in the cable locker, Eamonn Burke tried to get a signal through to London. He had no way of telling if his message had reached Whitehall, so he tried again and again. After several attempts, he stuffed the transmitter back into his rucksack and crawled through the forward hold, before re-entering the noisy engine room.

He had just stowed the transmitter behind one of the massive yammering diesel engines when suddenly the hairs on the back of his neck bristled. Burke sensed that he was not alone and spun round in a semi-hunched position to be confronted by the First Mate, flanked by two other members of the crew.

"So this is where you are!" the Mate growled.

"I was just coming…" The Irishman tried to finish hiding the transmitter.

"What have you got there?" the Mate demanded as he looked beyond the Irishman.

"Oh… it's nothing." Burke remained calm as he fought against the sudden rush of adrenaline and casually wiped his hands with an oily rag.

"Let me see!" The Mate brushed Burke aside and reached behind the engine. He opened the rucksack and pulled out the transmitting equipment.

"It's a radio set!" One of the men gasped.

"A what?"

"A signalling device," the man repeated. "I saw one like it when I was in the French Navy."

"Who are you working for?" the Mate demanded of Burke as he fixed his gaze.

Burke decided that silence would be more prudent.

"Then what the hell are you doing with a radio set?" The mate held up the undeniable evidence in front of Burke's face.

"I like messing about with electronics," came the weak reply.

"Down here in the engine room?" The Mate nodded for the other crew members to step forward and grab the struggling Burke. "We'll let the Captain decide."

Eamonn Burke was hauled along the deck and up to the bridge, where Bjorn Ramuldssen and Nasaf Rhullah were enjoying a shot of Norway grog.

"Captain we caught this man using some equipment that Saul here says is a radio set."

"Let me see…" Ramuldssen reached out with his massive paw and snatched the device from the Mate's grip.

"It's a radio all right," Nasaf Rhullah confirmed.

"Who *are* you?" Ramuldssen yelled at Burke.

"Who are you working for?" Rhullah screamed hysterically.

Burke did not reply. Ramuldssen struck him several blows across the face with the back of his hand. Blood trickled from the corner of the Irishman's mouth, but still he didn't speak. Ramuldssen snatched a knife from his belt.

"Let's see if this will help to loosen your tongue … while you still have one left.

Hold him!" Ramuldssen approached, wielding the knife menacingly. Burke struggled, but the sailors stiffened their vice-like grip. The Captain slashed him across the cheek, then held the knife close to the Irishman's eye. Burke jerked his head away from the gleaming point.

"I said hold him!" The awesome spectacle of Ramuldssen bearing down with his face reddening, and his Danish accent growing more pronounced, was enough to send an involuntary shiver down the spine of the most thick-skinned.

One of the sailors momentarily eased his grip on Burke. That was the one chance the Irishman needed. With another surge of adrenaline, Burke felt the rage of the betrayed and swung his head backwards into the sailor's face, wrenching himself free from the other man's grip. Ramuldssen lunged with the knife, but Burke side-stepped in one swift move. The Irishman lashed out and kicked Nasaf Rhullah hard between the legs. Burke dashed out of the wheelhouse and vaulted over the bridge's salt encrusted handrail. He landed on top of a large coil of rope and rolled over on the foredeck, with the demented Captain still screaming orders. Men approached from all sides. There was no escape. Eamonn Burke snatched up a small life raft and with one massive leap of faith he was quickly over the side of the *Norse Warrior* and plunging into the ship's foaming wake. Machine guns opened fire as the *Norse Warrior* steamed on, with bullets piercing the dark water all around him. A searchlight swung round and scanned the boiling waves as the ship sped away, but there was no sign of Burke's body.

"Ah … he's dead!" the Captain proclaimed.

"How can you be so sure?" Nasaf Rhullah was beside himself with fear and uncertainty.

"Even if we didn't hit him, nothing can survive in that water."

"But what if he actually managed to get a message away? We don't know who he was working for!" Rhullah's voice became hysterical.

The Captain slapped him across the face.

"Do you want to call off the mission?" Ramuldssen yelled.

"Of course not." The Iranian snapped back as he rubbed his cheek.

"Well then, we'll just have to take our chances." The Captain hauled his big frame back up to the bridge and gave orders to proceed at half speed. They were now five kilometres off the Norwegian island of Langoya and two hundred and fifty kilometres inside the Arctic Circle. Success was not just a simple matter of avoiding failure. It was always driven by a dynamic need to make all the right decisions, especially when taking corrective action and staring the possibility of failure in the face.

CHAPTER 19

RUSSIA : KOLA PENINSULA

STRANGE AND UNEASY FEELINGS kept troubling Alexander Volkov. He couldn't explain why. There seemed to be nothing but distrust and constant bickering about the most trivial matters of procedure between the environmentalists and nuclear scientists. Solitude was beginning to take its toll. The Russians argued with the Norwegians – and the Norwegians argued with Aletta Bjorkman: that is, when she would listen. The entire operation had by now degenerated to such a point that it could no longer be considered an international joint operation. Everybody insisted on doing their own thing, and constantly pulled in different directions. Nobody made any attempt to co-ordinate the results, or even tried to draw any logical conclusions from the plethora of data collected during the past few days. Volkov considered the whole exercise to be nothing more than a complete waste of time. A deep sense of foreboding accompanied his every waking hour.

The monotonous routine of life in these inhospitable northern climes was both dreary and boring. The Norwegians and the Finn had received regular supplies from their respective governments, but the Russians had to make do with whatever meagre stocks and supplies they could scrounge in Kolskiy Zaliv. Alexander Volkov desperately missed his family and the frenetic round of social life they used to enjoy in Moscow. He vowed that when his current tour of duty was over and he was able to return to civilisation, he wouldn't let the evils of drink get the better of him again... and he certainly wouldn't open his big mouth in the wrong place!

Lydia Ilychyova stirred beside him in the bunk. Volkov squinted at his watch, it was still only 04.00 hours; these arctic nights seemed interminable.

"What's the matter Sasha?" she murmured, still half asleep.

"Nothing."

"Can't you sleep?"

No ... it's OK." He climbed out of bed and wrapped a blanket around his shoulders "It's so cold in here. I'll stoke up the fire." Volkov placed a kettle of water on the hotplate, swung open the stove's black metal door, and piled in more logs to join the still glowing embers of the previous night. He prodded it back to life with a long poker and sent a shower of sparks swirling up the chimney.

"Come back to bed," Lydia purred. The Russian Officer had quickly seized the opportunity to move her things in with Volkov after his own scientist roommate had moved out a couple of days ago. This had left Aletta Bjorkman on her own, which seemed to suit the Finnish environmentalist fine. Volkov stared wistfully into the flames. He wished it could have been the young Bjorkman sharing his bed instead of the more mature and voluptuous Ilychyova. But... beggars can't be choosers, and at least he had a woman to keep him warm.

"Oh do come back to bed, Sasha," the naked Captain implored with a seductive pout. Even at this ungodly hour, Lydia still looked irresistible in the flickering firelight, as she teasingly patted the empty space beside her. Volkov responded to her tantalising invitation with a sigh of resignation. He pulled off his coarse night-shirt and lay back on the bunk, thinking of far away things. She purred and slid her leg across him, with her hand gently caressing his stomach and chest as she pushed her tongue deep inside his mouth.

Her warm body began to move rhythmically up and down over his heaving chest, with her heavy breasts swinging like pendulous melons before his eyes.

Volkov reached up and swept his fingers over the protruding rosebud nipples. Ilychyova shuddered and let out an involuntary groan. She threw her head back, and her tongue moistened the scarlet lipstick seeping into the crevices of her mouth as her long red hair fell across her shoulders. He could see her stomach glistening with small beads of silky sweat and he felt her vagina sucking eagerly at his penis. Volkov placed his hands round her once youthful waist to steady her rhythm. He was building to his own earth-shattering climax, and eagerly arched his pelvis under Ilychyova's writhing groin.

All hell broke loose. It wasn't the climax they had expected. A man in black combat fatigues burst through the door, wielding a sub-machine gun. Lydia Ilychyova instinctively reached over to the bedside table for her pistol, but a short burst of automatic fire sent seven or eight bullets ripping through her body and into the wall behind the bunk. Alexander Volkov watched in petrified silence as the expression on his lover's face turned from ecstasy to surprise. Everything moved in slow motion. She slumped forward on top of him, her warm blood flowing across his body and soaking into the blankets. Volkov's erection disappeared. He was momentarily stunned; pinned down by the sudden dead weight. He could hear the man rattling the bolt mechanism of his gun as he re-cocked the weapon and approached their bunk. The intruder appeared to be of middle-eastern origin: possibly Arab. Volkov lay completely traumatised as he looked back, unblinking, at the cruel unshaven face which now stared down at him. Lydia Ilychyova gurgled and gave a dying gasp. The Arab grimaced and placed the smoking muzzle of his gun to her head and squeezed the trigger. The Captain's brain exploded, sending bits of yellow gore and tissue splashing across Volkov's face. He felt the searing sensation of pain then waves of unconsciousness mercifully engulfed him as the bullet burst through his lover's mouth and entered his own head.

Earlier that same morning, the Iranian submarine *Zarand* had surfaced in the icy darkness of the Barents Sea, just off Kolskiy Zaliv. The Hamas death squad had launched their inflatable assault boats and silently came ashore a little further along the deserted and desolate coast. Approaching the isolated encampment, they had crept forward to study the open expanse of ground stretching out before them. After crawling up a long frozen slope towards the compound's outer fence, they had slowly elbowed their way through the thin patches of scrubby undergrowth to cautiously peer over the top. The main fence lay just twenty yards in front of them, with the barracks set a further fifty yards behind the perimeter. With weeks of sub-zero temperatures, the wire had become veneered with a clear film of ice smothering everything, except the rusty steel barbs. They were appalled at the camp's lax security. One of the death squad had crawled towards the fence and wrapped a piece of sacking around the lower strands of wire, to muffle the sound when it was cut. His comrade shuffled alongside on his elbows and pulled out a set of cutters. He pumped the handles, and the howling arctic wind obliterated the sharp clack of the jaws as they closed. Each member of the team had then slithered through the hole to take up his respective position, waiting for the signal to be given.

On receiving a silent command, four of the half-drunken Russian sentries had been grabbed from behind and their throats cut, as other members of the attacking squad had simultaneously burst into the barrack blocks, where they opened fire indiscriminately, shooting everyone that moved – except Aletta Bjorkman. The small handful of hapless Russian soldiers, still lounging around in a drunken stupor from the previous night's reverie, didn't stand a chance. Short bursts of semi-automatic fire had mown them down like ninepins. The darkly clad Hamas leader appeared in the doorway, where he grinned malevolently as Aletta Bjorkman was hauled before him. He tossed his gun onto one of the bunks before slowly circling around the terrified Finnish environmentalist, cutting away her night-gown and underwear with his bloodstained assault knife. Four of his men, laughing and joking to each other in Farsi, had then dragged the hysterical girl over to a wooden table and pinned her down onto it like a starfish. Bjorkman's pitiful screams and pleadings only seemed to stimulate the men's excitement into a more wild and demented sexual frenzy. Two of them held the writhing and helpless girl's outstretched arms, as they pressed her shoulders firmly down onto the table, while others she couldn't see, spread her legs and pressed upon her trembling thighs. The death-squad leader went first. He removed his belt and holstered pistol, dropped his trousers and pushed himself into the spread-eagled Bjorkman.

Awareness gradually returned to Volkov. He was still pinned down by the dead body of Lydia Ilychyova and could barely see through the veil of warm blood trickling into his eyes. A piercing pain throbbed within his head and with every beat of his pulse it almost sent him back into unconsciousness. Sasha fought against the blackness, and by some miracle found he was still alive. He froze and listened, trying to hear if the Arab was still present. Apart from the roaring and crackling of the log fire from within the stove, everything seemed to be quiet. But somewhere in the distance, he thought he could hear the sounds of pitiful screaming. Was he imagining things or was it just the icy Arctic winds shrieking through the camp? He reached up with his free bloodstained hand to push the hideously cold staring eyes and shattered jaw of Lydia's corpse away from his face. His splitting headache throbbed with every effort, as he rolled her lifeless form to one side and pushed his own aching body from the bunk. He breathlessly dragged himself across the room on hands and knees, gasping with pain, to haul himself up onto one of the chairs.

Volkov's hair looked matted and dishevelled. It was a sticky mass of sweat and congealing blood, and he was sure he looked much worse than Lydia's crumpled body sprawled across the bed. Perhaps the Arab had thought he was dead from the initial burst of gunfire and couldn't be bothered to waste another bullet. Waves of pain seared throughout his body as Volkov reached up and took down a small cracked mirror from the wall and looked at the matted hair clinging down the side of his face. He wiped away the oozing blood from above his left eye and winced when he saw the deformed bullet lodged in his cranium. Lydia Ilychyova's skull must have absorbed most of the bullet's velocity before it passed through her face. Bathed in the clammy sweat of shock, Volkov exhausted himself further by struggling to pull on some clothes, before making his way over to the door and staggering out into the snow-covered compound, clutching a blood-soaked dressing to his temple. He could see no sign of life.

Across the deserted compound, Volkov could see a shaft of pale yellow light shining from the grimy window of Aletta Bjorkman's hut. Perhaps she could help. He approached cautiously, stumbling towards the darker side of the hut, where he reached up and grasped a splintered window-sill to peer inside. He watched in horror through the frosted glass, as the Hamas killers systematically raped the Finn, each man taking his turn, some even going back for a second time. Volkov lowered his head onto the back of his frozen hands and sobbed quietly, as an overwhelming feeling of despair and hopelessness descended upon him. He felt sick and helpless, but gathering up all his remaining strength, he dragged himself across to the adjoining wooden barracks in the centre of the compound – and went inside. He eased open the inner door and reached out to prop himself against the door-frame, as the full magnitude of what had happened that morning confronted him in the row of gloomy lights down the centre of the barracks: it was like an abattoir. Blood and gore was spread all over the walls and ceiling. Dead Russian soldiers lay slumped all over the floor and across their bunks like discarded marionettes. He didn't need to look for any further confirmation as to the fate of the other scientists. Volkov staggered painfully through all the debris and carnage, as he made his way towards the radio room situated at the far end of the hut. Through the open door, he could see the radio operator slumped across his desk with wrecked radio equipment scattered all around. He realised that his only option was to make his way to Kolskiy Zaliv where he could raise the alarm. However, he also knew the sleepy town lay more than two kilometres away – and there was no serviceable transport left in the compound. Aletta Bjorkman had stopped screaming, and an eerie silence had now descended over the encampment.

Volkov left the soldier's shattered quarters and dragged his aching body back over to the environmentalist's hut where he peered through the frosted windows again. The Arab soldiers were sitting back with their feet on the table, laughing and smoking. He could see Aletta Bjorkman's battered and bruised body lying motionless across the table, with a growing pool of sticky and congealing blood spilling onto the floor beneath her head.

❖ ❖ ❖

Volkov could see beams of silvery light dancing about and probing the arctic darkness. He pressed his back against the hut and thought he recognised the familiar sound of Russian voices as a shaft of light suddenly swung round and fell upon him. He squinted and raised an arm to shield his eyes against the piercing light as he staggered towards the approaching party, where he slumped, semi-conscious, at the feet of a Russian naval captain.

Valentin Tarasov looked down at the crumpled man, and could see blood still oozing from his head wound. The Captain had decided to come ashore with Boris Lukin, Rem Bukato and Sharif Hamad, while the rest of the submarine's Iranian crew had remained on board to make final preparations for the mission ahead.

"Who *is* this man? Where has he *come from*?" Tarasov asked Sharif Hamad as he knelt beside the motionless form.

"I really don't know … he must be one of the scientific group."

"If that's true, then why has he been shot?" Tarasov was livid. "Your men were under the strictest orders to secure the compound, nothing more!"

Hamad felt uncomfortable. He realised something had gone wrong and strode away in the general direction of the long barracks.

"Captain … he's still alive!" Boris Lukin exclaimed as he bent down to examine the slumped form of Alexander Volkov. The Russian sailors picked up the unconscious environmentalist and carried him in the wake of the Iranian. Tarasov was speechless with rage when confronted with the appalling carnage inside the barracks, as he and Lukin carefully picked their way through the debris to place the shivering Volkov on one of the bunks. The Russians gathered up some blankets from the other bunks and gently wrapped them around the wounded man. Captain Tarasov straightened up and glared across at Sharif Hamad standing between him and the door. The Iranian offered no explanation and just shrugged his shoulders. The two Russians roughly brushed Sharif Hamad to one side, as they left the barracks to make their way towards a solitary light and the sounds of laughing voices coming from Aletta Bjorkman's hut.

"Oh my God…" Tarasov gasped and crossed himself as he stood in the doorway.

"Allah be our saviour…" whispered Hamad as he joined them. The Hamas death squad fell silent when the three men appeared and snatched up their weapons, grouping themselves into a defensive semi-circle. Tarasov came over and looked down in disgust at the mutilated young woman spread-eagled over the table. He could see that she had died a horrible and lingering death, and completely ignored the death squad as he moved over to gently wrap a coarse army blanket around the girl's lifeless body. The Hamas group shuffled back, but kept their weapons trained on Tarasov and Lukin as they gathered up Aletta Bjorkman and carried her through the snow towards the adjacent barracks, where they reverently laid her next to Alexander Volkov.

"This *is* the end." Tarasov declared to his companions standing on the other side of the bunk.

"What do you mean, *the end*?" Rem Bukato queried with an incredulous sweep of his hand.

"I mean, we go no further with these murderers." Tears glistened in the Captain's eyes.

"But…do we actually have any choice?" Boris Lukin asked.

"*We will make our own choice!*" Tarasov shouted.

"But surely they'll kill us *all* … especially if we refuse to go on," hissed Bukato, with the veins standing out and throbbing on his temple as he moved over to the door and anxiously looked out. No one had followed.

"I am certain they intend to kill us anyway," the Captain stated in a fatalistic tone.

"Then what are we waiting for? We're on Russian soil." Boris Lukin stood up defiantly. "Surely we can escape or at least get some assistance?"

"Look … we're here, *unofficially*, and in a Russian top-secret camp in the middle of nowhere," Rem Bukato reminded them. "The nearest civilisation is over in Kolskiy Zaliv, and that's still some two and a half kilometres away to the west – with probably nothing more than a small detachment of militia."

Having effectively joined up with a foreign power to invade Russia's sovereign territory, coupled with their forthcoming audacious plan to violate the *Cherkassy*, which by now would have been designated as an official war-grave, it meant their options were rapidly diminishing. If captured, they would undoubtedly receive an elaborate show trial to expose their treason – followed by execution by firing squad.

"Come, we must get away…" Sharif Hamad entered the hut, silencing Bukato in mid-sentence.

"Captain…" Lukin stepped forward and exchanged a glance with Tarasov before turning to face Hamad.

"These soldiers," he said with a sweep of his hand, "are our fellow countrymen, could we please have just a few moments to ourselves?"

"Of course," the Iranian agreed quietly and left the barracks.

"Captain…" Lukin continued in an urgent whisper, "we must bide our time, otherwise we're dead men."

"Perhaps we would be better off." Valentin Tarasov stepped carefully among the corpses, draping blankets over the dead soldiers.

"No!" Lukin followed and grasped his arm. "We must play along with these maniacs… until the time is right."

"And when will that be?" Tarasov asked wearily, "When the whole world is destroyed?"

"You're both crazy," Rem Bukato interrupted. "We knew what we were getting into. There's a good life waiting for us at the end of this. I know it. Why should we care about anyone? After all, nobody cared about us!"

"Have you no dignity left?" Tarasov roared.

"What use is dignity?" Bukato uttered scornfully, "when your pockets are empty?"

"I can see it didn't take you long to become one of them" Lukin scoffed.

"Well, what if I have? I certainly don't intend to be *used* by our *glorious* Russian Government ever again!"

"So you would prefer to be *used* by the Iranian's instead?" Tarasov mocked.

"Perhaps … but just this once!" he wagged a finger of admonishment.

"What makes you so sure they will keep their promises *and* pay us?" Lukin asked with derision. "Valentin is convinced they will kill us anyway."

"Ah, don't worry, they won't kill us." Bukato laughed with a dismissive wave of his hand. "We're far too valuable. They know we are the only ones who can train their forces … and don't forget the missiles," he added with outstretched arms, "who else could show them how to use the missiles? In any case, Sharif Hamad is not like one of those crazy Islamic fanatics, he's our friend and I trust him."

There was a soft knock on the barracks door and Sharif Hamad re-entered.

"I have sent for a squad from the submarine," he said. "We will give these people a dignified burial."

"Thank you lieutenant," Rem Bukato said in a sombre tone.

"It's the least we can do."

The Russians stayed together in the barracks for the next few hours, supervising the burial party and looking after Alexander Volkov as best they could. The environmentalist continued to be delirious, lapsing in and out of consciousness. Some of the time he remained lucid enough to give a staccato account of what had happened, but occasionally this became intermixed with wild rantings about Moscow, his wife and his children. The *Zarand's* medical officer patched up his head-wound as best he could, but confirmed it would be too risky to attempt removal of the bullet until his fever had stabilised.

An urgent message had been received from the *Norse Warrior* whilst they had been busy at the Russian encampment. The salvage ship had arrived at the rendezvous point some eighteen hours earlier where she had taken up her pre-designated position just a few kilometres to the north-west of the sunken *Cherkassy*.

American AWACs surveillance planes had already flown a number of provocative sorties over the salvage boat's position, and a combined naval task force was hovering nearby. There was no time to lose. They would have to go for the missiles whilst the world's attention remained firmly focused on the salvage vessel.

CHAPTER 20

Pakistan : Gwadar

THE SMALL COMMUTER JET FLARED OUT and touched down on the hot shimmering tarmac of Gwadar airport. Ross Lombardi wrinkled his nose and partially pulled down the window seat blind as he squinted to shield his eyes from the glare when he peered out at the surrounding dry, barren landscape. He just wondered where this godforsaken mission would take them to next and stuffed the crumpled in-flight magazine back into the seat pocket in front of him. Peter Lawrence sat beside him. Larry Tyson had flipped up the armrests in the centre section of the aircraft so that he could sprawl his big frame across several seats. Lombardi and Lawrence had been delayed an extra couple of days in Israel whilst they waited for Tyson to join them from Denver, before the assembled party had been able to fly on down to Karachi to take this connecting flight to Gwadar. Despite his earlier misgivings, Lombardi had actually enjoyed his brief stay in Haifa. Ruth Netanya was beginning to fascinate him. One minute she was the consummate professional, cool and detached, but when they were back in the hotel room, she became as passionate as any woman he'd known or dreamt about. Despite having worked on this assignment with her for the past few months, he still felt no closer to rationalising the contradictory elements of her nature. Maybe the sooner they wrapped this whole thing up, the sooner he could whisk her away on vacation to his Colorado hideaway.

Peter Lawrence gave a big sigh and put down his book. He had been struggling to read *The Man Who Never Was* by Janet Sayers, but found it heavy going. An excited Juliet Lucas had given it to him just before he had boarded the plane at Heathrow.

She had gone to great lengths to explain that it was considered an in-depth treatise on the theoretical psychology of men ... but more importantly, from a woman's point of view! Perhaps she was really trying to guide him through something with a much deeper significance? Lawrence had read the first quarter of the book over and over again, trying to find some hidden meaning or a deeper explanation, but still couldn't make head or tail of it. Perhaps he was missing something more subliminal? Lucas had desperately wanted to join everyone on this trip to Pakistan, but Adrian Dyson had specifically ordered her back to London where she could brief himself and Jeremy Sinclair on all the latest developments. Lucas had thrown one of her mild tantrums and sulked a bit, as she tried to convince everyone that she was as good as any man in the field. But ... orders were orders.

Larry Tyson yawned, stretched and lifted the giant Stetson off his stubbly face. Goddammit, the worst part of this mission was not the relentless fatigue or the loneliness, it was the incessant tedium that forced his thoughts inward. Having crossed several gruelling time-zones, he was still suffering from the effects of jet-lag and took every opportunity to sleep. The plane on this latest leg of the journey had been almost empty and as soon as they were airborne, Tyson had quickly moved over to claim three of the central seats where he could stretch himself out. He snored loudly for the entire ninety-minute journey. Before leaving Colorado, Ross Lombardi had informed him to have his men standing by and ready to move at a moment's notice. Things were definitely hotting up ... and it looked as if it wouldn't be long before the sparks would really begin to fly. Big Jake LeClair had set about recruiting a dozen ex-military personnel for the mission.

They were some of the roughest mixture of mercenaries, Desert Storm veterans and marine renegades imaginable – the sort of people that even the military establishment couldn't tame. Following their early discharge from the Marine Corps, they had moved to Colorado and set up their base at a secret location near Denver International airport and were able to reach anywhere in the world within twenty-four hours. Jake was of half Cajun extraction. A man of muscular build, sporting a huge black beard beneath a shaven head moulded like a bullet sprouting from his thick bull-neck. Despite a tough and almost sinister appearance, his grey penetrating eyes set deep within his dark weather-beaten face could still crack into a disarming grin that radiated a wealth of humour and goodwill. Explosives and demolition were his speciality. Tyson had known Jake for many years, almost as long as he'd known Ross Lombardi – and would trust either man with his life. The plane taxied up to the ram-shackled terminal building and as the engines spooled down the three men disembarked. They had come well prepared, with sheaves of documents to indicate they were an advanced team of construction engineers, carrying out an exploratory survey for a new multi-million dollar urban development scheme situated between Gwadar and the coastal town of Pasni. Their papers also confirmed they were employed by a fictitious company called *Near East Enterprises Inc* and reservations had been made for them in the name of that company at Gwadar's one and only hotel. It wasn't really much of a hotel; it was more of a hostel cum hang-out for foreigners called the *Sindhi Star*. The babble of traders plying their wares, coupled with the sweltering early morning heat and pungent smells was almost overpowering. No air-conditioning functioned within the hotel, despite it being situated on the same latitude as Riyadh and Taiwan.

An overhead paddle-fan barely moved above the front desk. Lombardi and Tyson didn't seem to mind the primitive conditions. Peter Lawrence on the other hand felt an overwhelming desire for the civilising influence of a mini-bar. After unpacking and taking a quick shower, they ate a primitive breakfast of unleavened bread and kebabs washed down with strong black coffee. Lombardi excused himself as he wiped his mouth with a napkin and pushed back his chair. He threaded his way through the crowded lobby and went over to the hall porter to make arrangements for them to hire a jeep for their drive out to the hydro-electric development on the Dasht Kaur River.

❖ ❖ ❖

Angry flies buzzed around their heads as the American project manager took them into his stiflingly hot Portakabin. He went over to an ancient refrigerator, yanked the door open and produced several iced cans of Doctor Pepper. It was all he had, but anything to slake their thirsts was more than welcome. Peter asked the manager if he knew where they could possibly find some good engineers and technicians in this part of the world. The man's casual reply confirmed the only skilled men he had ever come across on this project were some Russians.

"Hey, we don't aim to poach any of your guys …" Ross Lombardi quickly assured him.

"You couldn't, even if you wanted to" the man sniffed in reply.

"How so?"

"Well, we're nearly finished anyway. Mind you, we did happen to have a couple of guys called Medvedev and Sautov, but they moved on some time ago. It's a pity. They were good men too."

"Do you happen to know where they went?" Tyson lightly enquired.

"Afraid not," the manager said. "These Russians don't usually hang around for long."

"Would anyone else on the site perhaps know where we could find them?" Peter Lawrence added casually.

"Couldn't rightly say." The American site manager shrugged his shoulders. "Tell you what … why don't I put the word about that you're interested. Say, where can I get hold of you guys?"

Lombardi told him where they were staying.

"If I were still looking for Russian technicians…" the manager mused, "I think I'd try Moscow … or St Petersburg … or Minsk … or even Kiev. As a matter of fact, you'll be falling over highly qualified experts on every street corner. Most of them no longer have jobs and even those that do, simply haven't been paid for months."

"Not so easy getting them out though," Peter Lawrence suggested.

"Anything's possible these days." The manager gave a knowing wink, and casually shoved aside a pile of dust-covered files and reports stacked in different coloured folders, so that he could perch on the edge of his desk. He took off his hard-hat and saluted them with his can of Doctor Pepper as they began to leave the Portakabin which overlooked the nearly completed dam.

❖ ❖ ❖

That same evening, the Westerners decided to visit the *Arabian Night* bar in downtown Gwadar. It was a dismal, run-down place, with grubby white stucco walls and a broken neon light which flashed AR-B—N N-G-T intermittently above the door. The seedy decor inside also left much to be desired. The red flock wallpaper, peeling at the edges, housed myriad species of exotic bugs, while the threadbare carpets were splattered with booze and dried blood. Several of the rickety chairs had been re-covered with a dirty red velvet material and were scattered around the bare wooden tables, each one lit by thick blue candles jammed into whisky bottles. Liberal quantities of American beer was available, as well as a great variety of imported spirits and liqueurs. There wasn't much call for the few dusty bottles of obscure local wine which stood on the lower shelves of this establishment. Tonight's clientele consisted mainly of workers from the hydro-electric development project. They wisely drank only canned beer or spirits – it was much safer. In fact, the *Arabian Night* had only been opened by some enterprising local entrepreneur to support the needs of the joint-venture project.

The visitors pushed open the swing doors and braced themselves as wisps of heavy cigarette smoke drifted past them into the bustling street. The din of urgent conversation from groups of shabby figures, coupled with the clinking of glasses in the dimly lit room, confirmed this was as likely a place as any to find out what had happened to Yuri Medvedev and Victor Sautov. The three strangers approached the bar where Larry Tyson ordered a bottle of Jack Daniels and three glasses from the obsequious Pakistani proprietor who spoke fluent English. Ross Lombardi handed the man one of his business cards, which proclaimed in printed gold letters that he was the "Senior Vice President" with *Near East Enterprises Inc*. The American went on to inform the barman they were looking for some good technicians – especially Russians. He slowly looked round and made sure that everyone in the place overheard, before moving over to rejoin the others at one of the tables in a secluded alcove. Peter Lawrence noticed a lot of whispering and nodding in their direction, yet nobody came over.

They were well into their second bottle, when a tall skinny man suddenly appeared out of nowhere in the vacant chair beside Larry Tyson. It startled the big American. Tyson instinctively raised a balled fist and was about to strike, when the man flinched and held up his hands in a placatory manner.

"No, no … please …"

"Who the hell are you?" Tyson growled.

"My name is Salah Anbar. I am Iraqi."

"What do you want?" Ross Lombardi asked.

"I heard what you said …" Salah Anbar indicated towards the bar counter with a sweep of his hand. He was a young man with a thick but tightly trimmed beard, in his mid-twenties, although his face could have been that of someone much older. He smiled broadly and displayed a central gold tooth beneath a nest of fur and wore a red, Turkish-style fez on top of his black, close-cropped hair. "You are looking for the two Russians … no?"

"What two Russians?" Lombardi asked cautiously.

"If you want to play games…" The man rose from his seat and was about to leave. Lombardi quickly nodded to Tyson, who seized Anbar's arm, forcing the man back down into the chair. The Iraqi winced with pain as the others closed in to form a canopy.

"Now…" Lombardi whispered with menace, "what exactly do you know?"

"How much is it worth?" the Iraqi asked with as much bravado as he could muster.

"Five hundred!"

"Five hundred what?"

"Dollars!"

"American?"

"Of course!"

Salah Anbar smiled again as Larry Tyson released his grip on the man's arm. Ross Lombardi filled the uninvited guest's glass with a shot of Jack Daniels before pushing it over in front of the man. The Iraqi raised his arms in a gesture of polite rejection.

"Thank you, but no. My religion prevents me from consuming alcohol. However, a Coca Cola would be most agreeable." Lombardi signalled for the barman to bring over a coke. "I wondered how long it would take you Americans to realise what was going on." Anbar grinned as he sipped at the fizzy drink.

"Just what *is* going on?" Peter Lawrence asked.

"The Russians ... Medvedev and Sautov, you know about them?"

"Yes, we do" Lawrence played a bluffing game.

"Ah, but you don't know where they are now?" The Iraqi's eyes widened.

"Do you?" Lawrence asked.

"Of course." Salah Anbar responded in a hushed voice. "Very well ... they were missile technicians and Nasaf Rhullah knew that. Do you know about Nasaf Rhullah?"

"Yes." Lawrence answered patiently, careful to keep his voice low.

"Rhullah promised the Russians much wealth if they would work for him in Iran." Anbar continued.

"Work on what?" Lombardi looked at the Iraqi and arched an eyebrow.

"Missile launchers, of course ... mobile rocket launchers."

"Why would the Iranians want these guys, top men in their field, to work on their out-of-date systems?" Lombardi quizzed the Iraqi.

"You already know the answer to that, don't you?" The Iraqi grinned as he focused his attention on Peter Lawrence.

"Of course we do," Lawrence replied nonchalantly as he sat back and folded his arms. "We just want you to confirm it for us."

"It is very serious..." Anbar's jovial appearance now turned into a deep frown.

"They plan to adapt the rocket launchers so that they are able to accommodate the nuclear weapons which will be salvaged from the Russian submarine."

A stunned silence fell around the table. Nobody spoke for a few moments, then Ross Lombardi turned to the Iraqi. "Why are you prepared to tell us all this?"

"Sometimes it is more prudent to side with the devil," Anbar added with a sly grin. "We recognise our differences with the Americans and the Coalition Forces, but we are even more concerned if Iran should obtain a nuclear capability."

"You say you know where these men are now?" Anbar nodded.

"Are they with the missile launchers?" The Iraqi nodded again.

"How do you know these things?" Peter Lawrence remained sceptical.

"I am an agent of my Government. I was sent here as a result of some disturbing intelligence reports which we had recently received. I followed Nasaf Rhullah and discovered what he was up to. My Government has located the Russians and I was sent here to await your arrival. I know exactly where they are."

"Where?" Larry Tyson growled threateningly.

"Before I tell you that, I will need to see the colour of your money."

"Not here," Peter Lawrence whispered. "Back at the hotel." They gave Salah Anbar a room number and told him to meet them back there at midnight.

That night, the western agents contacted Benjamin Eshkol in Tel Aviv. The Israeli re-confirmed he could have an assault team ready to go into Iran within twenty-four hours. Lombardi had insisted that he wanted his own men and equipment, but eventually agreed on a compromise. The twelve members of the American squad would be supplemented by an Israeli group of the same size. Any larger force would attract too much attention.

"Can we trust this Iraqi guy?" Larry Tyson felt uncomfortable about the situation.

"Larry's right Ross," Peter Lawrence added. "It might be a trap."

"True. But we've got nothing else to go on," Lombardi said. "And besides, we're running out of time."

"Those Iraqis ain't got no love for us Ross," Tyson frowned, "you know that!"

"And we've only got his word he's an Iraqi," Lawrence mused. "He might even be an Iranian. He could have been left here by Nasaf Rhullah to confuse the issue."

On the stroke of midnight, the men fell silent when they heard a soft knock on the door. Larry Tyson put down his coke and went over to open it. He allowed the shadowy figure of Salah Anbar to glide into the room, before poking his head round the corner of the door to check the landing outside.

"You have the money?" Anbar wasted no time in asking, as he sat down and made himself comfortable.

"Yep. We have," Ross Lombardi confirmed.

"Good" the Iraqi held out his hand expectantly. "Then let me have it."

"Hey... not so fast!" Peter Lawrence stood up and approached the man. "How do we know you are who you say you are?"

"You will have to trust me," Anbar grinned.

"No dice!" Lombardi snarled.

"Here are my credentials." The Iraqi reached inside his jacket and pulled out a small bundle of documents. Larry Tyson made sure he sat between the Iraqi and the door while Peter Lawrence took the papers and made a telephone call to Benjamin Eshkol for verification.

"What are you doing?" Anbar looked uneasy.

"Just checking you out," Lombardi replied as he fixed a cold stare upon the man. "Relax! You've got nothing to worry about if you're on the level."

"How long will all this take?" The Iraqi was definitely becoming nervous.

"As long as it takes!" Larry Tyson replied.

"You in a hurry to go somewhere?" Lombardi asked.

"No. I am in no hurry." Anbar began to stroke his sweaty palms on his knees.

"Good. Then we wait."

It took the Israelis another forty minutes before they came back and verified Salah Anbar's details. Everyone jumped when the phone rang in the strained silence of the room. Peter Lawrence dashed over and snatched up the receiver from its cradle. He listened as Eshkol confirmed that Anbar was exactly who he said he was. Lawrence hung up without speaking a word. He turned to face the others.

"He's kosher," the Englishman said as he came over and offered back the credentials to Anbar.

"There..." the Iraqi breathed a huge sigh of relief and began to re-fold the documents with as much dignity as his sweaty hands would permit. He quickly placed them back into his pocket. "Now, can I have my money?"

"Not yet!" Ross took five hundred dollars from a drawer.

"What is the matter now?" Anbar wailed.

"How can we be sure this ain't a trap?" Lombardi waved the money enticingly in front of the Iraqi's face.

"How do we know you ain't in the pay of the Ayatollahs as well?" Larry Tyson bent menacingly over the man. "After all, you might be some dirty double-crosser!"

"I am not!" Anbar protested at such a suggestion. "Iran and Iraq are mortal enemies. It is not in our interest for the Iranians to have nuclear weapons. My country would be an immediate target!"

The three agents withdrew into a corner of the room and whispered amongst themselves. Salah Anbar watched them, and the door, with a worried frown. After what seemed like an eternity, they came back and stood around the seated Iraqi.

"We've decided to trust you," Peter Lawrence told the still nervous man as Ross Lombardi handed over the wad of money.

"And the information?"

"Here is a map…" Anbar quickly pocketed the money in exchange for a grubby piece of paper. "The precise location is marked with an X. It is a remote spot to the north-east of the *Dasht-e Kavir* desert. Security will be light, as the Iranians would not expect anyone to infiltrate the area." The Iraqi stood up, tugged his jacket straight with as much dignity as he could muster, and went over to the door.

Ross Lombardi followed.

"One more thing, before you go…" Lombardi gently placed his hand on the man's shoulder. "If this is a trick or if you're lying in any way, not only will you be killed but your whole family as well. You got that?"

"I'm not lying."

"You may think we won't be able to find you," Lombardi continued. "You may even believe we won't come back…"

"What I've told you is the truth."

"Nasaf Rhullah also thought we wouldn't find *him*." Ross Lombardi smiled malevolently as he reminded the Iraqi. "If we don't come back, there'll be others … and if necessary others after them, understand?"

"I understand. My prayers go with you." The door closed and Salah Anbar was gone.

Now they were in the unenviable position of having to risk the lives of some thirty odd people on the dubious word of a man they had only seen for a brief period, in a dirty bar at the far end of the earth.

CHAPTER 21

IRAN : DASHT-E KAVIR

ROSS LOMBARDI, PETER LAWRENCE AND LARRY TYSON had taken the first available flight from Gwadar to Ashkhabad in Turkmenistan. Upon arrival they were met by the Israeli team, led by David Weizman and Ruth Netanya. Benjamin Eshkol had decided at the last minute to remain back in Tel Aviv so that he could supervise and co-ordinate operations. Within the next few hours, the advanced group was joined by Jake LeClair and his contingent from Colorado. The Republic of Turkmenistan had been one of the first members of the former Soviet Union to break away and join the fledgling Commonwealth of Independent States. Consequently, the incumbent Russian military hierarchy still retained a powerful local influence. Even though they were no longer obliged to bow to the will of Moscow, they were nevertheless still able to obtain Central Government's approval for the supply of equipment and vehicles for the team's forthcoming mission. After much high-level political debate and soul-searching, the Superpowers had readily given their unofficial endorsement for a lightning raid into Iran. However, it was on the strictest understanding that if anything went wrong, the group would be entirely on their own. None of the respective Governments would be able to intervene or do anything to prevent the full wrath of the Islamic regime descending upon any captured personnel. To undertake such a dangerous and provocative mission would be the equivalent of engaging Iran in a deadly game of chess. If the mission failed, the politicians would have to think several steps ahead; they had to imagine all the possible ways in which a world press might react and seek to distort the facts surrounding their intentions.

The Americans had contributed by organising the supply of six M93 six-wheeled Fox nuclear, biological and chemical reconnaissance vehicles, mounted with automatic cannons. Five men were allocated to each vehicle, with just a driver for the sixth – to bring out the Russians – as well as any useful equipment which they might have. Ross Lombardi took command in the lead vehicle with David Weizman and Ruth Netanya following in the second. Peter Lawrence, Larry Tyson and Jake LeClair took control of the third, the fourth and fifth, with the empty vehicle bringing up the rear. Lombardi, Tyson and LeClair led their own men, while Lawrence and the Israelis divided up the remaining members of the Mossad special task force.

The International Rapid Response Force had gathered at an empty hangar on the far side of Ashkhabad airport, which was surrounded by old fuselages, tails and wing sections littering the bleak landscape. A last minute briefing had been hastily convened in one of the machine shops to check their route and weapons before the convoy set out towards the remote Iranian border. They passed millions of acres of parched and arid desert, miraculously brought back to life by the Soviet built Kara Kum canal. Vast fields of cotton and other irrigated crops stretched as far as the eye could see. The gentle rolling desert lowlands of the Karakum soon merged into the sweeping northern foothills of the Kapet Dag mountains. The Iranian border only lay a tantalising twenty kilometres to the south of Ashkhabad. The snaking convoy threaded its way through the treacherous darkness of the mountains and dropped into a wide valley on the other side. Here they crossed the river Atrak, before heading southwards between the towns of Quchan and Shirvan. The vehicles had been stencilled with Iranian Revolutionary emblems and, to anyone but the keenest observer, the convoy looked like a regular unit of the Revolutionary Guard out on manoeuvres.

The bone-jarring journey south proved to be uneventful, as they bumped and lurched along the old caravan routes carefully marked on the Iraqi map. The earlier terrain had been especially tough. It had taken them through the most difficult mountainous areas of the north, followed by a crossing of the swollen river Joyevn which brought them down on to a flat plateau for the final leg of their journey. The night air was freezing. There was nothing but a faint moonlight flitting between the growing overcast, threatening to dust the barren landscape with a fresh fall of snow. They finally arrived in the northern province of Khorasan, a sparsely populated area traversed by the Kavir-e Namak. The secret missile installation was clearly marked on Salah Anbar's map, with precise co-ordinates of latitude and longitude in degrees, minutes and seconds, between Khorramabad and Kashmar. Ross Lombardi brought the convoy to a halt while he stepped out to check their position with his global satellite navigation equipment.

Shielded by a dark jagged backdrop of mountains to their rear, the group slowly crested a piece of low rolling ground. Twinkling lights from the missile installation, six kilometres beyond a broad plateau, came into view – right on target. Lombardi heaved a great sigh of relief. They were dead on course. Salah Anbar was right, the Iranians were not expecting visitors. The convoy resumed its journey and approached as close to the perimeter as they dared before cutting their engines and rolling to a standstill. The main assault force climbed down from the vehicles and fanned out. They crouched in huddled groups with their respective team leaders for a final briefing, before silently advancing towards the northern end of the boundary fence, leaving only the drivers to look after the transport.

Lombardi and Lawrence were the only ones to have been given physical descriptions of the two Russian technicians. Both men dropped to the ground and scanned the area with their infra-red binoculars. It was almost midnight. The whole compound was bathed in a soft yellow light and a great deal of noisy activity was still going on. They appeared to be working round the clock and only one sentry had been posted. Lombardi scanned the darkness and counted at least a dozen military tents over to the south side: the place was crawling with well-armed Revolutionary Guards. The bored sentry had taken up a cosy position over by a clump of bushes, beyond the missile launchers, and was clearly finding it difficult to stay awake. Peter Lawrence lightly touched Ross on the sleeve and pointed. A stocky man in dirty overalls could be seen working on a mobile missile launcher beneath camouflage netting about twenty metres from their position. The man had close-cropped sandy hair and seemed to fit the description of

Victor Sautov down to the last detail. Lombardi nodded back in response. He quietly signalled for several men, including David Weizman, to approach the outer fence until they were as close as possible to the unsuspecting Russian. Sautov worked alone, studying a diagram with a hooded flashlight. Weizman spoke fluent Russian. It had been agreed that, if it were feasible, he would be the first to go in for the Russians. Ross gave a jerk of his head in the general direction of Sautov. Weizman took a deep breath as he surveyed the situation for a few moments, then nodded back. Lombardi's men crept forward and silently cut a hole in the fence for the Israeli to crawl through.

The camp lighting barely reached to the edge of the enclosure, but there was really only one way to do this. Weizman rose to his feet and strolled nonchalantly across the open ground until he stood behind the deeply engrossed Sautov.

Weizman peered over Sautov's shoulder at the diagram and whispered something into the technician's ear. Sautov froze momentarily before stealing a glance towards the darkness of the perimeter fence. Weizman spoke to him again as both men pretended to be studying a wiring problem. The Israeli nodded as if he had found a problem and traced a line across the diagram with his finger. He wiped his hands with a rag as he moved over to the fence and climbed back out through the hole. A moment or two later, Victor Sautov furtively looked around to make sure no-one was watching before quickly making his own way over to the fence and climbing through after the Israeli. The Russian was quietly grabbed on the other side and pushed to the ground by a waiting group, before being taken back to the reconnaissance vehicles by Lombardi and Weizman.

"Victor Sautov?" Ross Lombardi asked quietly.

"Yes," the Russian answered breathlessly.

"We're here to take you and Yuri Medvedev out."

"But who are you?"

"It doesn't matter who we are," Lombardi told him. "We've been given the OK by your Government."

"But what will happen to us?" Sautov was nervous of being taken back to Russia.

"It will certainly be a lot better than what will happen to you if you stay here, that's for sure," Weizman replied with the obvious conclusion.

"Listen…" Lombardi said, "we haven't much time. Where's Medvedev?"

"He's out there." Sautov pointed to the well-lit centre of the installation.

"Shit!"

"I know he won't come with us," Sautov told them in an urgent whisper.

"Why not?"

"He wants to stay," the Russian explained. "They've promised us a lot of money and a good life … and he *believes* them!"

"He's a fool!" Weizman hissed his contempt.

"I know that," Sautov agreed philosophically. "I've been trying to reason with him, but he won't listen."

"Look, get into the vehicle," Lombardi ordered as Weizman signalled for two of his Mossad team to stay with the Russian. "Well, what do you think?" the American was dubious.

"We're running out of time," the Israeli answered. "We don't have much choice.

I must go back and get Medvedev."

"But I can't allow you to go back in there on your own. It's far too dangerous!"

"There's no other way," Weizman insisted.

"But what if he won't come quietly?" Lombardi wrestled with all the options. He didn't want a fire-fight. He wanted to be in and out as quickly and as quietly as possible.

Back at the perimeter, Peter Lawrence had finally located Yuri Medvedev. Lombardi and Weizman shuffled forward on their elbows and trained their binoculars in the direction of his pointing finger. Medvedev was right in the centre. He was standing close to a small group of Iranian engineers studying some blueprints. They seemed to be having a heated argument. Medvedev suddenly snatched up a drawing and moved over to a table by the rocket launcher. He left the bemused Iranians to continue their lively debate as they adjourned to one of the tents. Before anyone could stop him, David Weizman had scrambled back into the compound. He rose cautiously to his feet and, with his hands thrust deep into his pockets, sauntered over towards Medvedev.

"Goddam him!" Lombardi whispered through clenched teeth. A restraining hand signal was sent along the line of waiting men. Positions were taken up and weapons trained on the interior. The reconnaissance vehicle drivers were ordered to stand by. All eyes remained transfixed as David Weizman continued, almost in slow motion, towards Yuri Medvedev. Nobody breathed. It seemed to take the Israeli an eternity to reach the table. Once there, he leaned forward and whispered something to Medvedev. The tension beyond the outer circuit was almost unbearable. Everybody watched in horror as the silent discussion became increasingly animated. Medvedev glanced towards the fence and shook his head. Lombardi and Lawrence both sensed it was all going wrong. After several tense minutes, David Weizman drew his pistol and pushed the barrel into Medvedev's ribs. He grabbed the Russian by the arm and began to lead him away. Medvedev's mind was in a complete whirl. The frightened man looked confused and offered no resistance as they strolled towards the waiting hole in the fence. It seemed as if Weizman was about to get away with it. Suddenly, one of the Iranian engineers came out of the tent and called after them. The two men stopped in their tracks but didn't turn round. The man called out again, but sensed something wasn't right.

Weizman again nudged Medvedev with his pistol and the two men continued towards the fence. The Iranian engineer started shouting at the top of his voice and raised the alarm. Several nearby Revolutionary Guards snatched up their rifles and aimed at the backs of the retreating men. The raiding party waiting out in the darkness of the desert, levelled their weapons and waited for Ross Lombardi's signal. Medvedev began to resist. He pulled himself away from Weizman and shouted. As he ran back towards the Iranians all hell broke loose. The soldiers hesitated momentarily before responding with a ragged fusillade of fire. David Weizman spun round from the impact as a hail of bullets slammed into his chest and head and his lifeless body slumped to the ground.

"No!" Ruth Netanya screamed as the entire Iranian military detachment blindly opened fire into the darkness on the north side of the compound. Some of the men were caught off guard and hit before Lombardi had time to give orders to return fire. Mission adrenalin took over as Ruth Netanya scrambled through the hole in the fence and crouched over David's shattered body. Clutching her automatic pistol, she fired wildly at anything that moved. Smoke and stun grenades were lobbed into the Iranian encampment. Jake LeClair had previously set demolition charges which now erupted and took away a whole section of the perimeter fence. Both he and his men spread out and poured through to the interior, whilst the Mossad men followed in a flanking movement. The Revolutionary Guards were quickly mown down in a withering crossfire.

Covered by his men, LeClair set plastic charges round the rocket launchers. Lombardi and Lawrence tried to find the terrified Medvedev, who had fled in the smoke and chaos. The Russian had naively sought refuge in one of the tents, which soon took a direct hit from incoming mortar fire.

By the time Lombardi had reached the smouldering tent, there was nothing left. What little remained of Medvedev had been blown to pieces; his broken body lay smouldering on the ground.

The Revolutionary Guards refused to surrender. Some of the surviving Iranian engineers had made a wild dash into the darkness of the desert. It would only be a matter of time before the alarm was raised. Gradually, the sporadic sound of gunfire died away and all that remained was the crackling of flames mixed with the shrieks and moans of the wounded. Lombardi realised the fires would be seen for miles. He moved amongst the carnage and ordered a head-count.

Three Americans had been killed and two others wounded. The Israeli dead came to five, including David Weizman, plus one wounded. Lombardi quickly snapped everyone back to their senses and ordered the bodies of their comrades to be loaded onto the reconnaissance vehicles. It was almost 04.00 hours before they were finally ready to leave. Everyone withdrew to a safe distance as Jake LeClair pulled out a radio trigger from his flak jacket. The exhausted group turned and took one last look at the complex, as Jake flipped the toggle safety cover open and detonated the charges. A succession of loud explosions rocked the night. Plumes of yellow-white flames leapt into the air, then died back again. Pieces of metal and debris rained down over a fifty-metre radius, followed by an eerie silence. The engines of the convoy burst into life and revved up in unison as they set off on the return leg of their journey. They had at least secured the release of one of the Russians, but more importantly, the missile launchers had also been destroyed. A good night's work, but the high price was nevertheless unacceptable. Lombardi would have preferred a mission without casualties, but such were the fortunes of war.

The journey back was fast and without incident. They kept to the bumpy dirt tracks of the stony *Dasht-e Kavir* and only used the tarmac roads to make up time whenever possible. Nobody took much notice of this strange convoy. Isolated farmers were already toiling by the qanat irrigation canals… long before dawn had broken. Horses and camels spooked in all directions as the stream of military vehicles passed. Most of the local Bakhtiani Arabs cursed under their breath at this early morning intrusion. The sun, a dull red glow, was just beginning to climb the Hindu Kush away to the east, as the convoy of mud spattered vehicles crossed back over the border into Turkmenistan.

An Aeroflot *Antonov AN-22 Antheus* cargo plane waited on the runway at Ashkhabad's airport. Puffs of white-grey smoke belched from the four massive *Kuznetsov NK-12 MA* turboprop engines as they started up and the contra-rotating propellers settled down to a steady idle. The first three reconnaissance vehicles raced onto the airfield and swung round to the back of the aircraft, driving straight up the lowered tail ramp into the thirty-three metre long cavernous interior. The remaining vehicles were abandoned at the side of the runway. Larry Tyson moved amongst the weary survivors and gave instructions for the dead to be removed and placed carefully into body bags. The lucky survivors reverently carried the anonymous misshapen bags up the ramp of the aircraft and laid them in two rows down the centre of the cargo hold. Ross Lombardi tried to console Ruth Netanya, but the Israeli agent was still traumatised by the killing of her friend and colleague. Lombardi went to the forward upper deck and slumped back into his seat. He rested his weary head against the vibrating side of the plane as he tried to come to terms with the crazy events of the last twenty-four hours.

The plane taxied round for a rolling take-off and accelerated down the runway.

It was soon engulfed in a clinging low grey overcast as it headed north-west, out over the Caspian Sea, for a secret rendezvous somewhere in southern Russia. By the time the giant aircraft had touched down at its final destination, the Iranian military authorities were already surveying the scene of complete carnage and destruction in the *Dasht-e Kavir* desert.

CHAPTER 22

UNITED STATES : WASHINGTON

CHRISTMAS WAS ALMOST UPON THE Nation's capital and the bustling streets of downtown Washington were awash with seasonal spending. Goodwill to mankind seemed to radiate from every smiling face – and a jovial white-bearded Santa Claus could be found within the entrance to every department store, ringing bells and calling for the hordes of excited children to drag their parents inside. Drew Dalton remained deeply engrossed with his innermost thoughts about the forthcoming meeting to which he had been summoned. He drove through the heavy traffic and a light dusting of early snow without even noticing all the seasonal excitement going on around the illuminated trees along Pennsylvania Avenue. The CIA man stopped his car outside the granite-faced Government Building and climbed out. His breath billowed into vapour clouds around his head in the cold night air as he stepped from the car. He tossed the car keys over to a young parking attendant waiting at the kerbside and entered the building through a pair of glass doors. By contrast, the air inside seemed to be hot and thick. Dalton continued across the main lobby area where he was casually saluted by one of the bored security guards. The man swallowed hard and stared straight ahead when the agent suddenly paused in his tracks and came over to the front desk to flash his ID badge in front of the man's face. Dalton had made his point. He continued over to the bank of elevators and stepped inside the first waiting car, before turning to fix a withering gaze upon the nervous guard. Dalton never took his eyes off the man as he pressed the destination button for the elevator to take him up to the sixth floor. The doors of the mirrored chamber quietly closed.

Drew Dalton was just one of the many thousands of anonymous Vietnam War veterans that time had forgotten. He'd seen far too many of his closest friends die needlessly in those bloody Asian paddy fields and jungles of this forgotten war on the other side of the world. He had become increasingly nervous about the prospects of embroiling America in yet another distant conflict from which she might find it difficult to extricate herself, but risks had to be taken and that was the name of his game. Dalton's colleagues at Harvard had always regarded him as a decent man of middle-income stock who was prepared to serve under any President, Republican or Democrat. He was a man who seemed to possess an almost religious style of conscience, something in sharp contrast with his contemporaries in the CIA. As a dedicated soldier, there was very little he wouldn't do to protect the United States, hence his use of freelance operatives such as Ross Lombardi. As a committed Christian, Dalton fiercely believed in the stabilising influence of the family unit which had helped to make his country great, and if necessary he was always prepared to lay down his life to make America just that little bit safer for his children. His second wife, Rachel, was a discreet and understanding woman. She didn't mind the long and irregular hours imposed by the job and always supported her husband in everything he did. During the Spring-offensive of 1975, Dalton had just returned to Saigon after being involved in some particularly fierce and bitter fighting near a small Vietnamese village called Plei Bo, close to the Cambodian border. He was only into the second day of his long overdue furlough when he received an earth-shattering cable from the States. The cold and impersonal message confirmed that Bonny, his first wife, had been killed in a car smash on Interstate 95 as she drove to their new home at Wheaton on the outskirts of Washington D C. They had been teenage sweethearts, right from the fifth grade and through to High School, before deciding to get married as soon as he had completed his basic training. Fate had ultimately played a cruel trick. It left Drew Dalton totally devastated and, although he loved Rachel and appreciated her unswerving loyalty, support and understanding, he could never forget those happy times with Bonny.

Senator Hefner T. Copeland waited impatiently inside a large meeting-room down one of the heavily carpeted corridors from the elevator on the sixth floor.

"Jesus, Drew…" Copeland began pacing the room as soon as Dalton entered, "I sure hope that dust up in Iran don't get out!"

"So do I, Senator!"

"What the hell was Lombardi thinking about?" The Senator lit up one of his Havana cigars and clenched it between his teeth. "Listen, I've spent more than twenty years on the Hill serving Uncle Sam and it's the end of my political career if this hits the fan … and yours too. That is, of course, if we're not locked up in San Quentin!"

"Ross did what he had to do Senator, and don't forget we *did* give him the green light."

"Sure we did … to go in there and bring out those stupid Russians, not to blow up half the goddam country and kill more than thirty Revolutionary Guards!"

"That's a slight exaggeration, Senator."

"Aw the hell it's not!" Copeland blew clouds of smoke about the room. He looked like a raging bull blowing steam from its nostrils.

"They left nothing behind," Dalton assured the Senator.

"How do you mean?"

"I mean nothing to link the raid with the United States or our Allies."

"They better not have!" the Senator roared. "The Ayatollahs can blame the Russians or the Israelis or whoever they like … just as long as it's not us! We don't want another Iran-gate embarrassment. The President would go ballistic."

"Look Senator…" Drew Dalton had just about taken all the flak he was prepared to take. "You can't have it both ways. You were present when we discussed the raid with Lombardi at Cheyenne Mountain. Those men risked their lives for the good old U S of A and the rest of the free world. Some were even killed for Chrissake! They did what they had to do. They followed their judgement and I fully support them. So don't go getting all hot under the collar!"

"I've had the President on the phone, Drew…"

"Look, the President gave his *unofficial* sanction – we all know that – so did the British and Israeli Prime Ministers – and don't forget the Russian President is in on it too!"

"OK, OK!" Copeland relented as he raised his arms in appeasement. "It's just that we expected it to be much *quieter* – y'know ... an in and out sort of thing."

"That was certainly the plan, Senator," Drew Dalton was prepared to defend Ross Lombardi to the last. "It just didn't pan out that way. One of those darn Russians raised the alarm. There was nothing else Ross could do."

"It's a hell of a thing, Drew." Hefner T. Copeland stroked his chin and looked out of the window and over towards the grassy park area of The Mall. He was Senator for North Carolina and an executive member of the National Defense Committee, which directly involved him in such delicate matters. Divorced three times, the Senator now had grown-up children in politics: one son was Governor of Maryland and two of his daughters were party activists here in Washington. The slightest whiff of scandal would certainly damage his career and also the careers of his children. He was also devoted to his four grandchildren, whom he loved dearly but saw little of. Copeland had every intention of retiring from politics at the next election, but still wanted to go out on a positive note. He was an incorrigible womaniser. His chequered past went right back to the Kennedy era when he was reputed to have forged dubious connections with the twin worlds of Hollywood and the Mafia.

Copeland would undoubtedly go to extraordinary lengths to maintain his squeaky clean image. He had managed to be one of life's survivors, despite all the mud-slinging and assassinations. He was a man who had been around a long time. He was used to getting his own way. Ruthless with enemies and determined with friends, the Senator didn't trust the CIA and especially not the FBI. His earliest misgivings went back to the bad old days of J. Edgar Hoover; someone he frequently called a 'depraved faggot' and 'child-molester'. Ever since the late Sixties, Copeland had managed to keep a private refuge down in New Orleans which he would often use for vacations. The whole place was surrounded by incessant rumours of wild drinking sessions and outrageous parties frequented by hordes of loose women. However, the Senator had been widely recognised as a shrewd and tough old cookie. He had the goods filed away on most of his enemies -just in case. Nevertheless, he was well aware the ravenous wolves of Washington were always waiting in the wings, watching for the slightest sign of weakness – even the smallest mistake. He knew they wouldn't hesitate to pounce and tear him apart.

"I guess what you're saying is right, Drew, it's just …" The red telephone on his desk began to ring, interrupting him in mid-sentence. The Senator moved round and snatched up the receiver.

"Yes, Mr President…" Copeland took a deep breath and nodded as he spoke.

"Yes sir! Whatever you say, Mr President. Sure thing … we'll keep on top of it." He hung up and breathed out a long sigh. "That was…"

"The President." Dalton raised his eyebrows as he finished the sentence for him. "I guessed."

"He wants a full report on that salvage boat up in the Barents Sea."

"The *Norse Warrior* …"

"Yeh, that's the one. What's the latest, Drew?"

"She's not doing anything … yet." Dalton sighed as he poured himself some coffee from the jug standing on the hotplate. "We've got all our stuff from Cheyenne Mountain beamed right down their throats. But they still haven't made a hostile move."

"Keep on them, Drew" Copeland ordered as he shoved his cigar back into his face. "Give 'em the works."

"If they as much as fart, Senator, we'll smell it."

"What do you really think?" Copeland asked with a sense of unease.

"Can they seriously bring up those damn missiles?"

"Don't look like it," Dalton replied. "Certainly not with the equipment they've got on board. The Norwegian coast-guards and the whole combined Russian observation team from the Kola Peninsula have been up there to investigate and they're still keeping an eye on things."

"And?"

"They've reported that the Norse Warrior's Captain claims they're up there to dismantle a whaling station on the island of Bjornoya. They got papers."

"A likely goddam story," Copeland laughed with derision.

"Do you really think it's true?"

"The Russians certainly don't! The Kola Peninsula team recommend full and continued surveillance – and that's just what we're giving them – round the clock."

"Good!"

"But what happens if they *do* make a move for the Cherkassy, Senator?"

Drew Dalton asked the loaded question.

"Our official line – and it's the Russians' as well – is that we can't lose, either way."

"How so?"

"If the Norse Warrior is legitimate, we've got no problem. On the other hand, if she's not, we have to wait and let her bring up the missiles ... and that would save the Russians the tricky job of doing it in the spring. On the other hand, if she is successful, everybody pounces on her like a cat on an unsuspecting mouse. The Russians get their weapons back and this guy Bjorn Ramuldssen and his crew enter into a plea bargain over who hired them. We go public, Iran is disgraced internationally and everybody wins! The President will be happy with the situation, just as long as we keep on top of it."

"I don't know. Something smells fishy about this, Senator." Dalton knew his doubts would provoke displeasure, which would soon translate into even greater displeasure from his superiors.

"What do you mean, Drew?"

"Well ... surely this Ramuldssen guy knows he's under surveillance? And that his vessel will be impounded as soon as he tries anything. It doesn't add up."

"Aw, he's just the fall guy, Drew," the Senator waved a dismissive hand. "The Iranians think they just got to send him up there. If he succeeds, they get nuclear missiles on the cheap. If he fails, its no skin off their noses ... or so they think."

"I don't know..."

"Where are they now?" Copeland lit up another cigar.

Dalton knew the Senator couldn't think straight without a cigar to draw on.

"Well Senator, quite frankly we're puzzled. Right now she's actually steaming away from the wreck of the *Cherkassy*. We figure that's because they either don't know the precise location, or they're trying to throw the Russians off the scent. But if they move into position, we'll be right with them. You can depend on it."

"What about Lombardi and his team?"

"Somewhere in Russia." Dalton smiled as the emphasis of the meeting shifted. "I'm not exactly sure where."

"Well, when are they due to come home?" the Senator demanded.

"Don't know that either, Senator."

"You don't seem to have much control over these people, do you? I like to have control, Drew … cuts down the error margin." Copeland blew more thick clouds of blue smoke into the air. "I sure hope these mavericks don't cause any more trouble."

"Ross is a good man, he gets the job done. I guess his methods are a bit unorthodox at times, to say the least," Drew Dalton sighed, "but then, the jobs we give him are usually the ones no-one else can do."

"What about the British?" Copeland rounded on the agent and was even more concerned that someone else might let the cat out of the bag. He trusted nobody.

"The British have their own guy with Ross," Dalton told him, "Peter Lawrence, remember, you met him in Colorado."

"Sure, sure, I remember the guy." A fugitive thought stole across the Senator's mind as he realised he would not be the only one to carry the can if everything went pear-shaped.

"So the British are up to their necks in this too?"

"So are the Israelis and the Russians," Dalton assured him.

"That'll make me sleep a bit easier." Copeland was visibly relieved. "At least none of them are gonna run off at the mouth and sink us in an international scandal."

"You got nothing to worry about, Senator."

Having listened to the unfolding story, the senator frowned as all the political and tactical problems flashed through his brain. The meeting concluded with both men swapping some small talk about their respective families and wishing each other a merry Christmas and a happy New Year. As their innermost thoughts began to drift away from the wild arena of political intrigue and the wider matters of the world in general, they concentrated on the season's festivities which still lay ahead. Drew Dalton looked forward to some well earned time off with his wife and children, while Heffner T. Copeland felt he had fulfilled his family duty by giving his secretary a list of presents to buy for his grandchildren. On New Year's Day he would head south to New Orleans for a small holiday. He certainly deserved it after all this crap.

CHAPTER 23

ENGLAND : LONDON

THE TOWERING STONE FACADES OF Horseguards Avenue looked grey and forbidding on this bleak mid-winter morning. Juliet Lucas turned up her collar against the blustery wind and gave an involuntary shudder. Her solitary footsteps clattered on the damp pavement as she scurried along to the inconspicuous building used by Jeremy Sinclair for clandestine meetings with his agents. She had not heard any news concerning the whereabouts of Peter Lawrence and the rest of the team for quite some time. However, whilst circulating at a Government cocktail party a couple of nights ago, she'd managed to overhear some Chinese whispers about a botched raid in the Dasht-e Kavir ... and the fact that there had been heavy casualties. Her heart was pounding and her mind was in a complete turmoil. She just hoped and prayed this unscheduled meeting with Jeremy Sinclair would at least confirm that Lawrence had survived and, more importantly, that she would possibly be able to re-join him. Juliet yearned to be back with Peter Lawrence. They had promised so much to each other during those earlier heated carefree moments. From the very first moment when she had met with Peter, she had readily succumbed to his easy-going ways and disarming manner, which seemed to make life so special and meaningful...but perhaps the truth was far more basic. Their initial relationship had been a deliberate and calculated career move on her part, but in the ensuing months she had nevertheless grown fond of the man. The ever-lingering thoughts of Peter that kept drifting through her mind were truly wonderful. During her waking hours, she embraced his memory with a warmth bordering on lust. It invaded every fibre of her being ... though true love was a concept she did not hold with or believe in.

Stepping into the comparative warmth of the government building, she hardly had time to remove her coat before a cheery security guard came forward to greet her. After briefly exchanging pleasantries about the appalling weather, he escorted her to a small, well-furnished room on the third floor where Jeremy Sinclair and Adrian Dyson were waiting.

Juliet entered the room and polite greetings were exchanged. There was a slight pause as the three waited for the guard to withdraw and resume his duties on the ground floor.

"Please sit down, Miss Lucas." Sinclair moved from behind a leather-topped desk and offered her a chair. "I expect you would like to know about Peter Lawrence, and possibly where he is?"

"He's *alive*?" Her pulse quickened as she half-spun round on the chair to confront Sinclair's smug expression bearing down upon her.

"Oh, very much so." Sinclair's cold calculating eyes met hers.

"Yes, of course I would like to know where he is." Lucas's voice trailed away.

Her true feelings couldn't be contained any longer as she turned her gaze towards the window.

"So would we!" Adrian Dyson interrupted gruffly.

"'You mean ... you don't *know*?" Lucas began to panic inwardly.

"Of course we *know*," Sinclair laughed awkwardly. "Well ... roughly."

"He's somewhere in Russia," Dyson added. "But we're not exactly sure where."

"But ... then how do you know he's alright?" Lucas enquired anxiously.

"We've had a communication from Rostov," Sinclair explained, "which confirmed the team had recently arrived there. Lawrence wasn't listed amongst the casualties so we can assume he's survived. However, we do know that an Israeli chap called Weizman was killed."

"Oh no!" Juliet couldn't help letting out a little gasp at this news.

"You knew him?" Sinclair mellowed when he sensed her distress.

"Yes ... yes, quite well."

"I'm sorry."

"Get on with it!" Dyson growled impatiently with his hands clasped behind his back, as he pretended to study one of the heroic paintings of an ancient sea battle.

"Yes, of course…" Sinclair coughed nervously. "Well, the group left Rostov two days ago en route for St Petersburg. But they haven't arrived yet – and what's even more disconcerting is the fact that the Russians don't seem to know where they are."

"And that's where you come in." Dyson turned to face Lucas. "You will leave immediately for St Petersburg to link up with Lawrence and obtain a full report.

Then you must return to London and give us a comprehensive briefing on the situation."

"And let us know what the ruddy blighters are up to!" Sinclair added.

"But why can't Peter do all that himself?" Lucas felt indignant at being brought back again so quickly.

"It is imperative for Lawrence to stay in the field with the Americans and Israelis," Dyson explained with a flourish of his hand. "This thing isn't over yet."

"But why can't I…"

"You have your orders Miss Lucas," Dyson interrupted. He was about to leave the room when his black telephone sprang to life, startling Lucas. Jeremy Sinclair moved over and snatched up the receiver.

"Yes?" he gave a weary sigh as he clasped the receiver with both hands. However, his weariness quickly faded as he looked from Dyson to Lucas and began to listen intently to what the caller had to say. Dyson and Lucas looked on with curiosity. When Sinclair had finished with the call, he replaced the receiver slowly into its cradle and thoughtfully drummed his fingers on the handset.

"Well?" Dyson asked impatiently.

"You're not going to believe this sir…"

"Try me!"

"It's Eamonn Burke, Lawrence's contact from Belfast…"

"Yes, of course I know *who* he is," Dyson snapped with exasperation, "He's on that bloody salvage ship."

"No sir, he's not."

"He's not? Then for goodness sake where the bloody hell is he?"

"He's at Paddington Green police station." Sinclair paused. "And he wants to talk to us about Russian missiles."

"Good God!" In one bound, Dyson tossed his overcoat over his arm and grabbed his hat and umbrella from the wicker stand by the door. "Miss Lucas, you had better wait here until we get back."

❖ ❖ ❖

The Whitehall Daimler glided past the imposing cluster of Ministry buildings and Government Offices as it headed towards Charing Cross. On this cold, windswept Sunday morning, Westminster had a haunted, melancholy look about it. Away in the distance Big Ben struck ten o'clock as they proceeded round the southern edge of Trafalgar Square with Lord Nelson glaring heroically down from his column. The vehicle sped along Pall Mall before turning up Lower Regent Street to continue its journey north-westwards towards Piccadilly Circus. The famous giant neon hoardings surrounding the Circus looked drab and decadent in the pale winter sunlight. A small group of Salvation Army volunteers were busily distributing food to a few shivering homeless vagabonds lurking in the shop doorways and the statue of Eros, the boy-god of love, reminded Jeremy Sinclair of his own peccadillo.

His mannerisms were perfectly suited to a game of bogus description. His languid, limping drawl and his foppish sartorial elegance created an accumulation of affections as if he was reproaching himself for not being put to more enduring ends. When approached to reveal his true secret, Sinclair would always react with the embarrassment, which is usually expected of a young maiden being tactlessly invited to lose her virginity. The Defence Department under-secretary had always been suspected of being a closet gay. This long-standing suspicion had posed no end of potential problems of security in his professional capacity at Westminster. During the past few years he had remained monogamous and was now settled into a long-term relationship, partly because of the AIDS epidemic and partly because he believed in total commitment. But despite all this, he was constantly haunted by the knowledge that he could never come out – and be himself. Such was the price he had been willing to pay for his ambitions.

Adrian Dyson fell silent as he opened up his briefcase and rummaged through some papers. He remained oblivious to the City's passing winter scenery, after all, it was something which he'd observed a thousand times before. Upon joining the army, the MI6 colonel had taken an early decision to remain unmarried and consequently lived alone. When asked why, his standard response was that he was already married to the Service.

A committed professional, he'd first seen active service in the Falklands war with Argentina, followed by the Iraqi conflict, and in more recent years, the collapsing cold-war of the Soviet Union. Being a recognised intellectual on a wide range of matters Soviet, it had always been rumoured that he had known Guy Burgess personally, although he never spoke of this openly. Underneath his cloak of cold professionalism, Dyson still harboured secret doubts. He sometimes wondered if he had actually made the right choice in life – or perhaps he should have studied law at Cambridge, as his father and grandfather before him. Perhaps he should have followed the more orthodox line by marrying and having children – possibly even grandchildren by now. Had he somehow missed out on the more important things in life? There were certainly times when he thought that was a distinct possibility, but then something like this Iranian thing came along: and he regretted nothing.

The Daimler zig-zagged its way through Portland Place towards Marylebone Road, where the Sunday morning church-goers were just beginning to emerge from the warmth of their places of worship. Finally, the vehicle pulled up at the back of Paddington Green police station. Identification cards were checked at the top security holding area, before the barrier was raised and they were allowed to proceed.

Adrian Dyson stepped out to be approached by a senior police officer who informed him that Eamonn Burke had simply walked into a local police station in Newcastle, where Burke admitted he was a known and wanted senior IRA operative. Burke had somehow convinced them that he had an important coded message for a special contact at a secret telephone number in London. That number had turned out to be an MI6 office in Old Queen Street and shortly afterwards, orders were given for Burke to be transferred down to Paddington Green.

 Since arriving, he had refused to speak to anyone – insisting that he would only talk with Peter Lawrence.

Eamonn Burke was brought to a secure interview room and seated opposite the pair of Secret Service people. He lit up a cigarette and sat back to observe them for a moment before speaking.

"Who are you?" Burke asked with a disarming smile.

"We're friends of Peter Lawrence" Jeremy Sinclair told him.

"Are you now," Burke replied in a supercilious tone. "And where's the great man himself?"

"In Russia," Sinclair said.

"Really? And how can I be sure of that?" Burke enquired coldly as he blew smoke rings in their direction.

"You can't." Adrian Dyson was becoming impatient with this cat and mouse game.

"And just who might you be?" Burke turned to the older man.

"Suffice to say that we know who *you* are, Mr Burke," Dyson replied. "And aren't you supposed to be still on board the *Norse Warrior?*"

"Well now…" Burke was surprised by Dyson's response and began to regain interest. "You seem to know something all right."

"We know everything," Dyson assured him with a cold stare. "Now, we really haven't got all day to sit around here chatting so, if you've got nothing to say…" Dyson noisily pushed the chair back and rose to his feet.

"I *was* aboard the *Norse Warrior*…" Burke snapped through clenched teeth. Dyson sat back down. "But I blew my cover and had to go over the side to avoid being killed."

"Over the side?" Jeremy Sinclair found this difficult to believe. "Into the Arctic Sea?"

"The Norwegian Sea to be precise," Burke corrected him sarcastically. "But we were well inside the Circle."

"And just how did you survive?" Sinclair asked in a condescending tone.

"I grabbed the small flat-pack liferaft which had been stowed on the fore-deck and used it as a shield when I plunged over the side." Burke went on to tell the story of the radio exchange between the *Norse Warrior* and the Norwegian coastguard. "I was picked up almost immediately." Before continuing, he paused to take a sip of tea and wiped his mouth with the back of his hand. "We were sailing right through the middle of a Norwegian fishing fleet returning to port and Ramuldssen didn't want to stop in case too many awkward questions were asked. Their whole mission would have been compromised." Burke went on to explain that when he went over the side, the liferaft had partially inflated and quickly slipped astern of the *Norse Warrior*. One of the nearby fishing boats had noticed this crumpled piece of orange coloured flotsam and moved over to investigate. When they finally dragged it aboard, they found Burke's shivering body tangled up in the collapsed canopy. Having revived him from the initial effects of hypothermia, they realised he still needed urgent medical attention and put him ashore at Bodo.

Burke sensed their doubts. He smiled and slowly raised his left hand in front of the sceptical duo to reveal the missing upper part of his index finger, which had been shot away in the skirmish. Having been discharged from the local hospital, he travelled south to Stavanger, where he boarded a ferry bound for Newcastle-upon-Tyne. Once there, he decided the quickest way to get the kind of attention he needed was to have himself arrested. The rest of the story they already knew. Burke paused to take the last dregs of his tea.

"You have some other information for us?" Dyson ventured.

"Sure I have…" Burke tipped back on his chair and smiled again, "but I want out of this place first."

"Oh really? And where do you want to go?"

"Back to Ireland," Burke shot forward as he replied, "where I can be of much more use. Don't forget I am probably the only person standing between you and a potential nuclear holocaust."

Dyson fixed the Irishman with a cold, calculating stare.

He remained thoughtful and silent for a while. It went against all his professional instincts to let this man go. Burke was a wanted terrorist and they had him at last. But he also knew the Iranian issue was much bigger than any domestic problem, especially in these days of cease-fires and peace talks.

"Very well," the MI6 man said at length.

"I can trust you now, can't I?" Burke maintained his provocative and cynical demeanour, but there was nothing they could do about it.

"Of course."

"OK…" Burke relaxed as he sat back in his chair. "The *Norse Warrior* is just a decoy."

"What?" Jeremy Sinclair was on his feet in a flash.

"The Iranians have their own submarine in the area and the Captain, Executive Officer and Weapons Officer from the *Cherkassy* are also aboard. They intend to salvage the missiles right from under your very noses… while you're busy watching the Danish boat."

"Oh my God!" Sinclair rubbed his brow and began to pace the floor of the interview room.

"When is all this supposed to take place?" Dyson asked coolly.

"Don't know exactly," Burke replied. "Probably right now, as we speak. I don't think they'll want to hang around too long, do you?"

"We must contact the Americans…" Sinclair began to panic, "and the Russians…"

"Calm down Jeremy!" Dyson snapped and took a deep breath.

"Mr Burke… exactly why did you think you could be more help to us back in Ireland?"

"Because that's where they're going to take the missiles – provided of course the salvage attempt is successful."

"But why Ireland?"

"They think it's far too risky to make it all the way back to the Gulf by submarine. There's an international airport at Knock in western Ireland which is mainly used by pilgrims who come from all over the world to visit a nearby Catholic shrine. Security is minimal. They've made arrangements to land the missiles on the west coast and take them overland to the airport, where a chartered cargo plane will fly them out to Libya – and from there on to Iran."

"Very interesting Mr Burke, but the Iranian missile launchers have already been destroyed." Dyson felt he had regained the advantage, "and what's more, the men who were going to adapt them have either been killed or captured."

"So what?" Burke exclaimed with derision. "Missile launchers and delivery systems are ten-a-penny – so are the people who operate them – you ought to know that. Once the Iranians get their hands on those missiles, nothing will stop them!"

"And what exactly do you think you could you do for us back in Ireland, Mr Burke?" Dyson leaned forward and placed his elbows on the table. He peered thoughtfully over his steepled fingers.

"Organise a surprise reception committee… But that's enough of all this talk! I'm not prepared to give any more information until I'm out of here!"

"Well, I think our options have been severely limited," Dyson said at length.

"Sinclair here will see to all the formalities. He will make the necessary contacts with the Irish Government." As the three men filed out of the interview room, Burke paused and jabbed his empty mug into the solar plexus of the young police officer standing by the open door. "Thanks sonny … and I did ask for *two* sugars."

The Irishman was whisked back to Whitehall for further debriefing, before being quietly spirited away by a group of faceless men standing by at the offices in Horseguards Avenue. Adrian Dyson and Jeremy Sinclair stopped off in Downing Street to organise the diplomatic side of the operations, before returning to brief Juliet Lucas.

Dyson and Sinclair startled Lucas as they burst back into the office and began their briefing.

"Miss Lucas, you will go out to St Petersburg, as arranged. You will take fresh orders for Lawrence and the others to continue by whatever local means are available and, by using their considerable initiative, they must attempt to apprehend the Iranians."

"And the Americans," Jeremy Sinclair reminded him, "Don't forget the Americans."

"Oh, of course, the Americans, thank you Jeremy. We will convey all this new information to the Americans and the Israelis. A joint task force must be assembled and dispatched to the Barents Sea immediately, just in case Lawrence is unsuccessful." Dyson rose to his feet to indicate the meeting was over and shook her hand warmly. Juliet quickly regained her composure and smiled inwardly as her anxieties began to evaporate. It was a serious situation and she was back in the thick of it. She couldn't wait to board a flight for St Petersburg. Quite suddenly, she found herself alone on the back seat of a taxi, heading towards Heathrow Airport although she couldn't help wondering if she was risking everything by taking this trip.

CHAPTER 24

RUSSIA : ST PETERSBURG

P ETER LAWRENCE PEERED OUT THROUGH the scratched window of the Russian Antonov AN-32 'Cline' as it banked over a thick plume of grey smoke belching skywards from the distinctive red and white-hooped chimney of the nuclear power station at Sosnovy Bor. The easterly approach to Pulkovo airport was a welcome sight. Despite all the frantic denials and cover-up, he still couldn't help wondering just how much radioactive iodine vapour had actually been released on that fateful day, 25th March 1992. The station's poorly maintained RBMK reactor had suffered a serious malfunction which caused a pressure surge throughout the system, followed by a catastrophic rupture within nuclear fuel channel number N52-16. The International Atomic Energy Agency based in Vienna had quickly issued a public statement and rated the accident as a '2' on their seven-point logarithmic scale: Chernobyl having achieved a sobering '7'. Thankfully, the over-stretched cooling system of Sosnovy Bor's tired and ancient reactors had worked satisfactorily. The plant on that occasion had been hurriedly shut down; which helped to minimise the effects of the radioactive cloud as it drifted northwards over Finland and Norway: Lawrence gave an involuntary shiver when he realised the world might not be so lucky next time.

Their long and tiring journey from the Iranian desert had taken almost a week. The team had been flown from Ashkabad to Rostov, where the Russian authorities had spirited them away to some meagre accommodation and medical facilities at a military barracks on the outskirts of town. David Weizman's body, along with those of the other Israelis killed in the Dasht-e Kavir skirmish, were quickly transferred to a waiting aircraft which had then flown them back to Tel Aviv for burial.

Ross Lombardi's own casualties were flown back to the United States. Following a couple of days well earned R & R in Rostov, the remaining members of the team were flown, by different routes, for a rendezvous in St Petersburg, with brief stopovers at Khar'kov, Voroneza and Moscow.

As they passed through immigration control, Peter Lawrence was surprised to see a smiling Juliet Lucas waiting on the arrivals side of the terminal. She stepped forward and kissed him lightly on the cheek before shepherding the rest of the team out to a fleet of waiting limousines for their journey into the city centre. The motorcade sped along *Moskovskij Prospekt*, and circled around the city's patriotic *Blockade Monument* before passing more monotonous and featureless apartment blocks. The cars bumped and splashed through the slushy puddles as they dodged around the clattering trolleys rattling from block to block, striking showers of sparks between the buildings. Rooms had been allocated for them in a safe Government building situated on *Krasnaja Ulitsa*, close to the Admiralty. It would have been far too conspicuous for them to stay in any of the larger international hotels and the smaller establishments were regarded as nothing more than notorious hangouts for pimps, drug-pushers and *Mafiozniki*. Juliet Lucas confirmed they were already late for an urgent meeting in the General Headquarters Building. They barely had time to dump their bags. After refreshing themselves, Ross Lombardi, Peter Lawrence, Ruth Netanya and Juliet Lucas were met downstairs by a young and impatient Russian naval attaché. He made an exaggerated show of looking at his watch and hurriedly escorted them from the building.

The party tried to keep up with him as he set off at a rapid pace along *Admiral Tejskij Prospekt*, and through the bleak Admiralty Gardens …sprinkled with the first winter's snow.

Crossing the vast expanse of *Palace Square*, they strode towards the fading grandeur of the yellow façade to the General Staff Building. The group shuffled through an entrance lobby to one side of the main Arch. The building was little more than a shadow of its former glory when it had been erected to commemorate Russia's victory in the Patriotic War against Napoleon.

Once inside, they traversed a bewildering network of odorous yards and muddy passages until they were finally ushered into a large cheerless room with lofty windows overlooking the Winter Palace. A semi-circular table covered with a green baize cloth formed a centrepiece, behind which sat several Russian naval officers and a plain-clothes intelligence specialist from the First Chief Directorate. Above them on the back wall, it was still possible to make out the faded shape of a huge hammer and sickle. It had once been hung in defiance, and for many years had stared out upon the very spot where the first shots of the Communist Revolution had been fired.

"Good morning, gentlemen … and ladies." A portly and distinguished man with a grey moustache stood up to greet them. He wore the uniform of an Admiral, complete with rows of ribbons and medals splashing colour across his chest and endless gold braid to the cuffs of his sleeves. Admiral Vasili Semyonovich Kuragin had graduated from the Naval Military School in 1962 and the Higher Naval College in 1966. He then moved on to the Naval Academy – where he also graduated with honours. His first staff appointment had been to the Academy of the General Staff. Some five years later he served with distinction as a fleet commander of a navigation group on board submarines, before being quickly promoted to Commander-in-Chief of the Red Banner Black Sea Fleet.

He was passionate about playing games of strategy such as bridge, billiards or chess.

"Congratulations on the success of your mission." The Westerners nodded without speaking and settled on the chairs provided. "However, I am afraid there is also some bad news…" The Admiral gestured towards Juliet. All eyes fell upon her.

She cleared her throat and stood to address the assembly.

"Within the past twenty four hours, Whitehall has fully briefed your respective Governments on the latest developments." She paused and cast her gaze towards Ross Lombardi and Ruth Netanya. "The situation in the Barents Sea has now become critical."

"But what's been happening that we don't already know about?" Peter asked.

"We have recently been able to confirm that the *Norse Warrior* is merely a decoy," Juliet replied solemnly as she looked around at their incredulous faces. "The ship has actually been standing off near the wreck of the *Komsomolets* to try and throw us off the scent. The real salvage attempt is still going to be made on the nuclear missiles of the *Cherkassy*."

"And just who's crazy enough to make such an attempt?" Ruth enquired.

"The Iranians. They have a modified submarine in the area." Lucas confirmed.

"OK, but surely they ain't got the necessary technology and know-how to pull off a successful salvage attempt." Ross remained sceptical.

"It's worse than that. We have been reliably informed the Iranian submarine is now commanded by three Russians…" The Admiral growled. "Valentin Tarasov, Rem Bukato and Boris Lukin."

"And who the hell might they be?" Lawrence was startled.

"The former Captain, Executive Officer and Weapons Officer of the *Cherkassy*."

"Holy shit!" Lombardi jumped to his feet. "How the hell did that happen? Were they kidnapped?"

"No. We understand they were enlisted willingly," Lucas informed the American.

"How come, for Christ's sake?" Lombardi fumed as he gave the Russians a withering look.

Admiral Kuragin turned to his people for support. "I am afraid we had no alternative. It was inevitable that we would have to discipline them for the loss of the *Cherkassy*." A naval officer piped up from the end of the table.

"Discipline them? How?" Ruth Netanya queried.

"They were court-martialled and dishonourably discharged from the service." The officer clutched at a sheaf of papers and lowered his head, trying to hide his shame and embarrassment.

"No wonder they went over to the bloody Iranians!" Lawrence's voice rose with frustration and anger.

"After her extensive refit, Captain Tarasov testified that, in his opinion, the *Cherkassy* still wasn't seaworthy enough to perform some of the more extreme manoeuvres," Lucas said in a matter-of-fact way. "But we have subsequently discovered that her officers were nevertheless ordered, under protest, to continue with the sea trials."

"It was not as simple as that…" The Russian naval officer tried to defend the integrity of his superiors.

"It was *just* like that!" Lucas snapped.

"But if this is true, *why* the hell did they take such crazy chances?"

"Obviously to do nothing more than impress the Iranian delegation on board."

Ruth Netanya was furious. She stared straight at the Russian Admiral.

"So you're now telling us these guys actually took the fall for nothing more than a bad decision from the Russian High Command?" Lombardi was beginning to get the full picture.

"Seems like that." Peter Lawrence agreed.

"Now the rest of the world has to join forces and clean up all this crap!"

"Do not forget you are representatives of your respective Governments and guests in our country," the Intelligence specialist said menacingly.

"Look … Good men, personal friends of mine, have died needlessly because of this mess." Lombardi faced up to the Russians.

The room was soon filled with the buzz of urgent voices.

"Gentlemen, gentlemen. Why don't we just compose ourselves for a moment." Juliet knew that an outright confrontation would achieve nothing. "If you'll allow me to continue…" She waited for the babble to subside. "Both America and Russia have despatched a special task force to intercept the Iranians and eliminate any further danger.

We have received fresh orders from MI6, the CIA and Mossad. We are to make ourselves available as a back-up force, should any containing action outside the jurisdiction of the official forces become necessary."

"Isn't there an advisory force based on the Kola Peninsula?" Lawrence queried.

"Sure … aren't they supposed to be monitoring the situation?" Lombardi added.

"Terminated!" The man from the First Chief Directorate said grimly.

"Terminated?" Lawrence's tone became hostile.

"What the bloody hell does *terminated* mean?"

"I mean they're all dead," the Intelligence specialist concluded, his armpits suddenly becoming wet.

"Dead? Jesus Christ!" Lombardi looked incredulously at the others.

"What the hell's going on here?"

"We recently discovered a raiding party from the Iranian submarine had come ashore near Kolskiy Zaliv. They killed everyone in the compound," the naval officer solemnly informed the doubting group.

"But didn't you also have a military guard up there?" Netanya demanded as she tried to contain her frustration.

"Of course we did!" the man answered indignantly "but they were taken by surprise."

"Well, this can only mean one thing. They're already on their way!" Lombardi exclaimed. "They obviously don't care any more! They've either retrieved the missiles or they're in the process of doing so right now – and I don't believe we can get to them in time."

"That is precisely the situation," Juliet Lucas fumed as she resumed her seat.

An eerie, death-like silence enveloped the room. Everyone remained motionless, deep in thought, as if they had been bewitched by some diabolical hoodoo.

"OK…" Lombardi finally broke the spell. "It's no good arguing amongst ourselves. What's the latest military situation?"

"A helicopter task force was dispatched from Archangel more than fourteen hours ago." Admiral Kuragin breathed a great sigh of relief now that the criticism had stopped and they were actually getting down to business. His officers took the initiative and spread out charts of the Barents Sea across the table.

"They should be landing in the compound near Kolskiy Zaliv as we speak."

"They are crack marine troops," the naval officer added with confidence as he pointed to the spot with a pair of dividers. "More than a match for any hostile force which may be encountered."

"Four kilo-class submarines and the destroyers *Neustrashimy* and *Dzerzhinsky* have sailed from Murmansk," Kuragin continued. "Their area of search will be concentrated between Norway and Iceland. Their orders are to seek and destroy. Meanwhile, the alternative escape route between the Arctic ice-pack and the northern Finnmark coast is being guarded by several yankee-class submarines, backed up by our aircraft carrier *Admiral Kuznetsov*. There can be no escape."

"The Americans are within thirty hours of joining up with the Russians," Lucas pointed out. "They have deployed the carrier *Alabama* from Newfoundland, escorted by two *Los Angeles* class hunter-killer submarines with orders to intercept anything coming south along the European Continental Shelf. We have already established the Iranian's eventual destination is Western Ireland."

"But, why Western Ireland, for goodness sake?" Lawrence queried.

"Believe me, we have obtained reliable information which confirms they are destined for the west coast of Ireland."

"Where on earth did you get that kind of information?" Lawrence sat back and folded his arms as he began to realise the answer to his own question.

"From one of your very own sources, Peter," Lucas confirmed with an impish smile.

"Eamonn Burke? But surely he's still aboard the *Norse Warrior*…"

"Not any more; he's back in Ireland."

"How?" Lawrence was puzzled

"It's a long story," Lucas smiled again, "I'll tell you on the way."

"On the way where?"

"We're going up to Andenes … it's a small place on the island of Andoya – where the Norwegians have their rocket range – just off the north-west coast of Norway. A frigate has been provided courtesy of the Royal Navy. Don't worry Peter…" she punched his arm mockingly, "you'll love it."

"What happens if the Iranians have already salvaged the nuclear weapons?" Netanya had saved the most provocative question until the meeting was beginning to break up. Everyone stopped in their tracks. The Russians muttered and looked uneasily at each other.

"Well…" Admiral Kuragin stared through the window before giving a measured response. "We cannot fire on her, that's for sure. We cannot risk a nuclear explosion."

"So you'll just let her go?"

"Certainly not!" The Admiral was indignant. He felt the rage of the betrayed. He was a man who would always march towards the sound of gunfire, but on this occasion he simply couldn't come up with a suitable answer for the Israeli Agent.

"So what will you do?" Netanya would not let him off the hook.

No answer was forthcoming.

"Just as I thought!"

"I guess that's where *we* come in," Ross Lombardi said quietly as he stepped forward.

"Oh. And what exactly can *we* do?" Netanya implored of the American. She was still consumed by bitterness and hatred about the death of her colleague and was in no mood to trust the American to come up with an acceptable play-it-by-ear solution at this stage of the crisis.

"Look… Let's get out there first," Lombardi advocated, "and see what's going on. Then we'll be in a better position to assess the situation."

"Ross is right." Peter Lawrence joined the exchange in support of his American friend. "When it comes to it, we may not actually have to do anything. The Iranian submarine problem may have already been dealt with."

"I damn well hope so!" Netanya flashed a look of pure hostility round the room, before striding through the door.

Back at the Government base in *Ulitsa Krasnaja*, the team made hurried preparations for their impending departure to Norway.

"Is Eamonn all right?" Lawrence asked Juliet.

"Oh, he's fine," she told her colleague. "and almost in one piece. He's organising a reception committee back in Ireland – just in case this thing gets that far."

"Good man!" Lawrence smiled, glad that Burke had survived.

The team were taken back to Pulkovo airport where they rejoined Larry Tyson and Jake LeClair as they reboarded the Antonov AN-32 'Cline'. It was snowing heavily. The aircraft shuddered like a tethered animal as the twin ZMDB Ivchyenko turboprops were throttled up for take off. The engines screamed louder as the pilot held the aircraft and went through his final pre-flight checks. The expanse of runway behind the prop-wash momentarily cleared of snow as the plane lumbered forward and took off into the white sky and settled into a north-westerly course out over the Gulf of Finland. Larry Tyson and Jake LeClair exchanged friendly banter with the other Americans. Ruth Netanya and her Israeli comrades stayed apart from the others. They maintained a hard-faced silence, partly in memory of David Weizman and partly in defiance of everyone and everything around them. Juliet Lucas sat alongside Peter Lawrence. During the flight they didn't speak much, but he felt her hand slip through his arm and her fingers entwine around his. He gave them a reassuring squeeze and smiled into her inexperienced but trusting blue eyes.

The weather deteriorated as the plane headed into increasing darkness and blizzards over Finland. Peter looked down upon the inhospitable snow covered patchwork of forests and wondered just how much radioactive fallout from Sosnovy Bor had found its way this far north. The trouble was, everything over this variegated landscape looked perfectly normal… and yet he knew there were bound to be "hot-spots" where nothing could live. Radiation was a sinister enemy that couldn't be seen. He also knew that its devastating effects were not usually felt until it was far too late.

The aircraft was being thrown about all over the sky and Lawrence was beginning to doubt whether they would be able to land at their destination. Then, just when it seemed they might have to abort the mission, clearer weather opened up over the Gulf of Bothnia to reveal the lights of Sweden. Violent snow squalls kept buffeting the plane as they crossed over Norway and made a rapid descent between the vertical sides of a craggy fjord. The old and battered military aircraft droned on as it flew out over the Norwegian Sea before circling back towards the island of Andoya, to make a precarious night landing at the small isolated airport.

The British frigate *HMS Cumberland* had sought refuge from this latest storm by moving into the lee of the island some four hours ago. Her dark grey shape now tugged and yawed at her bow anchor chain, just offshore from the small town of Andenes, which hung down to the ragged shoreline like some dirty lace shawl.

It was bitterly cold. An icy north wind had blasted in to whip up flurries of snow around the mysterious group of visitors standing in a huddled mass on the desolate quay, stamping their feet to counteract the cold. They turned their backs against the biting wind and shrugged their collars higher, as they looked down with apprehension at the small boat allocated to take them out to the waiting warship.

Once aboard, the team was ferried out by a local fishing vessel; they took it in turns to make a grab for the swaying Jacob's ladder hanging down the dimpled sides of the frigate. A team of naval ratings helped everyone aboard and ushered them down into the warm interior. After stowing their equipment, Juliet Lucas went back up onto the deck where she leaned against the ship's railings and pulled the hood of her parka tightly to the sides of her face. She looked out over the half kilometre stretch of dark waters which separated them from the sleeping town of Andenes, completely oblivious of the dramatic events rapidly unfolding right under their very noses, in the darkness of this cold Arctic night.

CHAPTER 25

Russia : Barents Sea

THE *ZARAND'S* COMMAND CENTRE WAS JUST beneath the conning tower and the atmosphere felt like a sauna. All the submarine's heat accumulated up here. The ventilation fans hummed quietly in the background without making any difference. All eyes were transfixed upon Rem Bukato as he peered over the sonarman's shoulder at the fuzzy cigar-shaped outline filling the console screen before him. A bead of sweat trickled into Bukato's collar as he turned to the group of expectant faces gathered in the control room. He wiped his brow. "She's here, Captain, I know it, I can feel her presence." Everyone throughout the boat glanced up towards the curved roof. The sea outside the hull was filled with an assortment of eerie creaks and groans, most of them coming from ice floes colliding and rubbing together more than a tenth of a mile overhead. The spooky noises unnerved the Iranians, but Tarasov knew it would mean there would be no warships up there to investigate their activities – at least for the time being.

Valentin Tarasov and Boris Lukin stood over by the chart table. At this time of year, the last thin tentacles of the Gulf Stream groped their way around Norway's northern coastline, and Tarasov knew they would keep the pack ice at bay before finally giving up their heat beyond the Kola Inlet. The Russians watched the navigator rechecking his plotted course for their intended escape. Time seemed like an eternity as everyone waited anxiously for the return of the advanced party of Iranian divers. Four of them had been sent out to set up strobe lights around the submarines and to reconnoitre the *Cherkassy's* wreck which now rested on the silty bottom of the Barents Sea only a couple of hundred feet to starboard.

The *Zarand* had settled into the darkness some six hundred feet down, over the Continental Shelf and about fifty kilometres due north of the Russian town of Kolskiy Zaliv. Sharif Hamad moved over to pick four Iranian divers from the waiting group scheduled to leave the sub for an initial reconnaissance. He jabbed each man on the chest and crooked his finger, indicating they were to follow him towards the improvised diving chambers. They followed in silence. Everyone knew these first divers were nothing more than eager volunteers. They were considered expendable. They were really nothing more than guinea pigs, testing for pressure and radiation levels before the main work party went out into the seamless black void.

Towards the stern of the boat, four of the *Zarand's* vertical missile tubes had been converted to form extra diving chambers to facilitate rapid deployment of men and equipment. The second diving team had been equipped with the latest piece of sophisticated underwater technology – the *"Newtsuit."* At 300kg, these yellow armoured scuba outfits were really more like mini-submarines than aqua-lungs. The reinforced aluminium body weighed next to nothing in the water and could be manoeuvred by four electric motors – two for horizontal movement and two for vertical. The self-contained battery pack provided enough heat and power for up to six hours of continuous use and the divers breathed on a re-circulating system which used oxygen purified by a soda-lime scrubber to remove carbon dioxide.

Tension mounted aboard the *Zarand*. On the surface, the *Norse Warrior* had been attracting a lot of attention and the decoy plan seemed to be working. Sharif Hamad remained in constant touch with the salvage boat, which slowly cruised a classical search pattern in an area of water about four hundred kilometres to the north-west of the *Zarand's* present position.

The *Norse Warrior* tossed and turned in the foaming seas above the wreck of the *Komsomolets*, which had gone down in similar circumstances to the *Cherkassy* on 7th April 1989. The *Komsomolets* had also been carrying nuclear weapons, which were never recovered, but these would now be far too degraded to be worth salvaging. However, the two nuclear tipped torpedoes she was known to be carrying, were badly damaged when her bow crashed into the seabed. They now posed a different, but more serious environmental problem for the world's oceans by threatening to leak four kilograms of plutonium – the most toxic radioactive element ever discovered, into the planet's food-chain. An urgent solution to this escalating crisis had now become the direct responsibility of St Petersburg's top secret Rubin Institute, who were also being closely monitored by Bellona, the Norwegian Environmental Group.

When the Iranian divers returned, the news was better than expected. Radiation levels outside the Russian submarine were high, but nevertheless acceptable. The *Cherkassy* had come to rest with the lower half of her bow partially buried in the soft silt. She was sitting almost upright, but with a five-degree tilt to port. Her mid and stern hatches were half open, but there was a massive hole in the exposed starboard side of her titanium hull which now provided an opportunity for further access to the Main Propulsion Battery Compartment. Several clamshell covers over the vertical missile silos behind the sail had become unlatched and eight of these had sprung wide open. Time was at a premium. They knew the world wouldn't be fooled by the *Norse Warrior's* subterfuge for much longer. Valentin Tarasov handed over to Rem Bukato, while he, Boris Lukin and two Iranian divers dropped down a ladder and onto the lower deck from the command centre. They worked their way aft towards the missile gallery sealed with an oval shaped door. Tarasov grasped the central wheel and turned it. The metal fingers around the perimeter retracted and allowed the door to swing inwards. Each man reached up and grabbed a polished rail above the door as he swung his body into the after section. Everyone felt elated and pumped up on adrenaline as waiting crew members helped them climb into their "N*ewtsuits*" and busily prepared the equipment for their forthcoming inspection of the *Cherkassy*.

The dark, forbidding waters of the Barents Sea were just above freezing. Tarasov's eyes narrowed as he powered himself across and tried to penetrate the inky blackness with the dancing oval light from his torch. He led the others closer to the slumbering behemoth, but kept a constant check for any abnormalities in radiation or pressure levels. The great hulk of the *Cherkassy* suddenly loomed into view through the plankton-laden waters. The Captain looked up through the clear canopy of his helmet and was dwarfed by the huge vertical rudder towering overhead. They rose slowly to avoid stirring up the silt and passed over the horizontal stabilisers and the twin bronze propellers with their five scimitar-shaped blades. When they hovered above the after access hatch, a ghastly sight met Tarasov's eyes which made his guts tighten. His torch suddenly focused on the decomposing bodies of his former crew clogging the hatch. He could still sense the wild panic these men must have felt as they had jammed themselves into the hatch in a vain effort to escape the *Cherkassy's* final death throes. One man's body was almost through to his chest. Another sailor's head protruded beneath him. Behind them, more desperately pleading arms with outstretched skeletal fingers reached upwards, clawing at the sea. It was a horrible scene, like something from the tortured paintings of Dante's *Inferno*. There could be no way to gain access here.

Tarasov waved Boris Lukin and the two Iranians away. The group propelled themselves over to the mid-ship access hatch of the conning tower. Here, a similar scene met their eyes. To try and gain access through more dead bodies would be gruesomely impossible. They powered onwards, over the dark void left by the escape pod when it was released. Perhaps they could gain access here? The forward torpedo-loading hatch remained firmly closed and was impossible to open from the outside. There could only be one other way in; and that was through a yawning gash blasted in the Main Propulsion Battery Compartment. Luckily, the *Cherkassy* had come to rest with a list on her port side ... otherwise the mission would have ended there and then.

Inside the shattered Battery Room, the decomposing remains of eight men from Swing Watch plus the two Iranian sailors who had also been condemned to a watery grave on Tarasov's orders, floated aimlessly amongst the debris. Their rotting faces stared accusingly at the Captain through wide, eye-less sockets. A tremendous feeling of guilt washed over him as he was confronted by the awful consequences of his decisions when in command of the ill-fated submarine. He closed his eyes and tried to block out the agony he had felt when he ordered the Battery and Torpedo Room to be sealed. He remembered the terrified face of the Watch Engineer pressed up to the closed-circuit camera; a face that would haunt him for the rest of his days.

The decision to seal off the area at the time of the disaster now posed a new problem. Tarasov trained his lamp on the main elliptical access door as the Iranian divers came forward with their cutting equipment. They manoeuvred through the floating debris and set about releasing the unyielding door of the Torpedo Room. Still fastened to the bulkhead was a fading picture of a beautiful woman gazing down upon them like an angel. Did angels really look so serene? Tarasov realised they might be about to find out. The whole process took longer than expected. The exhausted team had no option but to return to the *Zarand* as they began to hallucinate under the intense pressure and cold. Sharif Hamad wasted no time in giving orders for another group of divers to go out and finish the next stage of the job, but this time they were led by Rem Bukato, the Russian Executive Officer.

Tarasov briefed Bukato on the state of the wreck and advised him to enter through the damaged hull instead of the hatches. The second team entered the escape chambers and set off, whilst the first tried to recover from their ordeal by reviving their freezing limbs in the claustrophobic confines of the radio room filled with the stink of unwashed uniforms and the sharp odour of hot electronics.

On the surface, a terrified Nasaf Rhullah aboard the storm tossed *Norse Warrior* had noticed that all interest in the salvage boat had ceased. He stood on the bridge wing and thoughtfully ran his hand over his cheek, feeling the unshaven stubble. The intense cold spray finally drove him back into the wheelhouse where he rubbed his eyes, trying to clear away the endless fatigue as various options tumbled through his confused brain. The Iranian suddenly snapped into action. He snatched up the microphone and frantically reported this latest situation to Sharif Hamad aboard the *Zarand*, confirming his belief that the game was up. Rhullah had tried to keep the Danish Captain on station as long as he could, but Ramuldssen had made up his own mind and was now heading south at full speed. It was only a matter of time before the *Zarand* would have to do the same. Rem Bukato and the other divers returned shortly after noon.

The young Executive Officer reported that they had successfully cut their way through to the Torpedo Room, but radiation levels inside the bow area were extremely high. According to the World Health Organisation, the maximum possible dosage that any ordinary mortal should absorb in any 24 hour period is 1.3 milliroentgens. The level in the Torpedo Room was 15.00 milliroentgens or 11.53 times greater than the W.H.O. maximum – enough to fry a man's brains.

Tarasov gave a fatalistic sigh. That was that! They had tried and failed. Now it was time to go. In a way, he was relieved.

"We are going nowhere!" Sharif Hamad stepped through the entrance to the Control Centre. Behind him stood two of the Hamas killers, their guns levelled at the Russians.

"The mission has failed!" Tarasov retorted with a sweep of his hands to emphasis the point. "It would be suicide to go in there!"

"That is *precisely* what these men are here for," Hamad replied through gritted teeth.

"But they cannot do it alone…" Tarasov threw his hands into the air with frustration.

"I know that Captain." Hamad spoke without emotion. "You must go back with them."

"And what if I don't?"

"You will be killed right now!" The Iranian wasn't bluffing. The suicide squad cocked their weapons. An electrified silence followed, as Tarasov weighed up his rapidly diminishing options. If he went he would surely die. If he refused, he would die anyway – and so would Lukin, Bukato and Alexander Volkov, still lying critically ill in the submarine's sick bay.

"I'll go!" Boris Lukin offered before his Captain could reply.

"No…" Tarasov tried to intervene.

"It *has* to be me, Captain," Lukin turned to face him. "With all due respect sir, I am the Weapons Officer. No-one else knows the release codes for the missiles."

"That is, no-one except the Captain," Tarasov insisted.

"Maybe. But you cannot do it alone, Valentin. I can."

"It is true, Captain," Rem Bukato agreed as he stepped between the two men.

"No, I will not allow it!" Tarasov could not be persuaded. He remained adamant.

"It is no longer your decision!" Sharif Hamad stepped forward and turned to face Boris Lukin. "Get yourself ready. You can take as many of these men as you need."

Boris Lukin glanced away and looked deep into his Captain's eyes. They were no longer bright and sparkling, but seemed haunted and distant, as if Tarasov was resigned to the inevitability of his own death. The Russians had never fully understood the Iranians heightened fanaticism, which justified everything in the name of Allah. Tarasov and Lukin had been through so much together and knew they would not meet again. They kissed each other on both cheeks, before embracing and clapping each other's shoulders. They did not speak – there was nothing more to be said. Lukin broke away. He turned quickly and indicated for two members of the Hamas squad to follow him back to the improvised diving chamber next to the vertical missile tubes where they climbed into the waiting Newtsuits. When they had gone, Sharif Hamad gave orders for more Iranian divers to be deployed from the 'saturation' compression chamber and to position themselves over the *Cherkassy*'s missile hatches for the underwater transfer.

Boris Lukin powered ahead of the Hamas suicide squad and entered the submarine through the Main Propulsion Battery Compartment. Here they found torpedoes strewn around like giant matchsticks in the Forward Torpedo Room.

Five of the nuclear warheads appeared to be intact, but it was the lower one, damaged by the falling torpedo, which now discharged a deadly concentration of radiation into the enclosed area. Lukin realised that time was not on their side.

The harsh rasping sound of his breathing pounded within his head as he laboriously made his way through a gaping hole made by the exploding main sea-water valve during the original crisis. He pulled himself through to the Command Centre, which was largely undamaged. Although his body felt intensely cold inside the heated diving suit, he knew he would soon begin to burn up from the intense radiation and would therefore have to work quickly. Lukin over-rode the Captain's veto and set the controls for unarmed release. Overhead, the latest Hamas squad made their precarious way along the top of the slippery hull towards the sixteen vertical launch tubes, set in two rows of eight, abaft the sail. Several of the external hydraulically operated doors had been released and forced upwards during her final plunge and now exposed the missiles inner protective pressure caps. A separate team of divers had now moved in from the icy darkness and were systematically working their way along the hull to unlock these inner caps to reveal the menacing white nose cones of the missiles – shrouded in their waterproof launch canisters. Each warhead's smooth conical nose ended with a protruding loop at the very crown. The divers worked in well-organised teams as they attached large flotation bags to the handling loops of the one thousand seven hundred kilogram missiles. Armoured umbilicals from the *Zarand* snaked across the sea-floor and up the towering sides of the *Cherkassy*.

At a given signal, CO_2 began pumping into the flotation bags, until their tethers became taught against the unyielding mass of the missiles. Boris Lukin made several attempts to release the Sampson missiles by using the Main Launch Control. Nothing happened. The massive discharge of radiation in the immediate vicinity was beginning to take its toll and the numbing cold of the water no longer bothered him. He knew he was taking a huge dose of radiation and his body was beginning to cook, as if it were in a huge microwave oven. His skin tingled with the electrical charge of dying cells. Lukin left the launch firing panel and made his way along to the missile room. The remaining Hamas squad were also stumbling about and succumbing to the debilitating effects of radiation. Lukin noticed their glazed looks through the visors of their helmets. The Russian staggered around in the swirling debris as he moved over to examine the stubborn release triggers of the vertical tubes. They were almost welded with corrosion. Damn the incompetent shipyard, thought Lukin. A hurried refit and now several twenty five million rouble Sampson missiles were crippled by nothing more than shoddy workmanship and a two hundred rouble release mechanism. He directed the suicide squad to begin chipping away at the rust. It would be a long process – but it no longer mattered.

Boris Lukin knew that by staying too long they had effectively signed their own death warrants.

Back aboard the *Zarand*, Valentin Tarasov lay quietly on his bunk staring at the curved ceiling. The minutes ticked by like hours. Whatever little hope there might have been for Boris Lukin's survival had by now evaporated. Another flash signal came through from the *Norse Warrior*. She was encountering hostile warships as she steamed south at full speed. Nasaf Rhullah advised Sharif Hamad that they ought to be getting ready to make a run for it. To compound their problems, the *Zarand*'s sonar had picked up several submerged vessels heading in their direction. Although still some ninety kilometres to the north-west, they were soon identified as two rapidly approaching kilo-class submarines and Tarasov knew they would soon be in a position to launch an attack. The unmistakable high-pitched sound of destroyer's screws was broadcast throughout the Control Centre as they headed straight for the Iranian submarine. Both Hamad and Tarasov realised it would only be a matter of time before the might of the world descended upon them.

"How long are you prepared to wait?" Tarasov demanded of the Iranian.

"Until the final second!" came the determined reply "We still have time ... we *will* succeed!"

"How can you be so sure?"

"Because Allah is on our side!" Hamad felt the true burden of command as all eyes fell upon him, searching his sweat soaked face for signs of confidence or despair. He knew that a crew without strong leadership could not function. His drawn and haggard face betrayed his innermost thoughts. The threat of violent death had visited him many times before but had always been denied its prize. With eyes widened in defiance, he still found it difficult to keep fighting the overwhelming sensation of imminent death that crept over him. He began to marshal his thoughts for joining the blessed in paradise, when the long awaited signal came through from Boris Lukin.

"Allah the merciful has answered our prayers!" Sharif Hamad felt there was still hope. He quickly ordered more of his divers back out into the freezing waters of the Barents Sea.

Back on board the *Cherkassy*, the Russian Weapons Officer and the Hamas squad had done as much as they could to free up the release mechanism. The numbing effects from the intense cold were being rapidly taken over by radiation sickness. Three of the Arabs sank to their knees and slipped into unconsciousness as they were overcome by blinding headaches and uncontrollable vomiting. Boris Lukin had resigned himself to suffering the same fate. Fatigue racked every fibre of his aching body as he clawed his way through clouds of floating debris in the Ward Room and Radio Room, and made his way back towards the Command Centre. This was it! His strength was ebbing fast. If the missiles didn't release this time, it would be the end. Lukin had given considerable thought to sabotaging the whole operation, but had shared Tarasov's view about making a terrible mistake by enlisting with the Iranians. He also realised the devastating consequences for mankind if the Iranians acquired these missiles. But he also knew that if he didn't succeed, it would mean certain death for his Russian friends aboard the *Zarand*.

This was his dilemma – sabotage the mission and save the world or release the missiles and save his Captain. He realised there was no guarantee that the Iranians wouldn't kill Tarasov and the others, but at least he could buy his colleagues some time.

The intense exposure to radiation had finally distorted all sense of reality in Boris Lukin's brain. He turned the security keys and pressed the release buttons for a final attempt. This time, seven canisters containing sub-sonic, long-range SS-N-21 Sampson cruise missile were gently released from the *Cherkassy*'s vertical launch tubes and lifted by the flotation bags. Pairs of divers hovered above the gaping silos and trickled more air into the flotation bags. They slowly guided each missile canister as it rose from its launch tube – until it achieved neutral buoyancy and hovered in a vertical position just clear of the flooded aperture. Grasping the upright canisters suspended from the flotation bags, this surreal group of divers slowly powered themselves and their precious cargo across the dark void between the two submarines using the stabilising motors of their Newtsuits. Positioning the tail ends of the missiles over the corresponding open silos on the *Zarand* the whole process was then reversed. Mission accomplished,

Lukin's heart began to thud in mortal terror as he sank to his knees and prayed. All the Hamas divers were dead, including their commander. Boris Lukin was alone in a ship full of corpses.

It was not proving to be an easy task to load the hard won missiles back on board the *Zarand* . With a Russian Naval Task Force bearing down upon them at high speed, time was running out and Rem Bukato stayed close by the diving chambers to supervise the final stages of this delicate operation.

The Russian force had approached to within thirty five kilometres and was closing fast. Sharif Hamad and Valentin Tarasov both knew their kilo-class submarines would be equipped with long-range homing torpedoes and, once locked on target, there would be no escape. The approaching destroyers on the surface would soon have to slow down whilst the *Zarand* remained beneath the edge of the ice field. It could only be considered a short reprieve before depth charges would start raining down about their ears. It was 14.08 Zulu when Rem Bukato finally reported to the captain that all the missiles were secure and the divers back on board and locked in for the long process of decompression.

Valentin Tarasov gave orders for the *Zarand* to rise from the suction of the seabed and to move away from the wreck site at half-speed. His strategy was to take an evasive north-westerly course for the next few hours before turning south along the coast of Finnmark to make his way out into the Norwegian Sea. From there he intended to skirt past the Faroe Islands on their western side before heading out into the relative safety of the North Atlantic and on to their final destination off Erris Head on the western coast of Ireland.

The Captain now felt the full weight of every decision as he agonised over the inevitable consequences. He held strange feelings of mixed emotions, but most of all he was outraged with himself for being persuaded to carry out such chores for some other nation. He secretly wished they would be intercepted, and knew he would have to make some attempt at escape. In the meantime, he just hoped and prayed that the combined American and Russian naval blockade would snare their phantom submarine and its deadly cargo.

CHAPTER 26

THE HIGH SEAS

A LOW-PRESSURE FRONT HAD RACED THROUGH during the night. The shrieking winds had now moderated and were backing down to a force four, with layers of low cloud hanging like wet slate from horizon to horizon. As the salvage vessel slipped and yawed across the swells, the seas writhed and boiled in a confusion of whitecaps. Bjorn Ramuldssen wedged himself between the binnacle and the front of the wheelhouse as he took the *Norse Warrior* on a south-westerly course towards the coast of Finnmark. If their luck held for just a few more hours, they could hide amongst the myriad of craggy islands dotted along the western coast of Norway. At daybreak, two inquisitive Russian warships had suddenly loomed out of the rolling sea fog about half a kilometre off the starboard bow. Ramuldssen felt uneasy as the two ships suddenly veered away and steamed off in the general direction of Murmansk. He couldn't be sure whether they had been spotted and watched as the grey mass of the warships disappeared back into the swirling fog. He steadied himself against the ship's roll and then started across the slippery deck to haul himself up to the bridge. He needed to radio an urgent warning to the *Zarand*.

As far as Ramuldssen was concerned, his part of the job had been completed. It was time to get back to Esbjerg. The six-figure fee the Arabs had promised meant he could at least buy another boat ... or perhaps retire if he wanted to. The Captain stroked his bearded chin and mused over the various options. The crew's desires would be easily satisfied once they got back to the waterfront bars and amongst the whores. Nasaf Rhullah, on the other hand, wasn't celebrating. He didn't like the look of the Russian warships. He knew there was still a long way to go and his part of the mission would not be over until the cruise missiles were safely in Tehran.

"Come my friend …cheer up!" Ramuldssen boomed as he clapped the Iranian firmly on the shoulder with his huge paw. "We're going home!"

"Ah, but we are not there yet," Rhullah answered despondently.

"We've nothing to worry about, we're on legitimate business. We've done nothing wrong, so nobody will bother us."

"I am not so sure…" Rhullah replied hesitantly. "I think the Irishman might have survived."

"Impossible!" Ramuldssen roared with a dismissive wave of his hand.

"Then how did they get onto us?" the Iranian enquired.

"Aw, come on. They are just guessing!" Ramuldssen laughed. "They know nothing."

"I hope you are right…"

"Captain, we are picking up some interesting activity on the horizon some twenty-seven kilometres to the north-west. I think you had better come and have a look at this," called the First Officer. The Captain came over and peered down through the hooded enclosure of the radarscope. He watched as the scan painted three bright green blips – one large and two small. "They're coming our way … and fast," grunted Ramuldssen.

"Do you think they're looking for us?" the First Officer asked.

"Perhaps. But we can't afford to take any chances." The Captain took another look into the radarscope. The equipment was functioning well. The problem was, if he could see them, they could also see him. "Shut down the radar!" he snapped. "Let's hope they haven't picked up a strobe from our scanner."

For the next forty-five minutes, many anxious eyes remained focused on a rolling bank of sea fog some five kilometres beyond the *Norse Warrior*'s starboard quarter. Almost without warning, the Russian aircraft carrier *Admiral Kuznetzov* materialised through the fog bank. The big ship was steaming on a parallel course with the salvage boat and clearly making preparations to launch some of her helicopters.

"Where did that come from?" Nasaf Rhullah screamed.

"I don't know!" growled Ramuldssen as he brusquely pushed the Iranian aside and started bellowing a string of orders for all hands to stand ready. The drunken crew ran in all directions and fell over themselves in the confusion that followed. They grabbed their weapons and began to take up defensive positions behind the deck winch and engine room housing. The Tiblisi-class carrier narrowed the distance between the two vessels down to three kilometres and remained slightly astern of the *Norse Warrior*. Static began to crackle from the radio and soon gave way to a very clear message from the *Admiral Kuznetzov*.

"Heave to immediately and prepare to receive a boarding party."

Several minutes elapsed.

The carrier repeated the message and after a brief pause, Ramuldssen pressed the button on the radio mike. "Under whose authority?"

"Russian Naval Authority" came the terse baritone reply.

The next transmission from the salvage vessel was more formal – protesting against armed intervention on the high seas. The *Admiral Kuznetsov* responded without any further warning. A quick burst from one of her six AK-630 30mm guns mounted on a sponson projecting menacingly from the front edge of her flight deck sent a stream of tracer bullets flashing in front of the *Norse Warrior*.

Ramuldssen realised their options had suddenly become very limited. He might have known things had been going far too smoothly.

"I told you…" Nasaf Rhullah pulled himself forward and tried to restore his dignity as he looked accusingly at Bjorn Ramuldssen.

"Stop snivelling. We can still bluff them, " Ramuldssen cut the man short, "just like we did with the Norwegians."

"You are under arrest!" The Russian Captain's voice boomed from the speaker.

"Under arrest?" Ramuldssen retorted. "What for?"

"International piracy and crimes of espionage against the Russian people."

"Is this some kind of joke?" Ramuldssen protested.

"No joke," the Russian Captain confirmed abruptly, "my men are coming aboard and will take control of your ship. We will escort you to the port of Tromso.

The authorities have already been informed. Please give us your full co-operation."

"This is piracy!" Ramuldssen roared.

"It is you who are the pirate, Captain."

Two Kamov KA-29TB's dipped forwards as they spooled up their motors and took off from the *Admiral Kuznetsov's* forward flight deck. Each helicopter was fitted with four pylons containing 57mm rocket pods slung under their outriggers, and a four-barrel Gatling gun protruding menacingly from beneath the windscreens of their snub noses. The heavy pulsating beat of their main rotors clattered across the surface of the inky waters as the two heavily loaded helicopters approached just above sea level and closed rapidly on the *Norse Warrior*.

The lead pilot juggled with the helicopter's rotor pitch as he struggled to synchronise his approach to the heaving stern of the salvage vessel. Both aircraft pulled up and steadied into a hover, the downwash from their rotor blades whipping the sea's surface into a confused maelstrom.

Flight crewmen slid open the cargo doors on each helicopter, flooding the sparse cabins with an arctic blast. Winchmen could be seen assisting the first of the marines to come forward and stand in their respective doorways. With slings attached and machine-guns strapped to their backs, everyone was ready for a rapid descent.

"They are not getting my ship!" Ramuldssen hissed, and signalled for his men to take up positions.

"Give up, Captain," Nasaf Rhullah pleaded, "We are no match for them. This is suicide!"

"What! When the only alternative would be life in one of their stinking prisons? No thank you!"

"Look …" Rhullah tried to reason with the Dane. "My Government would not allow them to detain me for very long. A deal will be done … and I will insist you are part of it."

"And do you seriously expect me to believe that?" Ramuldssen scoffed. "You couldn't give a damn. You would just leave me to rot. Especially as you wouldn't have to pay me!"

"I give you my word…"

"No!" Ramuldssen snapped. He raised his arm and brought it down smartly, giving the signal for his men to open fire on the hovering helicopters.

The tail rotor on the nearest one was hit, bringing it spinning down on to the deck where the KA-29TB exploded into an orange fireball, which lit up the arctic sky.

The marines who had been standing in the doorway were thrown out by the centrifugal force and billowing flames shot along the aft deck of the *Norse Warrior*. The second helicopter pulled up and veered away to starboard, to place herself between the carrier and the salvage boat. The pilot swung the Kamov around until the head-up-display of his gun-sight stabilised and filled with the *Norse Warrior*'s rusty hull and weather-stained superstructure. He opened up at point-blank range with a devastating salvo of rockets followed by a rattling burst from his Gatling gun. Cannon shells hammered into the ship's wallowing side and bulkhead, blowing bits of her over a wide area of the Norwegian Sea. Nasaf Rhullah was killed instantly as red-hot shrapnel tore into his body and lifted him off his feet. His shattered corpse fell at the feet of Bjorn Ramuldssen, its eyes wide open with surprise and half its head blown away. The Captain yelled his defiance right to the end and stood amidst the shattered remains of the *Norse Warrior*'s bridge. He continued to fire at the avenging helicopter as the ship rolled over and threw him into the freezing waves, taking him to a watery grave.

"Depth 200 feet and stabilised, speed four knots," Rem Bukato called out.

"Up periscope," Tarasov ordered as he stepped up onto the control platform.

The high-pressure hydraulics strained against the unremitting sea pressure as the stainless steel tube silently rose 25 feet from its well, deep within the bilges. Tarasov snapped down the periscope grips and hooked his left arm over the extended bar. He focused and tilted the optics sixty degrees from the horizontal and rotated the scope through 360 degrees. A faint light was diffused through the thin pack ice above. They were moving into open water. Tarasov pulled his eyes away from the rubber cup surrounding the optics at the base of the periscope and frowned. The *Zarand* appeared to have successfully completed the first stage of her evasive semi-circle under the Arctic icepack and was now heading southwest into the open Atlantic.

Valentin Tarasov knew it could only be a matter of time before they encountered a strong defensive line of Russian and American warships filling the ocean with sonar pings. Squadrons of helicopters would soon be flying low over the choppy waters, dropping sonar buoys and dipping their sonar receivers on long cables into the depths. Tarasov was even more concerned about the deadly Russian Kilo-class submarines still in hot pursuit. He was puzzled as to why they had not launched an attack.

A triumphant expression of realisation swept across Sharif Hamad's face.

"The missiles!" he shouted excitedly.

"What about them?" Valentin Tarasov asked.

"Don't you see?" They won't fire on us because of the missiles!" Hamad repeated as if he'd found the solution to all their problems.

"But we haven't armed them …"

"They don't know that!" The Iranian laughed. "They must be afraid of causing a nuclear explosion."

"That may well be, but we can't stay submerged for ever," Tarasov reminded him as he returned to the navigation table to try and figure out their next move.

"When we surface, they will board us – and that will be the end of it."

"Then we must lose them!" Sharif had regained his confidence.

"Where? How?"

The Iranian lieutenant had no answer for the Russian Captain. Valentin Tarasov and Sharif Hamad both knew their only chance to shake off the unwanted escort would be if they made it to the open seas of the North Atlantic.

❖ ❖ ❖

Down the coast, just off the island of Andoya, the British frigate *HMS Cumberland* waited for orders. Ross Lombardi and Peter Lawrence were both becoming impatient. They had been aboard for almost 24 hours and there was still no news from the Russians about the Iranian submarine. After all, it *was* the Russians with all the big hardware out there scouring the Norwegian Sea. If their combined force of aircraft carriers, submarines and destroyers couldn't intercept and apprehend just one rogue vessel, then it was even less likely that Lombardi and his team could be of any positive assistance.

It was 05.00 Zulu on the second day when the *Cumberland* received a coded message from the aircraft carrier *Admiral Kuznetsov*. The Russian fleet had lost contact with the Iranian submarine somewhere between Iceland and the Faroe Islands. The *Admiral Kuznetsov* and her escort had been recalled to base at Murmansk, while the Kilo and Yankee-class submarines would continue with the search and try to pick up the scent. Peter Lawrence contacted London and orders were given for the *Cumberland* to set sail for Killala Bay off the west-coast of Ireland, where they were scheduled to meet up with Eamonn Burke and his small clandestine force. If the Iranians did actually manage to land the cruise missiles, Burke's forces were expected to stop the weapons from being flown out from the international airport at Knock. Should they fail, an alternative contingency plan had already been drawn up to attack and destroy the cargo plane as soon as it touched down in Libya.

Eight bells sounded across the cold waters of the fjord as Captain James Huxtable dressed hurriedly and stepped on to the bridge. The Officer of the deck handed a clipboard with the latest signals to the Captain, which he read and signed.

"Anything new from the *Admiral Kuznetsov* – headings, speed, changes, updates?"

"No sir. She has been recalled to Murmansk but the Russian subs are still in hot pursuit."

"Very well, Lieutenant."

A signalman came forward and offered the Captain a steaming mug of tea as he went over to the navigation table to review his calculations. Captain James Huxtable was in his late thirties, tall, slim and urbane. He had been a product of the Royal Naval College at Dartmouth some eighteen years earlier, where he excelled as a tactician. Upon graduation he had felt some initial disappointment at having to spend the first four years of his naval career in general administration before being posted to a sea-going command. Standing in the subdued lighting over the plot table, he was dressed in his service blue uniform with gleaming gold bands around the ends of each sleeve. Three rows of coloured decorations sat above his breast pocket.

"Prepare to get under way Lieutenant."

"Aye Aye Sir." The frigate slipped anchor, and sailed around the northernmost tip of the sleeping island and set a south-westerly course.

Peter Lawrence tossed and turned on the narrow bunk in his cabin as he felt the rhythmic vibrations of the ship gaining speed. He had been awake for the whole thirty six hours, ever since he and the rest of the team had arrived on board. He was exhausted, but since receiving the signal from London, he was too fired up with mission adrenalin to fall asleep. He just hoped they would be in time. If the Russians had lost the Iranian submarine, it could be anywhere. London had also confirmed that contact had been lost with Eamonn Burke. Yet somehow, Lawrence was looking forward to re-establishing this vital link. Perhaps when all this was over they could have a quiet drink together in some bar and talk about better things. It struck Lawrence that although they'd known each other for a long time, they only knew the military side of one another. They knew nothing about the man inside – the real personalities they both kept hidden. Maybe they had other things in common – a taste in music, sport or a liking for the same food – who knows?

There were sixteen members left in the team – two British, eight Americans and six Israelis. Once the team had been safely landed in Ireland, the *Cumberland* had strict orders to stand off into the international waters of the Atlantic. Peter Lawrence and Ross Lombardi leaned on the salt encrusted rail of the *Cumberland's* cold deck as they discussed the likely outcome of the forthcoming operation. They pondered all the options as they watched a watery sun sinking over the icy sea away to the west. Somewhere in that vast expanse of ocean lurked the *Zarand*.

Ruth Netanya had become increasingly aware of Lombardi's attentions during the past few days and realised that deep down she still felt something very special for the American. However, it was in those quieter moments that she sometimes wondered if it had all been a big mistake to become emotionally involved with the Agent in the first place. Such things made you sloppy – and you paid for sloppiness with your life.

Valentin Tarasov ordered the submarine to dead slow as the *Zarand*'s non-essential machinery fell silent, leaving just enough forward momentum to maintain depth control and the towed array deployed.

"Anything?" Tarasov asked the sonar man sitting at one of the consoles. The young man looked round to face the Captain and placed his hand on one of the earphones. His youthful face glowed in the red light of the command centre as he listened intently to the biological activity of the ocean. He paused, then shook his head as he returned to the bank of instruments and adjusted the cursor ball, listening to the broadband frequency. The ocean around them was empty. By using a standard series of sharp angles, turns and dives to clear the stern baffles, the submarine's blind spot, the *Zarand* had managed to give her pursuers the slip. The surface vessels had also disappeared and it seemed as if they had given up the chase. However, Tarasov and Sharif Hamad both knew that the Russian submarines would not give up that easily. They were still out there somewhere. The *Zarand* could be picked up again at any moment. Tarasov had been agonising for days about his own predicament and having weighed up all the options he decided that he certainly didn't relish the prospect of being captured by his own countrymen. If they had been so harsh with him for the *Cherkassy*'s sinking, how would they deal with him for daring to do this? No! it was still the best option if he were to continue using all his skills to help the Iranians get to Ireland. Once ashore, he could try and give them the slip and hopefully seek political asylum. The Irish would normally remain neutral in such matters, but Tarasov knew they also enjoyed very friendly relations with the Americans. Yes, that is what he would do. With such valuable Russian naval expertise they would surely welcome him with open arms.

The *Zarand* was just to the east of the Faroe Islands when the radar room reported to the Command Centre that one of the Kilo-class submarines had been detected fifteen kilometres to the north. Only a few people achieve the highly developed ability to detect these subtle sound waves, let alone recognise them. Despite his youth, the sonar man had quickly picked up the distinctive *swish-swish-swish-swish* of a *Kilo's* single six bladed propeller. There was no sign of the others: this one was on its own.

"Let's hope he hasn't heard us and we still retain the advantage," Tarasov commented as he ran his hands through his hair, wondering if their luck would hold. The deck vibrated as it inclined downwards when the helmsman pushed the yoke forward and took the *Zarand* deeper. As battle stations were manned, the deck levelled off and the control centre quickly filled with men seated at the various consoles in the attack centre. Sharif Hamad gave orders for number one and two torpedo tubes to be made ready.

"Captain Tarasov, I would suggest we shoot now," Hamad proposed, "otherwise he could counter-detect at any moment."

"Surely you are not going to fire on them?" Tarasov asked with horror.

"I have no alternative," the Iranian replied defiantly as their eyes met.

"You cannot…" Tarasov shouted. "This is pure madness!"

"You are no longer in command, Captain," Hamad told the Russian. "I am!"

Sharif Hamad gave orders for the torpedo's gyros to be spun up. He came over and watched the computations on the firing panel until the torpedoes were ready, tubes flooded and the outer doors open.

"Shoot!"

The sudden increase in air pressure caused by the launch blasted everyone's ears and the deck jumped beneath their feet. Two torpedoes leapt from their tubes and headed straight for the shadowing Russian submarine. Shock waves rushed back to the *Zarand* as both missiles struck their target. Everyone fell silent as they listened to the horrific sounds of tearing metal as the hull imploded – the unmistakable sound of a submarine dying.

"We must surface to pick up any survivors," Tarasov insisted when he had regained his balance.

"There will be no survivors," Hamad assured him coldly.

The Captain realised protestation was useless and reluctantly set a new westerly course. Their intention was to sail around to the western side of the Faroes and surface under the cover of a remote bay, before making the final southerly leg of their journey towards Ireland. Valentin Tarasov pressed his tired eye to the cold rubber shroud of the periscope's eyepiece as the *Zarand* approached the surface. He spun the periscope around, searching for the bottom of the waves and the dark shadows of any hulls overhead. As the tip broke through the surface, he focused the cross-hairs and rotated it several times.

They were about to round the northernmost headland for their final breakout into the Atlantic. There was nothing to be seen to the northeast... but when he swung round to face due east, he glimpsed what looked like a small warship between the troughs and at a distance of about two and a half kilometres. Rem Bukato came forward and identified the vessel as a British Broadsword Class (Type 22) frigate, but it was heading in a south-easterly direction, down the other side of the island and away from their current position. Tarasov snapped up the grips and downed the periscope. It was dangerously close. Fatigue was beginning to dull their judgement. They were plagued by a growing despair, familiar to anyone competing against a vastly superior force. Tarasov knew that his men were worn out and exhausted by the massive underwater salvage operation and would be prone to making mistakes. Such errors may be insignificant in detail, but invariably proved fatal for a submarine. A fugitive thought stole across Tarasov's mind. If things didn't improve, would he react like a seasoned submariner and unwittingly jeopardise both crew and vessel in a determined attempt to complete the mission?

They hovered in the water until the vessel had disappeared from their tracking equipment, before starting engines again and sailing on at full speed to the western side of the Faroes. Before they arrived, the Medical Officer came forward and reported that Alexander Volkov had died as a result of his head wounds. Valentin Tarasov went down to the sick bay and only had a few moments to say a few solemn words over the body of his fellow countryman before two Iranians brushed him aside and took it through to the forward torpedo room to be ejected through one of the tubes.

As they neared the uninhabited island of Rockall in the North Atlantic, the radar room suddenly detected the faint sound of an American Kittyhawk class aircraft carrier, ninety kilometres to the south. Tarasov was aware that all US carriers are accompanied by at least two nuclear submarines and a squadron of support vessels. He suggested it would be far more prudent to rig for silent running and sail further westwards out into the wild Atlantic, before making a final wide turn to sail back towards Ireland on a true easterly course. Nobody would be expecting them to approach from that direction.

"But that would put us way behind schedule."

"Better to be behind schedule than not to arrive at all."

"The Air Algerie charter plane will not wait if we are late."

"Well…" Tarasov's tone was sarcastic, "you decide. You're in command now!"

❖ ❖ ❖

It was 03.00 Zulu when the *Cumberland* made landfall off the western coast of Ireland. The ship heaved too and stood off about three kilometres from Killala Bay while the team made ready and went over the side in their inflatable dinghies. The desolate black shoreline of this area was remote, with not even the glimmer of farm lights to guide them in. Peter Lawrence and Juliet Lucas, along with four others, led the small flotilla in the first dinghy. About one hundred metres beyond the foaming surf breaking on the darkened shore, Lawrence was the first to see a small light flashing intermittently. He smiled to himself. Although he was a little rusty with his Morse code, he could still make out the message "*Welcome to Ireland Peter.*"

Eamonn Burke and a handful of others stood waiting on the rain-swept beach. Peter stepped through the clinging fronds of kelp defining the high-water mark and shook hands with the big Irishman. The other dinghies surfed ashore on the back of the surging waves to land on the shingle, where they were quickly deflated and taken off the beach by Burke's men.

"All's not well then, Peter?" Burke asked.

"Oh, and why do you say that?"

"Well, you wouldn't be here if it was!"

Two unlit trucks waited on a narrow side road leading away from the beach. The team hurriedly threw the deflated dinghies into the back before climbing aboard and setting off through the night for their destination near the international airport of Knock.

CHAPTER 27

IRELAND : MAYO

It was a cold and cheerless night and the sixty kilometre bone-jarring trip from Killala Bay seemed to take forever. The trucks bumped along the narrow twisting country lanes and back-roads where the tarmac surface had been worn into ruts and pitted with holes. The vehicles lurched and creaked as they passed Lough Conn and the many smaller lakes dotted around this desolate area. Juliet Lucas stared through the arc cleared by the wipers on the mud-splattered windscreen and noticed the barren and rocky terrain slipping by. Tiny fields enclosed by low stone walls were draped across the inhospitable landscape like a disjointed patchwork quilt. This was a wild and desolate land where only sheep and hardy cattle could withstand the unrelenting harshness of winter. They were on the very edge of Europe and at a point where it tumbled away into the boiling Atlantic. Only a few bare trees had managed to take root on these bleak and exposed slopes, and many were pushed over at a drunken angle by the incessant winds and rains that raced in from North America. Outside, wintry rain lashed down onto the potholed and bumpy highway as Burke's drivers kept the trucks well away from the larger towns of Ballina and Castlebar. The Ox Mountain's dark, rolling mass reared up away to their left as they crossed the River Moy. The fast moving crystal waters of the river boasted some of the finest trout fishing in Ireland – or so Eamonn Burke had claimed. Ross Lombardi liked the sound of that and made a mental note to come back and try his luck for some trophy fishing when this was all over.

"How much longer before we get there?" Juliet sighed.

"About another hour. Have you ever been to Ireland before?" Burke enquired.

"No."

"Down the N5 yonder lies the small town of Westport ... and the next town after that is New York!"

Their destination was a secluded country farmhouse about two kilometres to the north of Knock airport. It was built at the head of a boxed valley overlooking wide exposed pastureland where nothing moved but a few scrawny sheep. It had no electricity or other modern conveniences and the only water came from a meandering stream bubbling noisily to the rear of the house as it disappeared down to the mouth of the valley. A Solitary road followed the stream and was the only means of access to this remote group of farm buildings, so anyone approaching would be visible for miles.

It was 06.00 hours when they finally arrived. Peter Lawrence gave a weary sigh and wrinkled his nose as he glanced over towards the house. He sat back in the deep shadow of the lorry cab for a moment, looking about and assessing the situation. One of the curtains twitched and someone opened the front door. Eamonn Burke climbed down from the first lorry, crossed the yard and went in alone. The others tumbled out and stretched their tired limbs. Clouds of vapour surrounded their heads in the cold morning air as they stamped their feet and waited by the vehicles. After a couple of minutes, Burke reappeared.

"They're ready and they've been expecting us for some time," he told the group. "Come on, let's go."

Everyone shambled towards the door, where they were met by a couple of guards, the kind with dead eyes and bored faces. Lawrence, Lombardi, Lucas, Netanya, Tyson and LeClair filed through the small dingy hallway. Their hunger took over and lured them towards the kitchen, where a tantalising smell of bacon and eggs cooking on the Victorian cast-iron range greeted their nostrils. The dilapidated furnishings were simple but adequate. Everyone settled noisily around the scrubbed pine table and tucked in hungrily. Meanwhile, a shy red-headed colleen ushered the ten remaining Americans and Israelis into the front parlour where a separate welcoming cooked breakfast had been set out, complete with hot buttered toast and steaming mugs of coffee. Eamonn Burke collectively introduced his people, but without offering any names. They were dressed in camouflage kit, combat boots and armed mostly with Kalashinovs – a much favoured weapon of the IRA. The stone farmhouse was sparsely furnished. A peat fire burned over in the small iron fireplace and several dignified sepia photographs of previous inhabitants adorned the faded floral wallpaper. The surrounding land was rough and largely uncultivated. There didn't seem to be any farmer or farmhands, neither were there any animals and all that could be seen were a few pieces of old and neglected machinery rusting away in the muddy yard which gave only the barest pretence of agricultural authenticity. No special security measures were apparent and Peter Lawrence came to the conclusion that this must be a safe house or rendezvous for the IRA.

"Well then …" Eamonn Burke began gleefully as he rubbed his hands together, "How are you Peter?"

"As well as can be expected … given the circumstances."

"A fine looking bunch of people you have here," Burke continued. "And such a handsome pair of ladies."

Ruth Netanya flashed a hostile look in the Irishman's direction.

"Are we in time?" Lawrence quickly changed the subject as he chomped on a mouthful of food.

"So far, so good," Burke smiled. "I've got lookouts posted at the airport. No-one's arrived yet."

"Do we know their intended route?" Ross Lombardi queried.

"No, unfortunately not. Ah … Mister Lombardi…" Burke reached over and held out a hand. "Nice to meet you again. Sorry about your reception last time. No hard feelings I trust. Well now, all that we know is the Russians have evidently lost them and the Americans haven't yet been able to pick up the trail, so it's up to us now.

They could put ashore anywhere along the coast from Sligo Bay to Roonah Quay, but it's too large and wild an area to cover. We'll just have to sit tight and wait here for the time being."

"But how do you know for sure that they're actually coming here?" Ruth Netanya needed to be convinced.

"Because I risked my life for that vital piece of information, my dear." Burke leaned forward and smiled condescendingly at the Israeli. "I'm sure that under such circumstances you'll put your trust in me now, won't you?"

"What about the airport?" Peter Lawrence interjected, trying to avoid an acrimonious confrontation between Burke and Netanya.

"It's mostly used by American pilgrims coming over to see the shrine where our Blessed Lady appeared to young Bernadette, back in 1879." Burke crossed himself.

"Although it's got international status, the security still leaves much to be desired. God bless'em. All sorts of strange things are rumoured to be going on out there."

"Any idea how they're actually proposing to get the missiles out?" Lombardi queried.

"We have good connections with the Customs Authorities and we've been through all the scheduled commercial timetables and manifests with a fine-toothed comb. There's nothing that catches the eye ... except one!"

"And?" Lombardi fixed his gaze upon Burke, his lips set in a thin and determined line, confident that he was commanding the moment. He was becoming impatient with the Irishman's laid-back attitude.

"There's an Air Algerie cargo plane scheduled to take a consignment of communications equipment to Lourdes ... another place of pilgrimage in Southern France. From Lourdes, the plane is due to fly on to Libya – so what do you think?"

"Sounds promising. But who chartered it?" Netanya remained sceptical.

"Some company called Mauritanian Enterprises," Burke informed them, as he ran with this new thought and paced up and down the kitchen. "They have a small factory nearby, at Charlestown."

"Nothing else suspicious?"

"No, nothing, Peter."

"Well, if there are no other scheduled movements which could fit into the time-frame, I think that sounds like our target!"

"I've got men strategically staked out around the airfield and watching for the plane," Burke continued. "She's not due to land until

11.30 hours which will still give them plenty of time to refuel and load up the missiles."

Ruth Netanya's look of disbelief bordered on incredulity. "Surely we're not just going to sit around here on our hands while Iran quietly joins the nuclear power club! With those missiles, they could hold the world to ransom – and once they acquire such a capability, there's absolutely nothing that the US or Russia could do about it."

"No we are not! But for the time being there's nothing more we can do until we are certain that the missiles have actually arrived in Ireland." The Irishman waited a moment until he was sure that he held their attention, before breaking into a grin like a shark greeting its lunch. He clapped his hands together loudly and rubbed them with glee. "Well now, as we have got a bit of time to spare, why don't you all get some rest until my man gives us the signal?"

"Good idea!" Larry Tyson agreed, after stuffing himself with a good farmhouse breakfast.

"There's plenty of rooms in the house," Burke told them. "Just find a place that suits you and crash out."

❖ ❖ ❖

Sharif Hamad didn't like the fact that it would soon be dawn. Making a hostile landfall at night was not his preferred way of doing things. The submarine had crept cautiously into the sheltered waters of Clew Bay, between the Corraun Peninsula and Clare Island. So far they had been lucky.

"Depth."

"Thirty one fathoms" called the navigator.

"Take her up to periscope depth," Hamad ordered.

Up until now he had been harbouring secret doubts about the possible successful outcome of this mission, but now … he just wondered. When originally conceived, the whole thing had seemed such an audacious scheme, but right now it all seemed to make a twisted perverse kind of sense. His heart pounded with pride by the time the submarine had levelled off at periscope depth. Hammad snapped down the handles and pressed his eye to the periscope's eyepiece and spun it round to view the distant shore. Thank Allah for radar. It confirmed the *Zarand* had arrived at her pre-determined destination just five kilometres off the Irish coast. He swung the periscope back and forth until he settled in an easterly direction to where a solitary light appeared and blinked out a coded welcome.

He smiled with triumph. A succession of long and short flashes followed.

"Prepare to surface."

The ugly black leviathan glistened malevolently in the cold night air as a coastal trawler came alongside. The *Zarand* opened up seven of her clam-shell hatches which had been covering the vertical missile silos built into the sinister hump behind her sail. Eager crews from both vessels made fast with the mooring lines as they scrambled over the slippery topsides. When all was secured, they swung over the trawler's derrick and gently eased the eight metre shrouded Sampson cruise missiles out of their silos, one by one, and lowered them into the waiting fishing boat's hold. Sharif Hamad climbed down from the sail and quickly boarded the trawler with Valentin Tarasov, Rem Bukato, the half-dozen or so remaining Hamas killers and about twenty of the Iranian sailors. Once the last missile was safely stowed aboard, the trawler pulled away from the submarine and headed off towards a remote stretch of coastline towards the east. The submarine's twin propellers began to churn up white water around her stern and with a deep mechanical sigh, jets of vapour shot skywards as the *Zarand* opened her valves and submerged. She had orders to wait on the bottom for the next twenty-four hours and await the return of Hamad and the others. If for some reason they didn't make it, she was to find her own way back to the supertanker *Konari* which was waiting at a pre-arranged rendezvous in the Southern Atlantic.

Valentin Tarasov thought the language spoken by the trawler's crew seemed familiar. It was definitely Arabic – possibly Tunisian or maybe even Algerian. Then he suddenly remembered where he'd heard that dialect before! It was when they had briefly been ashore for their picnic at the oasis in Mauritania.

Rounding a jagged peninsula, the rusty trawler plunged and yawed its way into the calmer waters of a secluded cove. Tarasov braced himself against the wheelhouse. He glanced up at the sheer cliff face towering above and to a point where he could see a small group of people silhouetted in front of a lorry-mounted crane and two open-sided trucks. A puff of black smoke rose from the vertical exhaust stack as the crane's powerful diesel engine came to life with a throaty roar before settling down to a low-pitched growl. The operator jumped down from the lorry's cab and went round to the crane's control panel, where he revved up the engine again and began to extend the telescopic jib as it swung out over the edge of the cliff.

A ten-metre horizontal lattice steel boom, complete with a harness made from four wide straps suspended equidistant along its length, began its descent to the waiting fishing boat. This would be the most delicate part of the operation. After a few false starts they managed to synchronise with the pitching trawler, and the first Sampson cruise missile emerged from the dark hold and began its precarious journey to the cliff top. Here, many eager hands helped to stabilise the swinging weapon as they eased it into a specially constructed cradle mounted on the back of one of the waiting lorries. When the last missile was safely loaded, the heavy-duty tarpaulin sides of the vehicle were rolled down to conceal the sinister cargo.

The transporter had been transformed to look like any other legitimate heavy goods lorry, with "Mauritanian Enterprises" boldly displayed on the canvas sides. But time was ticking away, and Sharif Hamad knew the Air Algerie cargo plane would be arriving in just a few short hours. He ordered the rest of his team aboard and the two trucks set off due east towards the airport. Valentin Tarasov's instincts for survival took over. His brain was feverish with frustrations, plans and stratagems as he was pushed and pulled by the agonising decisions he would have to make at daybreak. He was still desperately waiting for the right opportunity to make a break for it, but none came. Tarasov was roughly bundled into the back of one of the trucks, where he was made to sit between two of the Hamas militiamen. Rem Bukato was similarly guarded at the other side of the vehicle and occasional furtive eye contact between the two Russians confirmed their mutual understanding of the current situation. Tarasov was convinced they had outlived their usefulness and wouldn't be boarding the plane with the Iranians.

It was more than two hours since the missiles had been loaded and they were now approaching their destination. Some valuable time had been made up once the lorries had rejoined the N17 and as they passed through Glentavraun, Knock International Airport finally loomed into view. Tarasov turned to peer through a join in one of the tarpaulin sheets and could see the Algerian charter plane parked some distance away from the main terminal area. The Captain cursed under his breath. It was too exposed. It was going to be virtually impossible to make a successful escape from such a remote spot. The only buildings close by were some old deserted warehouses. His mind raced through all the possible options as he shaped his thoughts and strategy. Perhaps he could make a break for it and find some suitable cover in there. He was caught between two worlds – Russia and freedom – the first he had well and truly left behind, whilst the second had still to be attained, although the only world he completely understood was that of a professional sailor.

After a cursory examination of their documents, the trucks were allowed to proceed around the perimeter and make their way towards the waiting cargo plane.

"But, how did you manage to arrange all this?" Tarasov asked Sharif Hamad with an incredulous sweep of his arm. "With some help and co-operation from our Mauritanian friends ... and as a result of a very special relationship we enjoy with certain members of the Irish Customs and the Garda," the Arab replied.

"The Mauritanians have a small factory producing electronic equipment at a place called Charlestown, not far from here – set up with Iranian money of course and very generous tax concessions from the Irish Government."

"Clever!" Tarasov acknowledged.

"I thought you might appreciate it," Hamad smiled benignly as he waggled his raised hand to signify infinite mystery before winking and tapping the side of his nose with an index finger. "It makes importing and exporting so much easier, don't you think?"

❖ ❖ ❖

At 13.00 hours, Eamonn Burke's lookouts radioed back to the farmhouse to inform them that the Algerian charter plane was still refuelling near hanger number four.

"Right!" Burke called out. "Time to go!"

The team assembled in the farmyard and stood over by the trucks for a final briefing as they quickly gathered their kit together and checked their arms. Everyone climbed aboard and the convoy quickly sped off towards the airport.

As the remote side of the airfield came into sight, the vehicles slowed down and coasted to a halt in a small copse skirting the perimeter fence about a quarter of a mile away from the disused buildings. The group tumbled out of the trucks and began their approach through the thick cover of bushes and scrub, where they were able to circle round to the far side of the old warehouses behind hangar number four. They could see the plane was still being serviced and its crew anxiously scanning the main approach road for a sign of the missiles. The team crouched and took up positions behind the warehouse's shattered windows.

"Where are they?" Peter Lawrence whispered to Eamonn Burke.

"Late ... obviously."

"You'd better be right, Eamonn," Lawrence hissed.

"Now have I ever let you down before?" the Irishman grinned and spread his hands to give the impression of wounded pride.

"No ... but there's always a first time."

The Air Algerie plane had completed its refuelling and was standing by, but there was still no sign of the Iranians. The plane's crew jumped at the slightest sound and Burke's team kept their heads down as they went through the various possibilities and rapidly diminishing options. Everyone sat on the floor, hugging their raised knees, and with their backs firmly pressed against the wall. The rear cargo doors of the plane had been swung open to reveal its cavernous interior and the whining sound of the loading ramp's hydraulic servos began to reach their ears as it was lowered. Burke indicated for everyone to stay down as he turned and cautiously peered over a shattered windowsill. It was becoming clearer by the minute that the Iranians intended to save time by driving the missiles straight on board.

The Algerian crew would have to be taken out – and quickly! Ruth Netanya and her agents had drawn the short straw. They gathered up their weapons and began quietly picking their way through the heaps of discarded furniture and other debris which lay scattered around the warehouse as they made their way towards a shaft of daylight filtering through an open doorway at the end of the building. This would be the closest vantage point from where they could take stock of the situation.

About twenty metres of open ground separated them and the Algerians. There was no time to loose and Netanya silently indicated that she would lead her team by creeping forward along the blind side of the aircraft. The Algerian flight crew were anxiously looking at their watches and scanning the vast expanse of the airfield from where they expected the missiles to approach, when the Israelis suddenly pounced from behind and dragged them back into the warehouse where they stripped the hapless crew of their uniforms.

A rapid surge of adrenaline instantly united the Israelis as a cohesive team. Everyone shared the same deep convictions – and knew that in such moments of extreme danger each would provide appropriate back-up and deliver the goods. Theirs was a murky world in which partnership and trust were vital for mutual survival.

Netanya and three of her men quickly dressed in the outfits and made their way back out to the waiting plane. They were busily pretending to make a pre-flight inspection of the cargo plane when the transporter finally came into view, followed by the two escorting trucks. The convoy slowly circled around to the back of the Algerian aircraft, with the lead trucks veering to the left and right of the ramp as they came to a halt beneath the giant wings. Sharif Hamad jumped from the cab of the first lorry and began to shout orders as the rest of the squad tumbled out. Netanya and her men climbed aboard the plane on the blind side and made their way towards the cockpit. The missile transporter briefly paused at the base of the ramp with a hiss of brakes whilst the driver struggled to engage one of the crawler gears to enable him to drive the deadly load up into the vast cargo hold.

"Get ready…" Ross Lombardi ordered, as the last of the Hamas squad disembarked from the trucks.

The Iranian sailors had separated from the main group but remained huddled together beneath one of the giant wings, intending to re-board one of the lorries for the return journey back to the submarine. Valentin Tarasov and Rem Bukato could be seen struggling violently as they were roughly man-handled from the trucks and fell to the ground before being dragged away towards hangar number four by two of the Hamas killers.

"Drop your weapons!" Lombardi yelled over a portable loud-hailer. "This is the CIA!"

The Iranians instantly signed their own death warrants as they spun round and blindly opened fire, spraying bullets in the general direction of the warehouse.

The team inside responded with a co-ordinated fusillade – killing several sailors with the first volley. Ruth Netanya and her men added to the general confusion and mayhem by firing down from the aircraft. The Iranians quickly realised they were caught in a deadly crossfire and Sharif Hamad frantically screamed orders for the Hamas squad to make for one of the trucks. He kept firing from the hip as he ducked and weaved towards the vehicle where he dived into the cab and started the engine. The Russian's escort began to panic. They came running back from hangar number four, clutching Tarasov before them and using him as a shield as they made their way towards the retreating truck. Ross Lombardi noticed a solitary Iranian break away from the main group and climb onto the port wing of the aircraft where he made his way along to the cockpit. The terrorist had snatched a grenade from his belt and had almost reached his objective through all the mayhem, when Lombardi took careful aim just as the pin was pulled. The crosshairs of his scope focused on the man's ear as the American exhaled and squeezed the trigger, sending a high velocity bullet screaming through the Iranian's head. The man's knees crumpled as he dropped the grenade from his lifeless hand. It clattered over the leading edge of the wing and tumbled to the ground, with his body falling on top of it, smothering the explosion.

Ruth Netanya instinctively flinched back from the rain of blood and gore as body parts spattered against the side of the aircraft. From within the deep shadow of the cockpit she looked over towards the warehouse window from where the shot had come and saw Ross Lombardi with his rifle still held in the aimed position.

Sharif Hamad made good his escape and sped away across the tarmac with several of his surviving guerrillas on board and Valentin Tarasov lying on the floor of the truck. Realising they had been abandoned, the remaining Iranian sailors quickly threw down their weapons and surrendered to Eamonn Burke's advancing men. Peter Lawrence leapt into action. He ran over to the second truck, wrenched open the door and dragged the driver's lifeless body out onto the ground. Lombardi and Burke raced over and jumped into the cab from the other side as Lawrence gunned the engine with Larry Tyson, Jake LeClair and a few more of the American agents scrambling into the back before the vehicle shot away in hot pursuit of the Iranians.

Ruth Netanya and her men stayed with the missiles while Juliet Lucas stood by to deal with the irate airport authorities, now cautiously arriving at the scene of carnage. Eamonn Burke's second in command came alongside and assisted Lucas in calming everyone down by assuring them that both Dublin and London were aware of the situation. Juliet's eyes met those of Burke's officer with a knowing smile that underlined her admiration for his political skills and timing. This brief moment of triumph was completely overshadowed when Rem Bukato's crumpled body was discovered in hangar number four. He had almost accomplished his dream and made it to the free world, but he had been shot through the head.

The two trucks hurtled along the pot-holed country lanes and grass tracks. Everyone was bounced around so much that no-one could get a clear shot.

"I know a short cut…" Eamonn Burke shouted to Peter Lawrence. "Take the next left and turn through that farmyard. There's a gate at the other side … we'll be able to cut them off!"

Lawrence swung the heavy vehicle around at such a speed that two of the wheels lifted and the truck almost went over. He careered through the farmyard, scattering chickens and geese in all directions.

The bewildered farmer was busy digging out a tree-root with his tractor in one of the adjacent fields when he stopped to watch in amazement as the bizarre drama unfolded on his premises. The gate at the other side of the farmyard was firmly closed and Lawrence could already see the Iranians making their turn into the bottom of the lane at the other side of the farm. If he stopped to open the gate they would simply fly past.

There was only one thing for it.

"Hold on!" the Englishman shouted, as he gripped the wheel and charged towards the heavy five-barred gate, taking it out into the lane with a loud crunching sound and a grating of metal on metal as the lorry's radiator was ripped out. The Americans picked themselves up from the floor, grabbed their weapons and tumbled out of the back to take up defensive positions behind the steaming vehicle.

Sharif Hamad saw the road was blocked and tried to turn round, but the lane was too narrow for the big truck. Hamad was prepared to fight to the death. He had no family or other ties that would whisper caution in his ear, entreating him to survive to fight another battle. He would join his fanatical comrades in paradise this very day!

Larry Tyson and his men shot the tyres to pieces as the fleeing Iranians spilled out of the truck, with the Hamas Death Squad still holding Valentin Tarasov as a hostage.

"Hey! Who's that guy?" Ross Lombardi asked.

"It must be the Russian, the submarine Captain," Eamonn Burke suggested.

"We can't afford a stand-off" Lombardi hissed "We haven't got the time."

"Wait…" Eamonn Burke raised his hand. "I've got an idea. Who's your best explosives man?"

"Well, I suppose it's got to be Jake LeClair," Lombardi replied.

"Hey, Jake come on over here will ya," Burke said. "We've got a little job for you."

The two men crouched behind one of the stone walls and made their way back into the farmyard and out across the field towards a somewhat bemused farmer.

Burke had a brief exchange with the man and persuaded him to loan them his tractor, after convincing him he'd be well compensated by the Government for any damage or loss. Burke and LeClair wasted no time. They climbed up into the cab and drove the vehicle back out of the farmyard and along the lane so that they could approach the entrapped Iranians from behind. As the vehicle advanced, they raised the front loading shovel for protection.

"What have you got?" Burke asked LeClair above the noisy clatter of the diesel.

"Nitro compound," replied the American, "Explodes on impact … makes a lot of noise."

"Ah … one of my favourites," the Irishman replied with a knowing wink.

"When I get as far as the Russian, let them have it!"

Burke brought the tractor to a halt about ten metres from the terrorists and jumped down from the cab. Seizing the moment, he realised that fear and wonder under such circumstances could sometimes prove to be a powerful combination. Burke peered over his cupped hands as he slowly lit up a cigarette and forced his features into a smile through the rising cloud of smoke. He found it difficult to gauge their intentions – and could only assume the worst. He began walking slowly towards them. The Iranians stood firm, brandishing their weapons and shouting hysterically at the approaching Irishman. Burke shrugged the shoulders on his big frame and spread his arms in appeasement as he jabbered away in Gaelic. The Iranians were temporarily distracted and looked at each other in bewilderment, not knowing what to do with this strange turn of events. The first explosion erupted in the road between Burke and the main group of Iranians, just as he came alongside Valentin Tarasov. The blast temporarily stunned the Hamas guard who staggered and released his grip on the Russian. Burke seized the opportunity and leapt forward to make a grab for Tarasov, pulling him across a low stone wall and into the adjacent field.

Jake LeClair continued to lob explosives into the middle of the Iranian force from behind the tractor's digging attachment as Ross Lombardi and the others opened up with a withering fire from the other side.

Behind the stone wall, Burke and Tarasov lay face down in the mud as bullets whizzed and whined overhead. The Hamas suicide squad reacted in the true nature of their calling by refusing to surrender. Some remained defiant to the last, as they stood up to return the fire and made deliberate targets of themselves. There could be no escape – it was a complete death-trap.

Sharif Hamad saw the wink of muzzle flashes and little puffs of smoke as bullets whizzed and whined all around him. He stood and gave a defiant maniacal laugh as a bullet exploded in his upper chest. Hamad placed his hand over the entry point and looked down in disbelief at the blood beginning to ooze through his fingers.

Suddenly, four more bullet holes exploded in his body and one ripped through his leg. "ALLAH!" he screamed as he threw his arms to the heavens. He was a dead man whose body refused to drop. It continued to function on shear fanaticism.

A look of surprise, followed by a fleeting expression of regret washed over Hamad's face as he pitched forward and died, sucking his own blood.

Within a matter of minutes, all the Iranians were dead. Some would say these sacrifices in the name of Allah were considered to be glorious and holy, but that was just a lie. Their luck had simply run out.

When the smoke had finally cleared, Eamonn Burke could feel a cold sweat break out under his arms, in the middle of his chest and between his legs as he cautiously peered over the wall. Lombardi, Lawrence, Tyson and the others were advancing down the lane towards the scene of carnage, guns still at the ready. Jake LeClair had emerged from behind the shot up tractor and approached from the other side. Eamonn Burke turned back to the Russian Captain.

"Valentin Tarasov, I presume?" The Irishman gave a disarming grin as he held out his huge paw. Tarasov looked dazed and bemused, but quickly wiped his muddy hand down his jacket before accepting a handshake from this strange looking man who had just saved his life.

CHAPTER 28

Russia : St Petersburg

CLOUDLESS BLUE SKIES HAD TRANSFORMED the whole ambience of St Petersburg and provided the city with an awesome sense of space on this quiet winter morning. Snow-covered rooftops and monuments shimmered in the early sunlight, and even the city's baroque architectural facades seemed to smile benignly at the rest of the world. Two elegant golden spires dominated the city's famous skyline: the Peter and Paul Cathedral and the Admiralty.

The Admiralty building was at the very heart of the place, in every sense of the word. It had been there right from the beginning, and at a time when the city was nothing more than a simple fortified harbour nestling on the windswept Neva marshes, with all the main avenues radiating from its powerful axis.

One of Peter the Great's earliest decisions, some three centuries ago, had a profound and lasting effect upon his ambitious plans for the expansion and layout of the new St Petersburg. Having decided to move Russia's main naval dockyards to the banks of the river Neva, a large rectangular structure surmounted with a wooden spire, had been hastily erected as a focus for the enterprise and became the site of the Admiralty's first Headquarters Building. From those very earliest days, the yards around the building expanded as needs dictated, with bridges, moats, warehouses and all kinds of secondary buildings springing up. Now, even with the dawn of a new millennium, this majestic successor of that humble beginning was still arguably one of the most important landmarks of Russian history.

Jeremy Sinclair gazed thoughtfully through the snow-spattered windows of the car as they drove along the quarter mile length of the building. He possessed a deep, but passionate sensitivity for the wondrous architecture of St Petersburg, and always researched the building's he was about to visit.

As the Government Zil passed along the *Admiraltej Skaja*, between the river Neva and Falconet's triumphant statue of the Bronze Horseman, Sinclair's concentration suddenly became more focused as he studied the function and purpose of the short wings at either end of Zakharov's re-designed building. They seemed to embrace the great river, harmonising the whole design concept and the very function of the Admiralty.

The old canals and docks were filled in long ago, and the once bustling shipbuilding facilities had subsequently been replaced with anonymous business premises and faceless Government establishments. Only this great classical edifice remained of what was, in a bygone era, one of the most evocative symbols of Russian naval power. The sailing ship weather vane swinging at the top of the spire, still looked defiantly out over the chilly waters of the Baltic estuary as it cast its shadow of supremacy over Decembrists Square and the Winter Palace: but that is just what it was – a shadow. Perhaps the whole thing was nothing more than a sad reflection upon the true reason for their latest visit to St Petersburg.

The limousine bounced and splashed through the slushy puddles of the pot-holed driveway; and didn't even pause as the Admiralty Guard snapped smartly to attention and presented arms. The vehicle just continued under the great archway cut into the lofty rectangular tower, surmounted by its cupola and gilded spire soaring defiantly towards the wintry heavens.

At the main entrance, writhing sea-nymphs clamoured with outstretched arms to grasp a globe of the world, heralding a very different meaning for the diplomat.

The British had always held the belief that they were the supreme masters of the sea – so too did the Russians – particularly in St Petersburg. Exotic dolphins cavorted at roof level, and a quartet of dignified statues depicted the four seasons, the winds, shipbuilding and astronomy. In fact, the entire architectural ensemble exuded a brooding malevolent form of power and confidence as if proclaiming that Russia was still *the* major sea power. Was it still true – or was this just another elaborate lie?

Sinclair and his party were escorted to a lavishly furnished room within the huge interior. They were running late. The Americans and Israelis had already arrived. Drew Dalton and his aides sat to one side of a large oval table, and casually looked up from a mountain of documents they were studying to acknowledge Sinclair and his team as they entered. The Americans knew they faced an uphill struggle with a disgruntled-looking Benjamin Eshkol and his Mossad delegates, whereas the Russians had been quick to take the moral high ground. Admiral Kuragin had clearly positioned himself to chair the meeting, with several other high-ranking naval officers strategically seated to protect his flanks – each accompanied by their respective advisors.

Jeremy Sinclair had been actively lobbying in Whitehall. He had made a specific request for Juliet Lucas to attend this delicate summit as a key member of his diplomatic team, and she now sat beside him, busily spreading out documents and folders as they prepared to face up to the Russians. Delegations from Norway and Finland were also seated at various points around the table. The usual assortment of brightly coloured bottles of soft drinks were set out in neat rows down the centre. Jeremy Sinclair offered his profuse apologies for the delay, blaming it upon the city's traffic congestion as they drove in from Pulkova Airport and the continuing festive New Year celebrations, with dozens of drunken *Dyed Moroz*'s and *Snegurochka*'s adding to the usual chaos.

"Can we just get on with this?" Benjamin Eshkol growled impatiently. Nobody offered any objection and one of the Admiralty aides rose to give an in-depth report on the *Cherkassy* situation. He assured the assembled group that all the hi-jacked SS-N-21 Sampson cruise missiles had been accounted for… and at this very moment were being safely de-commissioned on Russian soil.

He went on to inform his sceptical audience that such an episode could not, and indeed would not, ever happen again.

"We all faced oblivion. The entire world was placed in jeopardy!" Eshkol bellowed, before the man was able to finish his carefully prepared soliloquy. "You people simply don't seem to realise the seriousness of what has happened!"

"The whole situation was under control at all times," Admiral Kuragin interjected with annoyance.

"Was it hell!" Drew Dalton sided with the Israeli. "My Mossad colleague was merely referring to the enormous effort and sacrifice our respective countries have had to make in order to bring this whole ridiculous fiasco under control."

"Do not forget, we too have made sacrifices," the Admiral added solemnly, "We also lost many good people on the Kola Peninsula ... as have our Norwegian and Finnish comrades." He nodded in their direction.

"The Kola Peninsula expedition was nothing more than a half-baked operation and totally inadequate for the task!" Eshkol ranted on. "Those people were inexperienced, ill-equipped and totally disorganised!"

"Remember ... you are still a guest in our country, Mr Eshkol!" Bottles jumped and glasses rattled as Admiral Kuragin slammed his hand down onto the table and rose to his feet, glaring at the Israeli.

Kuragin was a driven man, a product of the old Soviet Regime. He found it frustrating and difficult to come to terms with the new order of things. He had risen quickly through the ranks to make his mark as one of Russia's top front-line strategists. Until recently, he had been Supreme Commander of her once mighty northern fleet – which was still armed with a formidable arsenal of cruise missiles – programmed and targeted to attack any hostile intruder above, on or under the oceans of the world.

"Gentlemen, gentlemen..." Jeremy Sinclair's eyes had been travelling back and forth between the two protagonists as if he'd been watching a tennis match. He leapt to his feet. "These wild and emotional outbursts will get us absolutely nowhere. Could we at least try to be a bit more positive and forward-looking?"

The British Diplomat smiled his soothing balm around the table before sitting back down again. This unexpected exchange gave the Russian aide an opportunity to gather his thoughts and retrieve the floor. The officer concluded his report by confirming this meeting had been specifically convened at the request of all the countries involved in the *Cherkassy* affair, and reminding everyone that they were expected to draw up a co-ordinated, and workable plan to ensure such a crisis could never be repeated.

"We all know *why* this crisis occurred in the first place!" Eshkol looked on defiantly at Kuragin and placed his palms firmly on the table as he pushed himself to his feet. "It's because you people keep dumping your nuclear cast-offs all over the Arctic." His face became flushed as he waved an admonishing finger. "You are completely irresponsible and without scruples!"

"Benjamin, please…" an Israeli advisor pleaded as he tried to restrain him.

"Please, schmeez…" Eshkol hissed scornfully. "Why don't we just speak the truth? Otherwise nothing will be achieved."

"I doubt if anything meaningful will ever be achieved," Jeremy Sinclair whispered to Juliet Lucas, "whether we speak the truth or not. Best thing we can all do is at least be civil to each other."

"Who says we are dumping nuclear material in the Arctic?" one of the Russian officers asked defensively.

"You see?" Eshkol shrugged and threw his hands in the air with frustration.

"Mr Chairman…" Drew Dalton stood up. "If we're gonna keep playing this game of denial and counter-denial, then we might as well all pack up and go home right now!"

"How dare you speak to Admiral Kuragin like that!" an indignant naval Commodore roared from the top of the table.

"Everyone knows there are literally hundreds of obsolete nuclear submarines and other warships rusting away – all the way from Murmansk to Kamchatka!" Eshkol continued with a sweep of his hand. "Most still have their nuclear reactors in place and god knows how many are still armed!"

The atmosphere became electric, with Russians shouting at Israelis, Americans shouting at Russians and the Scandinavians shouting at everyone in the room. Eshkol almost made himself hoarse as he tried to appeal for calm so that he could make himself heard again over the hysterical babble. "No one must forget, that whilst this ridiculous situation remains unresolved, the rest of the world is still faced with the real prospect of another major military and ecological disaster!"

Jeremy Sinclair sat back, folded his arms and raised a quizzical eyebrow. He gave a weak smile of resignation as he looked across to a bemused Juliet Lucas and raised his index finger to beckon one of his aides to come over. He whispered something into the man's ear and pointed to Admiral Kuragin at the head of the table. "*Whenever politics and common sense collide, high-command always freezes like a rabbit caught in the beam of a headlight,*" he thought to himself.

The British aide gave an obsequious nod and set off around the turmoil, heading straight for the Russian. The message received, Kuragin's face glowered with suppressed rage and the veins on his temple began to throb. He stood momentarily rooted to the spot, then drew his Tokarev from its holster and fired a single round into the ceiling. A hushed silence descended upon the conference room, as bits of delicate and priceless plaster-work cascaded to the floor.

Delegates were momentarily stunned. They rose to their feet, dusted themselves down and stood open-mouthed. Taking his cue, Jeremy Sinclair straightened his tie, cleared his throat, placed his hands on the chair's arms and calmly pushed himself to his feet.

"Gentlemen... thank you. Please resume your seats."

The Englishman turned to Juliet Lucas, who handed him a sheet of paper.

"Now that I have your complete attention, perhaps we could get down to some more serious business?

This problem, as my friend Mr Eshkol quite rightly points out, is a global one. Therefore, it is only right and logical that we must be prepared to apply a global solution." Sinclair went on to outline a comprehensive plan which had been drawn up by their respective governments, whereby the Russians *might* receive substantial technical and financial aid from the West, in order to assist them in safely decommissioning and storing their obsolete fissionable material. This latest startling revelation only caused further dissension, with the Israelis stating that they would not be able to justify the allocation of such huge resources to their electorate and, in any case, they didn't believe this problem was their responsibility. On the other hand, the

Americans were quite happy to go along with the plan, as long as they were able to maintain overall control. Meanwhile, the Russians were only too pleased to accept financial assistance from whatever source – providing the West didn't go around poking its nose into their nuclear backyard. Another acrimonious shouting match erupted, but this time Jeremy Sinclair just gave a sigh of resigned despair and allowed the madness to take its own course.

The heated verbal skirmishes rumbled on for several hours, with each side fending off a constant barrage of interruptions and derision from the other opposing factions whilst everyone continued to trot out their old familiar hackneyed clichés and platitudes.

In the end, Sinclair's predictions had come true; nothing constructive was achieved. The Israelis stormed out, whilst the Norwegians and Finns remained totally ineffective and were completely sidelined. They merely paid lip service to the Russians. Having completed the formal part of their presentation, the British delegation began to gather up their documents and withdrew discreetly; leaving the Russians and Americans the dubious honour of formerly shaking hands to give the public impression that something meaningful had actually been resolved. Everyone knew that such proposals were always wrapped up with the usual hollow promises of further talks – but at a diplomatic level.

❖ ❖ ❖

That same evening, in a grand gesture of appeasement, the Russians hosted a small reception at the Beloselskiy-Belozerskiy Palace on nearby *Nevsky Prospekt*. Everyone attended, except the Israelis. They had become totally disillusioned by the outcome of this fiasco, and were already on their way back to Tel Aviv.

The imposing red facade of the Palace was an incredible shade of crimson, with Corinthian pilasters imparting a feeling of robustness and vitality to its sinuous window surrounds. The sturdy balconies were supported by a broad and bearded figure of Atlantis, who looked down upon the approaching guests.

Jeremy Sinclair paused briefly on the palace steps and began to admire this architectural masterpiece. He couldn't help but feel the overwhelming sense of power and history peeling off these ancient walls, where St Petersburg's once profligate aristocrats had been embroiled with endless plots, intrigues and assassinations ... only to suffer a similar fate, once their evil deeds had been accomplished.

Juliet Lucas stood alongside Jeremy Sinclair within the main reception area as she sipped a glass of Dom Perignon and took delicate forkfuls of Beluga caviar.

"I'm intrigued. What was so special about the information that your aide gave to Admiral Kuragin," she asked. "I mean ... to make him react the way he did?"

"He was informed that Valentin Tarasov was still alive," the diplomat replied as he scanned the room full of guests.

As if on cue, Admiral Kuragin could be seen approaching through the crowd, with a broad gold sash cinched tightly around his ample midriff and an impressive array of medals festooned across the chest of his number one dress uniform.

"Tell me more about Tarasov!" The Russian spoke in a low voice, so as not to be overheard.

"You'd better ask my colleague, Miss Lucas." Sinclair made the introductions. "She was one of the last people to see him."

"Captain Tarasov was saved by one of our team in the field," Lucas explained. "He then spoke of seeking political asylum from the Irish authorities."

"And did he by any chance *receive* this asylum?" the Admiral almost spat out the words as he glanced over his shoulder to make sure that no one was within earshot.

"I don't really know..." Lucas stiffened visibly as she thought carefully about her next response, "but *I do know* he was taken away by the Irish para-militaries who assisted us with the re-capture of your missiles. After that, I didn't see him again."

"We have tabled the appropriate er... *diplomatic* questions to the Irish Government," Jeremy Sinclair added with a sigh, "querying his asylum application."

"And their response?"

"They *say* they never received any such application." Sinclair shrugged.

"*Then where the hell is he?*" the Russian demanded through gritted teeth.

"We can only assume that he is still out there with the paramilitaries," Lucas added.

"This is outrageous! Are you trying to tell me he's in the hands of *terrorists?*" boomed the Admiral, then quickly lowered his voice as heads began to turn in his direction "Do you think you can get him back? *We want him here!*"

"One of our agent's is very close to the paramilitaries," Sinclair whispered, "He is trying to set up a suitable rendezvous at this very moment."

"Can any *diplomatic* pressure be applied?" the Admiral whispered back.

"Let's just say that ... we may have some leverage." Jeremy Sinclair smiled over the edge of his raised glass and took a sip of champagne.

"Excellent!" The Admiral beamed and clinked glasses with the Englishman, "I trust you will keep my people informed?"

"Most certainly, Admiral." Sinclair gave a polite nod as he watched the Russian turn and mingle with the other guests.

"So... what do you think of all this intrigue and high-level international diplomacy?" Sinclair asked his female companion.

"It's very exciting! Just like being in the field, sir!"

❖ ❖ ❖

Later that same evening, Juliet Lucas returned to her room at the Astoria Hotel on *Bolshaya Morskaya*. She undressed and tried to summon up the image of Peter Lawrence as she slipped between the cool sheets of the big double bed. Since returning from Ireland, she felt their mutual passion had not been diminished in any way. She still hung onto a strange mixture of desire and respect for him, and realised it was probably as close to love as she was ever going to get. She longed for this strange but pleasant feeling to last, but deep down she knew it would be nothing more than a transient relationship. Peter Lawrence was essentially a field operative, who always tried to stay out of the limelight and would probably remain an active agent until he retired or was killed. Juliet gave a deep sigh. She was gradually coming to terms with her other ambitions. St Petersburg had been her first official taste of the diplomatic high-life, and she was determined it wouldn't be her last. Her emotional desires were finally succumbing to her personal career ambitions. Peter Lawrence had been a man for the moment, and Juliet instinctively knew she would soon outgrow the relationship. Sooner or later, she knew she would have to make the agonising choice between her career and this enigmatic man. That might not be today or tomorrow, but she knew it was inevitable, just as surely as night follows day. Before leaving Belfast, they had agreed that when she returned to London, they would both take a much needed weekend break in the Lake District. It all sounded wonderfully romantic, but the champagne was now beginning to take her away from the hard surface of reality as it delivered her into contented sleep.

CHAPTER 29

Israel : Tel Aviv

Ruth Netanya had always considered Tel Aviv to be a vibrant symbol of the modern Israel. It was a big sprawling city, with a ribbon of high-rise buildings jostling each other for a breath of fresh air along the water-front. The ceaseless, frenetic crowds made this place not only brash and tacky but also very expensive! Netanya disliked the place. It sapped her energy and patience. She would much rather be amongst the excitement of Haifa, or even in the familiar surroundings of her birthplace, the holy city of Jerusalem. But orders are orders, and Benjamin Eshkol had insisted she was to join him here.

Eshkol and his political friends from the Knesset had been shuttling back and forth through the corridors of power as they tried to coerce a wavering group of sympathetic Arabs into denouncing the Iranians. However, despite their valiant efforts, everyone still suspected it would all turn out to be just another futile gesture. The Arabs who really mattered would not actually be represented at the meeting. Eshkol was still in a bad mood after his recent trip to St Petersburg.

At least one good thing had happened in the past few days. Netanya's long overdue leave had finally been sanctioned, and she looked forward to getting away for a well-earned break. She needed some time and space to unwind – and maybe to reflect upon the past couple of months, but above all, she needed time to straighten out her true feelings. The recent spate of violence and killings had finally taken its toll. Everybody had thought that Netanya was a tough woman and hard as steel, but nothing could have been further from the truth. It was merely a self-inflicted shallow façade, and nothing more than a defence mechanism.

It had been created for the protection of her intractable image and only came into focus when duty called. Anything less would have been letting her colleagues down. However, her private persona was not so tough. She constantly struggled with all the emotional turmoil and the pressures of the job, which often brought her to the very brink of her mental endurance. If there was one single criticism that stood out above all others, it was perhaps that she was inclined to become too personally involved.

The cool evening breeze raced through Netanya's hair as she drove her open-top sports car southwards, across the *Yarkon River*. She turned right at the junction with *Yehuda ha Maccabi* and threaded her way through the early evening traffic where she followed *Shelomo Ha Melekh* for several blocks. Darkness had cast its all-embracing mantle over the city as Netanya passed *Dizengoff Square* to avoid the crowded maze of elevated pedestrian walkways converging overhead. The water sculpture in the middle of the square was out of commission, as usual. With the dawning of a new millennium, Tel Aviv had become firmly established as the traditional home for at least a third of Israel's entire population. In Hebrew, the very name conjures up its true meaning: "the hill of the spring." The ancient book of *Ezekiel* describes this as a most sacred place. It is where the holy prophet had a vision and raised his outstretched arms towards the heavens when a collection of dry bones came back to life on their return to *Eretz Yisrael*. Very appropriate, thought Netanya, because despite its skin-deep panache and pretentious frivolity, it nevertheless remained such a sterile place. A city continuing to play the strumpet for its cross-section of *avant garde* Israelis, foreign tourists and assorted hangers-on.

Netanya put her foot down and sped past Independence House where the declaration of the establishment of the State of Israel had been proclaimed by the Provisional Government on 15th May 1948, and headed towards her ultimate destination – a safe Mossad building on *Derekh Shalma*. Whether she liked it or not, most die-hard bureaucrats still considered Tel Aviv to be the Capital of Israel. The city was at the very centre of diplomatic activity, and home to many Foreign Embassies. No matter how much she tried to resist, the unrelenting and persuasive thoughts of Ross Lombardi kept gently probing away at her sub-conscious. Netanya's last brief encounter with the American was when he had saved her life during the skirmish with the Iranians at Knock airport. Since that time, and as a result of the earlier operations in the *Dasht-e Kavir*, she had been able to gradually reconcile their strange enigmatic relationship when she realised that David Weizman's death wasn't his fault.

It could have been any of them: Lombardi, the Englishman, Peter Lawrence … or even herself. Life and destiny sometimes moved in strange and mysterious ways, but sentimentality was an unacceptable luxury in their line of business. Netanya parked her convertible at the rear of the building and entered through the back door. Having displayed her identification to security, she crossed the spartan lobby and took the stairs up to the second floor. No one was about, but her attention was caught by a thin shaft of light accompanied by a mixture of exotic voices cascading from an open doorway off the deserted landing. Netanya approached, knocked politely, and entered to find Benjamin Eshkol engrossed in heated debate behind a large pile of documents spread out across a polished rosewood table.

He was flanked on either side by a couple of Mossad colleagues who were being harangued by an unknown junior politician, and several Arabs within the room glanced casually in her direction as Netanya paused briefly in the doorway. She looked around at the gathered officials, and instantly recognised two of them from press photographs and previous meetings. During the past few months, the outside world had reluctantly been forced to acknowledge this duo as the most senior leaders advocating a non-violent approach to the Middle East problem on behalf of the various Palestinian and Lebanese factions.

Behind the scenes, Mossad had been quietly manipulating them for years and usually trotted them out on such occasions when they wanted to re-assure the world that not all Arabs were homicidal maniacs. As leaders go, they effectively had little or no influence with the paramilitary groups and these exercises were just a publicity stunt for the world at large. Eshkol stood up as Netanya made her way round to his side of the table and welcomed her with paternal kisses on both cheeks. She placed her briefcase down on the floor and pulled up a chair to take her place at the table.

"The Russians have no intention of doing anything..." The men had obviously been discussing the Russian nuclear problem before her arrival and Eshkol now continued where he had left off.

"Well, what on earth did you expect them to do?" one of the Arabs asked with an incredulous sweep of his hand.

"I expect them to clean up their own mess!" Eshkol turned on the man. "Ever since the break-up of the former Soviet Union, the Russians have *still* been dumping their obsolete ships all along the northern coastline. It's like a nuclear graveyard up there! They don't seem to care..."

"Was Ross Lombardi in St Petersburg?" Ruth Netanya calmly interrupted his tirade.

"Who?" Eshkol shifted uneasily in his chair. He was annoyed at being sidetracked.

"The American ... Ross Lombardi?"

"No!" he snapped. "Drew Dalton was there. Why?"

"No particular reason..." Netanya looked away.

"Then can we just get back to the real issues?" the Israeli politician asked.

"Of course..." Eskkol shuffled his papers and flashed a disapproving glance at Netanya. "They don't seem to care... apart from the more obvious dangers posed by pirates and salvagers, there's also the ecological issue. It's an absolutely terrifying time-bomb, just waiting to go off ... and remember, it's also one where the entire world would feel the inescapable consequences." Eshkol paused for breath and took a drink of iced water.

"This whole incident cannot go without appropriate condemnation from all the Arab organisations in this area," the politician insisted, as he looked towards the Palestinian and Lebanese delegation across the room.

"Of course ..." one of them replied as he expanded his hands in a gesture of appeasement. "We shall make a statement to that effect, but we hardly exercise any influence with the Iranians."

"Hardly any influence ... period!" Ruth Netanya muttered, under her breath.

"In any case..." the man continued, "Tehran has already issued an official statement to the effect that this incident was regrettably caused by nothing more than a breakaway group of Hamas extremists, aided by a renegade band of Russian sailors who hi-jacked one of their submarines."

"That is preposterous! And they expect us to believe that?" the Mossad agents laughed openly.

"They do not care whether you believe it or not," another Arab added solemnly over steepled fingers.

"So long as it is accepted by the international community ... which seems more than likely to be the case."

"I'm not talking about "official" statements," the Israeli politician scoffed. "You people have your own underground network. You must forcibly denounce this action to the various sections responsible – and fast! Get word to them on the camel telegraph if you have to – but make it clear that you don't approve."

"We will do what we can," the Arab leader promised with a polite nod, knowing their actions would be futile.

Ruth Netanya had waited patiently. She loudly cleared her throat, to attract some attention. Eshkol turned and realised he had quite forgotten the reason for her attendance.

"Yes, of course..." The Mossad chief brought the meeting to order and requested Netanya to present her own account of the *Cherkassy* operation. They all knew about such carefully crafted public statements, but this latest official report from one of the actual agents involved was intended as just a bit of window dressing exclusively for the Arabs benefit. She picked up a dossier and scanned the table before proceeding. The Arabs and the politician sat as if mesmerised.

Having concluded her briefing, she tried to deflect the host of inevitable and unanswerable questions coming from the group. As the probing questions died away, the Arabs and the politician re-opened their folders and started to thumb slowly through the documents and photographs. Netanya's leave period was scheduled to commence just as soon as this ordeal was over. She had made plans to stay in Tel Aviv overnight, before driving down to Jerusalem for a long overdue visit to her parents. Netanya was busily gathering up her briefing documents, when the telephone sprang to life.

One of the Mossad agents reached over and pressed the handset to his ear.

"It's for you…" the man shrugged with curiosity as he handed her the receiver.

"Yes?" she cupped her hand round the mouthpiece and spoke softly, surprised that anyone should call her on this number. Netanya twiddled with the phone line as she half turned away and remained silent for a few moments, listening intently to the mystery caller. She gasped with surpressed excitement and a wide smile broke across her face. Everyone in the room paused and watched the interruption with concealed amusement.

"I'm in Tel Aviv…" Netanya continued, "I'm almost finished here… Yes, I can make the airport in about an hour…" She jotted down a few notes. "OK, that's plenty of time … see you there." She hung up. There was an electrified silence as the men studied her beaming face.

"Well … who was that?" Benjamin Eshkol couldn't contain his curiosity any longer.

"Ross Lombardi," Netanya answered coquettishly.

"Who?"

"The American … remember?"

"How on earth did he get this number?" Eshkol tried to remain calm.

"I don't know," Netanya shrugged nonchalantly.

"*Zeh yoter midai!*" Eshkol shouted. "Now the whole world knows the secret number of a Mossad safe house. Why don't we just list it in the Yellow Pages? What is happening in this crazy world? What does this Ross Lombardi want?"

"To take me on vacation," Netanya answered with a pleading look. "Can I go now?"

"*What?*" the Mossad chief was taken aback and almost speechless by the woman's forwardness.

"I'm meeting him in Washington. My plane leaves in three hours."

"I want your report – in writing – for the Knesset…"

"It's already on your desk at the Defence Ministry."

How could he refuse? Before Eshkol had time to respond, she kissed him on both cheeks and rushed through the door.

"Go! Go! Don't mind me…" Eshkol sighed and waved like a dismissive father as he turned back to the bemused delegation. "*Women*: they just don't make good agents." Everyone nodded in agreement. "They always allow men to take advantage *and* they think with their hearts instead of their heads!"

"There is little else for us to say at this moment," one of the Arabs commented, when everyone had regained their sense of decorum. "We will do as you ask."

"Very well…" The Israeli politician shook hands with each Arab as they filed from the room. "*Shalom* and good luck to you."

The Arabs responded with appropriate *Salaams* and a polite nod.

When they had departed, the Israelis re-convened for their separate agenda.

"What a bunch of ineffectual yes-men!" one of the Mossad agents laughed.

"They may be doves…" Eshkol said sullenly, "but they are better than nothing."

"It's the Arab hawks we actually need to confront!" the other agent commented.

"Sure. But they won't speak to us." His colleague voiced the obvious.

"Nobody seems to be even remotely interested in preventing a crisis like the *Cherkassy* incident from re-occurring," Eshkol mused, almost to himself.

"Except us!" He rubbed his furrowed brow. "I am so tired of such ineffectual bureaucratic mediocrities running our Government and our country. After all, what does this great nation of ours really symbolise? I will tell you. It symbolises the hopes and aspirations of all those who came to escape persecution!"

"True. But what can we do alone?" the politician asked.

"Well… what if we were to launch a nuclear missile at a Russian city?" Eshkol replied coldly to the man with this question of his own.

"Are you mad?" the others cried with derision at such an outrageous suggestion.

"From inside Arab territory!" he concluded. "Let me remind you that suspicion and proof would be two entirely separate matters."

"Benjamin, please..." the politician raised his hands and turned his head away, shocked at such an idea.

"That way, at least..." Eshkol continued, "Moscow would have no alternative but to blame those rag-heads and wipe them from the face of the earth *and* it would save *us* the trouble. We could just sit back and let the world get on with it!"

"Please Benjamin, this is no joking matter" The politician ceased to smile.

"I am not joking!"

Several moments of silence followed as Eshkol quietly surveyed the collection of ashen faces gathered in the room.

❖ ❖ ❖

Ruth Netanya strolled along Dizengoff Street. There was still time to kill before she would have to leave for Ben Gurion Airport. Ross Lombardi had confirmed that her ticket was already paid for and would be available for collection at the departure desk. He also went on to inform her that he had some unfinished business in Washington, but he would nevertheless still be able to meet up with her at Dulles International Airport for their onward flight to Colorado. Ruth paused at one of the brightly coloured pavement cafes and ordered a coffee. She put down her load of last minute shopping and settled at one of the tables where she wistfully stirred the strong black beverage as she watched the mixed parade of night-life passing by. Only as recently as two weeks ago she would have spat down the phone at the American. However, since then, he had saved her life and suddenly everything had changed. She was torn between a strange mixture of guilt and sadness as the memory of David Weizman began to fade. In her mind, she could still see David's ephemeral image waving good-bye, as he trod the heavenly pathway of the *Torah derekh*. She realised that people in her profession must be prepared to accept such loss without question. Death must become as everyday an experience as eating, drinking and breathing. It must not be asked for, but neither must it be feared.

CHAPTER 30

USA : Washington & Colorado

Larry Tyson had fought his way through Washington's early morning commuter traffic and now waited anxiously for Ruth Netanya in the crowded arrivals lounge of Washington's Dulles airport. Ross Lombardi had requested his friend to meet the Israeli, as his own rendezvous at the White House was taking a bit longer than expected. The big man stretched above the group standing in front of him as he watched the American Airlines jet touch down and taxi back towards the terminal building. Excitement rose as the plane's engines spooled down and the jet-way manoeuvred into position over the front passenger door. Tyson decided to edge his way forward by easing his massive frame through the milling crowd.

"Excuse me Ma'am … Oh I'm sorry, I didn't see your bag down there … Pardon me Sir…' until he found his way to the front, just as Ruth Netanya emerged from the covered walkway. Having discarded her unflattering military fatigues, Netanya now looked quite different. She appeared more feminine and more radiant, dressed in a pencil-slim skirt and casual jacket.

"Miss Netanya…" Tyson approached the Israeli, nervously clutching his Stetson.

"Yes?"

"Remember me … Larry Tyson?"

"Ah … yes of course, you're Ross's friend." Netanya smiled up at the big man.

"That's right" Tyson stuck the big white hat back onto his head and pumped her hand. "Ross asked me to come over and meet you."

"But why isn't he here?" Netanya searched the sea of faces, visibly disappointed that Lombardi hadn't come along himself.

"He offers his apologies, but he's been delayed at the White House." Tyson quickly tried to put her mind at ease. " Come on ... let me take your things. We'll meet him there."

"At *the* White House?" Netanya gasped with excitement.

"Sure, why not?" Tyson grinned.

Ruth Netanya took an immediate liking to Washington. She thoughtfully studied the Capital City through the car's window as they drove in from the airport.

Larry Tyson played the perfect host. He gushed with patriotic pride as he pointed out the various landmarks and gave a full narration of their historical significance. It reminded her of Paris, with its stunning buildings, manicured lawns and neat avenues of trees. The City's main streets and boulevards appeared even wider and more grand, than those found in the French capital. It all seemed like a dream.

She couldn't believe she was actually here at last. They both fell silent as they passed the Vietnam War Memorial. This sobering reminder of the fifty-eight thousand American soldiers who died during that bloody Asian war quickly brought her back to reality, but somehow couldn't really dampen her spirits on this clear winter day. The sun was shining and everything in the world seemed to be bright and new. The Lincoln Memorial looked quite imposing to the Israeli, with its high stone columns and wide steps.

A fugitive thought crept across her mind. The Americans seemed to have a disturbing habit of killing off some of their finest statesmen: the Kennedy brothers, Martin Luther King and even Lincoln himself. Her pulse quickened and adrenaline surged when the White House came into view. It wasn't quite as big in real life as she had imagined, but she was nevertheless impressed by its symbolism.

An early morning queue of hardy tourists turned their backs against the biting westerly wind as they waited patiently for the first public tour of the day. The crowd shuffled their frozen feet and stepped aside. They looked on with mild curiosity, wondering just who these exalted visitors were, as Tyson's car drew up to the gate. He rolled down the tinted window as a security guard appeared alongside. After verifying Tyson's credentials, the guard instructed him to keep to the right of the main gardens and drive towards a side entrance. Once inside, Netanya's initial impressions of the White House began to change. Despite all its elegance and grandeur, the general warmth and comfort radiated a feeling of domestic efficiency.

Elaborate and colourful arrangements of freshly cut flowers could be seen cascading from ornate vases and bowls scattered throughout the building and their strategic positioning provided a subtle filter for the soft lighting which seemed to cover everything in a light golden hue.

Every room they passed through appeared smaller than expected, but nevertheless still retained that kind of lived-in feeling. Tyson led the awe-struck Israeli into the State Dining Room, then onwards through the East Room, and paused only briefly to explain the function of each as they went through. Probably one of the most intriguing things that managed to capture Netanya's attention was the range of dignified Presidential portraits which lined the walls of the White House and brought the place to life. She paused in front of Jack Kennedy's famous picture with his head bowed, hiding his face from view. She was puzzled.

Larry Tyson explained the artist had never met his subject and he therefore decided to paint it with the President's face obscured rather than do it wrong: it was such a sad and melancholy picture.

The portrait's poignancy had caught Netanya completely off guard, and she found her thoughts drifting back to David Weizman. The big cowboy had also sensed the moment, and when they reached the Blue Room, with its varnished woodwork and oval shape he tried to bring her back to reality. "You hungry?"

"Famished" replied Netanya with a deep sigh as she looked down at her watch.

Her long and tedious flight from Tel Aviv had taken more than fourteen gruelling hours, including a brief stop-off at Shannon. As soon as they were airborne again, Ruth Netanya had quickly settled down to catch up on some sleep for the trans-Atlantic crossing and consequently missed out on the usual unappetising in-flight meals. But with Washington some seven hours behind Israel – she was certainly ready to eat ! Larry Tyson lead her through to one of the adjacent reception rooms where a hearty breakfast of coffee, scrambled eggs and pancakes smothered in maple syrup awaited them.

He wasted no time in wolfing down a double helping for himself and Netanya began to lighten up and relax in the company of this big affable cowboy.

The Middle East, Russia, and all the other problems, both personal and professional, somehow seemed to evaporate for the time being. Tyson's boyish charm and innocent patter had managed to weave a temporary spell… as he went on to enthral her with endless tales about himself and Ross Lombardi.

❖ ❖ ❖

Senator Heffner T Copeland blew clouds of rich Havana smoke from the cigar firmly clasped between his fingers. He stood in one of the conference rooms located next to the Oval Office, and looked thoughtfully through a French window at the first light dusting of snow sprinkled across the White House gardens.

Although the President was still away on his state visit to South Africa, he had nevertheless thoughtfully left behind a couple of close personal advisors to attend the Senator's own hastily convened summit. Ross Lombardi and Drew Dalton were also present, and calmly seated at a highly polished table, drinking coffee.

"You know we got that Iranian sub, the…" Copeland jammed the evil smelling cigar back between his teeth and snapped his fingers as he gazed into the middle distance, trying to think of the name.

"The *Zarand*," Lombardi politely jogged his memory.

"Oh yea, that's right … the *Zarand*. Anyway … we tracked her all the way from the Norwegian Sea and down the western coast of Ireland into Clew Bay, where our submarines set up a blockade and forced her to the surface.

The *Alabama* took over control from there, and we now have her impounded down at the Parris Island Marine Base for a full technical evaluation."

"But what happened to the crew?" Lombardi addressed the Senator's back. "And all the other sailors we captured at Knock airport?"

"It seems that nobody was prepared to accept any responsibility for what had happened," the Senator gave a dismissive shrug, "So the Irish Government deported them all back to Iran."

"I guess they'll get it in the neck when they get back," Drew Dalton seemed to state the obvious.

"You ain't kiddin…" the Senator laughed. "I reckon they've already been shot."

"Hey wait a minute… those guys were just ordinary sailors," Lombardi wasn't amused. "They were just obeying orders."

"Ain't it the same the world over?" Drew Dalton philosophised. "Anyhow … all's well that ends well, as the British would say."

The Senator turned away from the window and pointed directly at Ross Lombardi with his cigar wedged between his fingers, "Just don't do anything stupid like that again!"

"Like what, Senator?" Lombardi was taken by surprise.

"Like that goddam raid into Iran! Jesus man … shooting and blowing up half the country. It was the most reckless thing I've ever heard of!"

"Aw come on now! You know I ain't the first person to organise such a raid on Iran, Senator." Lombardi was offended and sat on the edge of his chair, his blood pressure starting to rise. "And what's more, I was *successful*, which is more than can be said for the other clowns!"

"Just don't do it again, OK?" one of the White House men joined in.

"Surely you appreciate the Government's sensitivity on such issues?"

"OK, OK," Lombardi said with raised hands. "But let me give you all another little sensitive issue to think about. Of the one hundred and thirteen Russian Northern Fleet nuclear submarines which we already know to have been taken out of commission at Severodvinsk, only a third have so far been dismantled … and ten of them have actually been waiting for more than 15 years!

Unlike ours, the Russian subs have *two* nuclear reactors, and *each* of these reactors contains some *250 fuel rods.*

Now, the one and only place in the whole of Russia with the appropriate facilities, and enough technology to process this spent uranium, is the closed nuclear city complex at Chelyabinsk 65 – and even that's more than fifteen hundred kilometres away in the Urals. Several high security trains a year used to make the long and difficult journey to transport this uranium, but the Navy now owes the Chelyabinsk complex billions of roubles...and cannot pay. Consequently, trains have stopped running.

But wait a minute ... it gets worse! The Northern Fleet Commander recently had to take an armed guard to conduct some very forceful negotiations with the Director in charge of the local power utility company as the man constantly threatens to cut off electrical power to the navy's decrepit submarines. You see, what you people just don't seem to understand, *or appreciate,* is that without a continuous and uninterrupted supply of electricity to power the vital pumps which keep circulating the cooling water, a reactors core temperature will spiral out of control. This would then cause the fuel rods to swell and jam in their conduits, leaving them firmly wedged ... *and highly radioactive."*

The starkest truth was beginning to emerge. It was a frightening picture. The Russian nuclear de-commissioning programme was out of control.

Senator Copeland broke the lengthy silence that followed.

"All very interesting Ross, but just tell me ... How long would it actually take to make an inventory and complete the decommissioning process for them?"

"If money and resource was no object, I would estimate between 100 and 150 years."

The Senator took out a handkerchief and dabbed his forehead. He could see his political career turning to ashes.

Lombardi looked at his watch and uttered a mild curse. "Excuse me Senator, if there are no other pressing matters? Look ... I've officially been on leave since mid-night, so d'you think we could wrap this whole thing up...I've got a very special young lady waiting for me."

"If she loves you, she'll wait a little longer," the White House aide interjected.

"Oh, there's just one other thing ..."

"What's that?" Lombardi blew out a long exasperated sigh.

"That guy Tarasov ... the Russian submarine Captain ...What actually happened to him?"

"That's a darn good question Senator, but I really don't know!" Lombardi replied, with his own curiosity suddenly aroused.

"Aw...come on Ross, you gotta know," Drew Dalton said. "After all, you were over there with him for Christ's sake."

"Well... I think it was one of the senior IRA guys who actually got him."

"Holy Christ!" The Senator almost choked on his cigar stub.

"They took him away somewhere," Lombardi shrugged. "Peter Lawrence reckoned the man was going to try and seek political asylum. But I thought you guys would have heard something from the Irish Government by now?"

"And who the hell's this Peter Lawrence?" the Senator queried.

"He's a member of the British SAS," Drew Dalton gently reminded him. "You met him in Colorado."

"Oh, sure, sure ... And this other Irish guy, what's his name?"

"Burke, Senator."

"Yeah ... and just who exactly is Burke working for?"

"He's a senior IRA commander," Lombardi confirmed.

"So you're now trying to tell us *he's* the one who's actually got the Russian?" The White House aide looked directly at Lombardi for confirmation.

"I guess so." Lombardi gave a conceited smile.

"Get our people on to Dublin and London right away," the aide instructed his colleague, "and find out just what the hell is going on – and more importantly, what they're doing about all this."

"OK!" the White House man gave a decisive nod to affirm his understanding of the instruction, gathered up his papers, and left the room.

"Now may I please go?" Lombardi asked again.

"What about your men, Ross?" Drew Dalton showed genuine concern.

"Oh, I guess all the survivors will have made their way back home to the mountains by now ... all except for Larry Tyson. Why, he's waiting for me right here. We're planning to shoot off to Dulles and catch the two o'clock flight for Colorado."

"Say, where can I get in touch with you?" Dalton asked.

"You can't! Lombardi rose to his feet, buttoned his jacket and made for the door, "I'll get in touch with you!" He threw a casual salute, and left the room.

❖ ❖ ❖

Aspen's nearest international airport connection was located some thirty miles to the north-east of Denver. Ruth Netanya purred with contentment as she settled down for the scheduled three hour internal flight, kicked off her shoes and curled up alongside Ross Lombardi. No one said much – everyone was too exhausted.

Upon arrival at Denver, Lombardi and Tyson checked through and collected everyone's luggage from the baggage carousel before parting company under the airport's spectacular tented roof, with much hand-shaking, bear-hugging and back-slapping. Larry Tyson hefted his bags and came forward to kiss Netanya on the cheek before heading off up north to a bar he knew near Fort Collins.

"There's a little lady I know up there..." he told them with a knowing wink, "runs the Spur 'n' Saddle roadhouse. I've been promising a visit and I guess now's as good a time as any."

They hopped onto one of the airport's shuttle buses and set off to retrieve Ross Lombardi's electric blue Thunderbird from the long-term car park. Soon the couple found themselves heading west, past Arvada and Golden and up into the snow covered Rocky Mountains along Interstate 70. The air up here beyond the "Mile High" city was crisp and fresh. It made Netanya feel light-headed – or perhaps it was just the thought of being with this wild enigmatic character, as they headed even higher into Aspen's wild timber country.

The first stage of the journey took them as far as Copper Mountain. Here, Lombardi turned south and made his way through Leadville to join Highway 24 before continuing on down to Twin Lakes. The higher they drove the more rugged the country and it was clear the Thunderbird wouldn't be able to take them much further. The winter sun was just dipping below the crest of the Rockies when Lombardi pulled into a roadhouse called the White River Saloon.

Netanya shivered in the cold mountain air as they left the warmth of the car, and crossed the parking lot to step through the swing doors.

"Ross, you old varmint!" A large middle-aged woman in blue denim dungarees and a wide brimmed Stetson pushed back over her silver hair came flying across the room and threw herself onto the unsuspecting Lombardi. She held his head in a vice-like grip, kissing him full on the lips.

"Annie…" Lombardi gasped, tearing himself free. "Ruth, this is Annie. She owns the place."

"Hiya Ruth, honey," Annie beamed as she warmly shook the Israeli's hand.

"Annie looks after my Jeep – she keeps it round the back," Lombardi explained. "It's the only thing'll get us up to the cabin this time of year."

"Hang on there Ross…" Annie punched him on the arm. "This little gal looks mighty hungry to me. You kids ain't goin' no-wheres until you've had somethin' to eat."

"We really need to get up there before nightfall…" Lombardi tactfully tried to decline Annie's hospitality.

"You hungry, dear?" the woman asked Netanya, ignoring Lombardi's excuse.

"Very!" the Israeli answered.

"There you go! You've been outvoted by us women, so you just sit yourselves down!" Annie would brook no further argument. The couple sat by a roaring log fire while Annie served up the biggest couple of steaks Netanya had ever seen.

"Say, what'll you guys have to drink?"

"Milk for me please Annie," Lombardi answered "I'm driving."

"I'm fine with milk too," Netanya quickly added.

The couple ate heartily, and washed the meal down with a couple of glasses of iced cold milk from the big pitcher sat on the table before them.

Lombardi soon cleared his plate, wiped his mouth with his napkin – and politely excused himself. He went out the back to prepare the Jeep for the final leg of their journey up into the mountains.

Darkness had fallen, but Lombardi knew this terrain like the back of his hand.

They drove in silence over the freshly packed layers of snow as Lombardi picked his way carefully over the frozen ruts left by other vehicles. Thirty-five minutes later, Lombardi suddenly turned off the main highway and proceeded up a steep twisting track clinging to the mountain's craggy contours. This bumpy and tortuous trail eventually lead into a box canyon where the dark outline of a log cabin loomed into view. The Jeep's tyres became embedded in the deep layers of fine drifting snow as it rolled to a halt by the side of the building. Netanya peered hesitantly through the windshield. The place looked desolate and cold. She certainly didn't feel inclined to leave the womb-like warmth and security of the Jeep.

Lombardi gave a reassuring smile as he reached over and touched her hand.

"It's OK Honey." Their eyes met briefly, and her fleeting wave of unease began to evaporate as he pulled himself away and went inside to turn on the lights. It was not long before he had a good fire going, which made the cabin look warm, safe and inviting. Netanya emerged from the Jeep and stepped into this silent wilderness area nestling beneath a sparkling necklace of stars. She clutched at her collar and headed through a powdery layer of knee-deep snow, as she made her way towards the cabin's inviting glow. Netanya gave an involuntary shiver when she paused at the base of a short flight of steps leading up to the cedar-wood decking spanning the front of the building. She stamped her feet to remove the snow, which had covered her boots, before entering Lombardi's inner sanctum. He stood to one side, watching her pause by the doorway and taking in the room, before walking over to the roaring log fire.

He fell in behind, and gently massaged her shoulder. Radiance and contentment fluttered across Netanya's porcelain features as she reached up and covered his hand. She began to relax for the first time since leaving Israel.

CHAPTER 31

Northern Ireland – Belfast

Cold and sleety rain drifted across University Road towards the River Lagan. It was typical mid-January weather for Belfast. Peter Lawrence looked out at the dreary city and wished he could back in Israel. At least it would be warmer. Even with the radio turned down, he could still pick out the occasional clipped messages coming through the static. His young military aide drove the unmarked Mercedes northwards towards the junction with Lisburn Road, and then made his way along the Dublin Road for a short distance, before turning eastwards into Ormeau Avenue. Lawrence had been worried all morning. He'd never met Eamonn Burke in this part of the city and he didn't know what to expect. To stay alive in this business, he knew it was best to stick to well-tried routines and procedures. Lawrence didn't like the unexpected. It usually meant you were out of control – and control was often the difference between life and death. He pulled his collar up round his ears before stepping out of the car.

"Peter…" the MI6 man whirled round, hand instinctively reaching inside his coat. "Jesus, man… you *are* jumpy." Eamonn Burke visibly flinched as he partially raised his hands and took a step back.

"Eamonn… what the bloody hell do you think you are doing?"

"I said I'd meet you here, didn't I?" Burke had recovered his composure and gave a grin. Sure… but we should be following established procedures!" Lawrence looked up and down the desolate street to see if anyone was watching.

"Not any more!" Burke laughed "All the serious fighting's been done over in Stormont right now … that is, apart from the occasional sectarian murders, kneecappings and beatings. Nobody's really interested in the likes of you and me any more, Peter."

"I don't agree," Lawrence snapped back. "This is bloody dangerous!"

"Aw, come on…" Burke tried to defuse the situation by curling his big arm around the Englishman's shoulder. "Don't be so touchy … let's go and get ourselves a drink."

Lawrence eased himself from the Irishman's grasp. He poked his head back through the car's open passenger window to arrange a pick-up time and place with his driver, before rejoining Burke on the deserted pavement. The Mercedes pulled away, with vapour spiralling from the exhaust as it drove off down Ormeau Avenue and disappeared round the corner into Cromac Street.

"I don't like this one little bit, Eamonn," Lawrence continued, "we're too exposed."

"Nonsense!" Burke took him by the arm and led him across the street to O'Leary's public house. It was approaching midday and the lounge bar was almost empty, apart from a few old men sitting at the counter watching television.

Lawrence hesitated by the door and looked the place over while Eamonn Burke went over to the bar and ordered two large Irish whiskies.

"What's the matter? Don't you trust me, Peter?" Burke shook his head in mock disbelief. He watched the Englishman following his natural instincts, checking out the toilets and the public bar. "After all we've been through?"

"Can't be too bloody careful in this game," Lawrence replied coldly.

"Look here …" Burke said in his usual disarming way, as he placed the drinks on a small wooden table facing the door. "You and I both know this is an unofficial meeting, so why don't we just try to be a little bit more sociable with each other and have a nice quiet drink together."

"You know why I'm here." Lawrence felt the hairs bristling on the back of his neck. He couldn't take his eyes off the door.

"And there was I, beginning to think we had actually made some progress…" Burke sipped at his whisky and lit up a cigarette.

Lawrence's adrenaline began to subside as he came over and sat down at the table. "It's not *you* I don't trust, Eamonn," he explained. "It's all the others. So this isn't one of your usual safe places?" Lawrence looked the place over again.

"No," Burke replied. "But I just thought it would be better if we met on neutral ground … man-to-man kind of thing. What d'you say?"

"Social calls aren't really my scene," Lawrence replied, "But on the other hand, I've got my instructions."

"Why always so serious?" Burke tut-tutted. "Aw come on, lighten up man. More positive results can always be achieved in an informal atmosphere. All this political rhetoric and other clap-trap gets us nowhere. Another whisky?"

"I'll get them." Lawrence sprang to his feet. He felt much safer if he kept moving and went over to the bar to order a couple of doubles.

"Any more developments over this Iranian thing?" he casually enquired of Burke as he returned with the drinks.

"I thought *you* might be able to tell *me* something" the Irishman replied.

"All I've heard…" Lawrence conceded in a hushed tone, "is that London and Dublin are quite chuffed. The Americans are falling over themselves, kissing everyone's arse with eternal gratitude, and I can tell you there's a lot more mutual back-slapping going on in other quarters as well."

"Tell me Peter… Do you think any good will actually come out of all this?" Burke was hopeful, but didn't expect miracles.

"Absolutely! It's becoming clearer by the minute and by the day that Dublin will be able to negotiate some very favourable concessions from all the latest Peace Talks," Lawrence conceded. "But surely, that would suit your lot, wouldn't it?"

"Mm, I suppose so …" Burke mused. "Tell me now, have all the others gone home?"

"Yes."

"And your young woman … What's her name again?"

"Juliet Lucas."

"Aye, Miss Juliet Lucas," Burke smiled benignly. "A fine *colleen*! How is she?"

"She's OK," Lawrence confirmed. "She decided to stay back in St Petersburg when I left for Belfast … and incidentally, she's *not* my young woman."

"Ah, come on now, Peter."

"She's a colleague," Lawrence insisted, "a professional colleague."

"You can't fool me!" Burke's elbow gave a knowing nudge, "I've seen the two of you together…"

"Look, it's none of your business!" Lawrence was becoming irritated by all this facile small talk, and besides, he wasn't in the mood to discuss Juliet Lucas. He knew their transient relationship wouldn't last. She was being groomed and cosseted for far greater things. It wasn't a good thing to have too much emotional baggage in this game, as it made one vulnerable. How could anyone in his profession reasonably expect any self-respecting woman to settle down to marriage and raise his children? Every time the phone rang she would jump. She could never be sure where he was or when he was coming home – or more importantly, if he was ever coming home. No, he intended to maintain complete control of his own life and destiny. Perhaps Her Majesty's Government would one day shower him with her bounty, and provide him with a suitable reward for all his years of loyalty and dedication. However, he wouldn't hold his breath! Deep down, he realised that Burke was just trying to ease the tension, but the bad feeling he had woken up with earlier this morning just wouldn't go away.

"Let's get down to some more serious business," Lawrence said, when Burke had returned from the bar with two more whiskies.

"And what business might that be?"

The Irishman lit up another cigarette, and blew endless clouds of smoke to join the thin layers already hovering beneath the nicotine stained ceiling.

"Valentin Tarasov," Lawrence whispered, looking round to make sure no-one was listening.

"Who?"

"'You know bloody well *who*, Eamonn," Lawrence hissed. "Don't play games."

"Oh, you mean the Russian? He's dead."

"What do you mean, dead?"

"Committed suicide," Burke replied, in a matter-of-fact manner.

"Now, why on earth would he go and do a stupid thing like that?" Lawrence wasn't buying it.

"Ah well now, I suppose he finally realised that he'd jumped from the frying pan into the fire." The Irishman was obviously reluctant to discuss this particular topic. "One hostage situation to another, you might say."

"How the hell did he do it for Christ's sake?" Lawrence pressed for more details.

"How should I know?" Burke's reply contained a hint of irritation.

"You mean, you didn't actually *see* the body?"

"Listen, Peter…" Burke banged his glass down on to the table. "My second-in-command out in Mayo took charge of the Russian."

"O.K., O.K. What's his name and where can I contact him?" Lawrence kept up the pressure.

"You know I can't tell you that…" Burke scoffed, "I'd be dead in half an hour, man!"

"Eamonn…" Lawrence softened his tone, "Tarasov is a hot piece of property at the moment. We want him, the Americans want him, the Russians want him … *everyone's* looking for him. Now can you handle that sort of pressure?"

"Let me explain my situation to you Peter…" Burke flicked the cigarette butt onto the bare wooden floor and hunched over his drink. "Certain people in my organisation didn't take very kindly to the fact that I helped MI6 … and I mean certain *powerful* people. They didn't quite see the wider picture. My lieutenant in Mayo brought them Tarasov as a peace offering … otherwise I'd have been made into dog food by now, you understand?"

"I'm beginning to get the picture," Lawrence sighed.

"I no longer command the same level of respect that I once did back in the nineties. I simply don't have that indisputable power any more … and you know how necessary that is to make things happen over here." The Irishman virtually spat the words out. "And that's why we're meeting here, in this open bar, instead of one of the traditional safe places, with the usual security."

"Look, I'm sorry, Eamonn…"

"So, you see …when they *tell* me that Tarasov is dead, I have no other way of establishing whether it's true or not."

"Can you put me in touch with someone who can?" Lawrence tried to coax him.

"I could try…" Burke rose to his feet, "but it's lunchtime and all this talking has given me a raging appetite. D'you fancy a bite to eat, Peter?"

"Why not?" Lawrence gave a deep sigh and nodded resignedly.

The two men emerged into the grey Belfast day. The sleet had eased, but it was still cold, with a stiff westerly wind blowing across the city. They walked up Ormeau Avenue and turned north into Linenhall Street. Lawrence studied the stark outline of City Hall at the end of the road, with its white facade and copper dome. The building seemed to dominate the city skyline and looked down upon their progress as they threaded their way through endless hordes of shoppers, huddled against the driving rain. Lunchtime crowds began to spill out from the shops and offices, filling the cafes and pubs around the area. Lawrence just couldn't shake off the uneasy feeling that had dogged him all day. As they strolled past a rain-spattered shop window, he thought he saw the reflection of a dark-coloured car kerb-crawling behind them. He spun round, but could see nothing; nobody was there.

Perhaps it was just his vivid imagination playing tricks, or perhaps he needed a rest. A wave of exhaustion suddenly swept over him as he thought about the holiday he had promised Juliet Lucas. No matter how hard he tried, the bad feeling he had woken up with just wouldn't go away. His deep-rooted Service training had always taught him to trust his instincts. Something wasn't right and he knew it.

Eamonn Burke crossed the street and pushed open the frosted glass doors of a small noisy brasserie that was rapidly filling with lunchtime customers. He led Peter down into the soporific fug of the cellar bar where he selected a table in the far corner of the room so that no one could come up behind them.

"Fancy trying some of the local cuisine?" he asked with a disarming smile.

"When in Ireland…" Lawrence replied casually.

Burke snapped his fingers with an air of superiority and a waiter appeared at the table as if by magic. He set about ordering the local speciality of *bagun, cabaiste agus caulcannon* which he then went on to translate for his guest as gammon and green-cabbage, mixed with mashed potatoes, onions, pepper and buttermilk. To help wash it all down, he ordered two bottles of room temperature Guinness to be poured into half-pint tulip glasses.

"It's the only *real* way to drink Guinness," Burke explained with a satisfied gasp as he wiped the back of his hand across his mouth. He couldn't help noticing that Lawrence was picking and prodding at the meal set before him.

"Well, what d'you think?" Burke asked through a mouthful of food as he eagerly tucked in to the pile on his plate, washing it down with more large slurps of the malty porter.

"Oh… excellent!" Lawrence replied with forced enthusiasm, as he looked round at their fellow diners. The clientele consisted mainly of young office and shop workers from the surrounding commercial district, with their lively chatter ebbing and flowing above the subtle background of eighteenth century French baroque *chansons*. Lawrence thought this could be *any* restaurant in *any* city in *any* part of the world … But it wasn't – it was Belfast. Thirty years of wearying bloodshed and high-profile military presence had all but gone from the streets, leaving a new and vibrant optimism buzzing throughout the business community. Most people were tired of the conflict and genuinely yearned for an end to all the senseless killings. They were just beginning to believe in some sort of future: However, this was still Belfast!

With the meal finished, Burke ordered a couple of Irish coffees and lit up another cigarette. The men fell silent, each lost deep within his own innermost thoughts.

"Sorry if I was a bit snappy earlier," Lawrence apologised as he idly stirred his coffee. "I just *can't* seem to settle today."

"I understand. I expect you're just a bit anxious to get back to Miss Juliet," Burke smiled. "Can't say as I blame you."

"It's not really that serious between us…" The subtle warmth of the Irish coffee began to have an effect upon Lawrence. "It's just a physical thing … you know."

"Ah, but they're always the best kind of relationships." Burke raised his glass. "Here's to you Peter … and Miss Lucas," he toasted.

"And here's to you, Eamonn," Lawrence responded.

"I'll drink to that!" The men touched glasses and drank back the thick creamy coffee. "Two more?" Burke suggested.

"Not for me." Lawrence put his hands up in a gesture of polite refusal, "I've got to go. But thanks for the hospitality anyway."

"Aw come on Peter it's nothing … after all, that's what friends are for?"

"Eamonn…" Lawrence became serious again.

"Yes?"

"Try and get them to give up Tarasov – even if it's only his body." The Englishman's steady and sober voice contained a note of warning.

"I'll do my best," Burke promised as he stubbed his cigarette into the ashtray.

"Just remember, your people are dealing with much more than Protestant bully-boys here." Lawrence lowered his voice to a conspiratorial whisper. "This is way out of your league, man. You're going to have the whole of the CIA, MI6, Mossad, FCIS, Islamic lunatics and Christ knows who else sniffing round here if you're not careful …"

"I'm not exactly the flavour of the month, especially with my own people Peter … never mind anyone else."

"All the more reason to get clear of it – and fast." Peter Lawrence stood up. He pulled on his raincoat and was about to depart, when one of the waiters came down the stairs and approached their table.

"Peter Lawrence?" the man enquired.

"Who wants to know?" Burke's eyes narrowed.

"Someone upstairs asked for a Peter Lawrence," the waiter replied "That's all I know. I'm just the messenger, so there's no need to get uptight with me."

Neither had a chance to respond. The waiter raised his eyebrows and shrugged his shoulders before busily returning to his duties.

"I *told* that bloody driver…" Lawrence fumed.

"Hold on a minute, Peter…" Burke caught his arm. "Did your driver know we would be coming here?"

"Hey, wait a minute! I didn't even know we were coming here myself," Lawrence replied with alarm. The two men looked at each other and froze.

A thousand unanswered questions swooped and collided within their minds. Each man instinctively reached inside his coat to ease the safety catch off his gun. With fingers lightly curled around the hair-triggers, they cautiously moved up the steps and looked uneasily around the ground floor. Nobody appeared to be waiting and every table in the restaurant was taken. Waiters dressed like a barber shop harmony group could be seen bustling back and forth to the kitchen.

Eamonn gave a discreet nod to Peter when he noticed the young man who had brought the message downstairs, busily taking a diner's order. He moved over and lightly touched the waiter's arm.

"Where's this person who's been asking for Peter Lawrence?"

"Gone…" the young man said, as he looked up from his order pad.

"Did he say who he was?" Lawrence added.

"No. And it was a *she*," the young man replied "Why not ask over at the counter?"

Burke and Lawrence exchanged glances, before threading their way through the crowded tables towards the cashier seated behind her desk, just inside the door.

"Excuse me. We understand somebody came in looking for a Mr Peter Lawrence?" Burke asked the young woman.

"Oh yes … that's right," the girl replied, "But she was in a bit of a hurry and couldn't wait."

"Did she say exactly *who* she was?" Lawrence enquired.

"Are you Mr Lawrence?" The girl tapped her pen irritatingly on the side of the phone as she awaited confirmation of a credit card transaction.

"Yes…" Lawrence replied cautiously.

"Oh, it was your wife, Mr Lawrence." The credit card confirmation buzzed into life as the girl reached down and picked up a black briefcase from behind her counter. She held it out towards the two men. "You forgot your papers this morning."

"RUN!" Burke screamed, as he shoved Peter Lawrence headlong through the door and out onto the glistening wet street. In little more than a microsecond, an ear shattering blast, coupled with a blinding flash, hurled the two men through the air to land on the opposite pavement. The last vivid sounds that Burke could remember hearing were the dreadful screams coming from the injured and dying, followed by the piercing wail of sirens somewhere in the distance. Then darkness descended, as he collapsed in a pool of blood and muddy water in the middle of Linenhall Street.

Peter Lawrence tried to drag himself across to the crumpled body of his friend, but couldn't move his legs. He cursed as he rolled over to look back to where the brasserie used to be. Traumatised diners, their clothes in shreds, were staggering out through the raging fire and billowing clouds of acrid smoke onto the broken glass and bloody pavement. Some were dreadfully injured. They choked and gasped from blood spilling back into their shattered lungs. Emergency services were quickly on the scene as anxious crowds from the nearby streets began to gather. Lawrence gasped in agony as he lay with his outstretched arm just a few feet away from Burke. The Englishman tried to fight the powerful and overwhelming sensation of falling which threatened to envelop his mind. He was surprised to find there was no searing pain… just a sense of euphoria. The scene of carnage became brighter and brighter until all he could see was a brilliant white light. His inner resolve kept telling him that it was not yet time to die, but other uncontrollable sensations were trying to persuade him that perhaps it was.

The sounds of hysterical screaming and shouting gradually died away to be replaced by silence. He could fight it no longer and felt himself floating away on a plateau of complete serenity…

CHAPTER 32

England – London

THE PALE WINTRY SUN DIPPED BEHIND Admiralty Arch as if drained by its game of hide-and-seek with the solid grey clouds hanging like wet slate away to the west. Flocks of scrawny pigeons stood in huddled rows on the narrow ledges and cornices of the Government building as they looked down upon the approaching limousine.

The all pervading dismal London atmosphere tended to reflect upon Drew Dalton's latest mood as he sat in the back of the big car, heading along the Strand from the Savoy Hotel.

Dalton was afraid this would all turn out to be nothing more than just another talking shop. He hoped he was wrong. But, he'd nevertheless been around long enough to realise that such political conflicts of interest inevitably led to inaction and apathy. Senator Hefner T. Copeland sat beside him, with two top White House insiders sitting on the fold-down seats opposite. Officially, they were on a low-key diplomatic mission to Westminster – a loosely defined visit to foster goodwill and co-operation in the area of foreign affairs. Wild and exaggerated rumours had been circulating for some time, but nobody wanted to be the first to put forward an official statement about the seriousness of the situation or allow any information to get into the hands of the media. All hell would break loose if that happened. The four men remained silent and deep in thought about the forthcoming meeting, as the government limousine cruised elegantly along Whitehall and made its way towards the Houses of Parliament.

The President had personally briefed them in Washington less that twenty-four hours ago. He was absolutely furious that the whole incident had come within an ace of becoming an international disaster, and now expected immediate action.

The US delegation had been left in no doubt that they had better return with some concrete proposals – otherwise they would be subjected to early retirement and the full wrath of Uncle Sam.

The limousine rolled through Parliament Square and turned left into new Palace Yard. Security was tight, but the American delegates were expected, and arrangements had been made for them to proceed with the minimum of delay. Dalton pulled himself over and stared up at the imposing face of Big Ben as the huge clock struck 3.00pm. This grand Victorian Gothic seat of Government known as the Palace of Westminster covered an area of eight acres, had over eleven hundred rooms, one hundred staircases and more than two miles of passages.

The last of the Americans had just emerged from the car as a nervous Jeremy Sinclair stepped forward to escort them into the building via the Member's Entrance.

They had decided it would be more prudent to avoid the open public spaces of Westminster Hall. Sinclair shepherded the group through Cloister Court, before turning left to skirt around the octagonal Central Lobby with its lofty vaulted stone roof and four arched entrances. Each doorway of this important reception chamber was flanked on either side by regal statues of ancient Kings and Queens of England, benignly looking down upon the ordinary subjects seeking an audience with their respective Members of Parliament. Sinclair ushered his American guests along Peer's Corridor lined with pictures of the Stuart period. Those adorning the west wall illustrated the virtues of the Royalists, whilst those on the east depicted the Parliamentarians. Sinclair's pace slowed. He sensed he was losing his visitors, and turned at the end of the corridor to see them staring in wonderment at the portraits. He allowed them just a few brief moments to absorb this significant piece of British history before taking them along the Law Lords Corridor and through a maze of passageways, which Drew Dalton thought would never end. Their pace quickened.

They passed a solemn statue of Sir Charles Barry at the bottom of the Committee Staircase, which they ascended, two steps at a time, past a ghostly line of marble busts. Pausing briefly on the top landing, they were suddenly confronted by an impressive portrait of Queen Elizabeth, majestically looking down upon them. They averted their gaze from the painting and avoided eye contact with each other, as a universal feeling of unease about the awesome responsibilities associated with this latest summit began to descend upon the visitors...

Sinclair kept urging his followers to keep up, as they scurried along the gloomy corridors towards an impatient Adrian Dyson standing in front of a large oak panelled door, making a theatrical gesture of looking at his watch. After brief introductions, Jeremy Sinclair started to apologise for their delay, but on seeing Dyson's face, he left the sentence unfinished. Dyson turned and paused before the heavy timber door. He squeezed his eyes shut for a brief moment's contemplation, took a deep breath, pushed the door open and strode in. Jeremy Sinclair and the Americans quickly followed in his wake, as everyone entered the large meeting room on the first floor overlooking the Members Terrace and the River Thames.

Comfortable furnishings lined the perimeter, and a huge circular table dominated the centre. The Georgian oak-panelled walls were hung with a series of portraits by Pickersgill, Herbert and Mendoza, impassively overlooking this auspicious international assembly.

The Prime Minister's Press Secretary could be seen seated in such a position that it was clear he would be chairing the meeting, flanked by two senior MI6 people. Benjamin Eshkol sat to the Press Secretary's left, escorted by a couple of senior Knesset advisors, and the three most senior Russian naval officers, accompanied by two political aides from Moscow, sat on the right of the Chairman. Once Dyson, Sinclair and the Americans had seated themselves opposite the Chairman, the meeting got under way. The Press Secretary coughed politely, and rose to address the assembly.

"Gentlemen, to answer the burning question which is foremost in your minds, we have been summoned by our respective Governments to try and find a discreet way of assisting our Russian colleagues to safely de-commission their obsolete nuclear submarine fleet'. He slowly glanced around the room over the top of his glasses: he had their attention. "Unless there are any pressing questions at this stage of the proceedings, I believe it is vital for you to be fully briefed on *all* the circumstances which surround the unfortunate *Cherkassy* affair"

Historically, the Western Superpowers had believed, in their arrogance, that such problems could simply be resolved by playing for time. Although it was a policy that appealed to many, there were still others in government that feared the consequences of procrastination.

"I thought this was supposed to be a secret venue?" Benjamin Eshkol remarked.

"It is," the Press Secretary assured him.

"But what if the general public were to find out just how serious this whole situation is? We could have a global panic on our hands. There might even be rioting in the streets."

"This place is probably one of the most secure in England, Mr Eshkol." Dyson emphasised his confidence in the security by aiming a sobering expression of authority in the general direction of the Israeli. "You could hide a regiment within these walls – and there is absolutely no chance of anyone listening in."

"We all have official cover, I presume?" Drew Dalton enquired casually as he glanced at the multi-national delegation seated around the table.

"Of course!" Jeremy Sinclair stood up. "Nobody will query your presence."

"Good!" growled Senator Copeland, as he leaned forward and steepled his hands on the edge of the table. "Then let's do like the man said and get on with it!"

A rumble of voices echoed around the stately room as a variety of languages and accents affirmed their concordance.

"Everyone here knows the entire civilised world has just recently had a *very narrow escape*," Dyson stated, when the noise had died down. "We must ensure it doesn't happen again!"

"And just how do you propose we do that?" Benjamin Eshkol's jowls began to quiver.

"By eliminating the problem at source," Drew Dalton answered, as all eyes focused on the Israeli.

"Fine words…" Eshkol blustered, "but we need more than just words!"

"YES, you are quite right. *We need money!*" a Russian naval officer retorted.

"It's entirely your own problem," Eshkol scoffed as he turned and wagged an admonishing finger at the man. His aggressive approach surprised the Russian. "You people are just downright irresponsible – you have been totally negligent."

"We are doing everything we can," a Kremlin aide protested.

"*You are doing nothing!*" Behind Eshkol's outward appearance of political aggression lay an astute politician endowed with a solid egotistical intolerance of anyone else's problems.

"Gentlemen, gentlemen ..." Adrian Dyson appealed for calm. "Our task is to work together to find a solution to the problem, not to allocate blame."

"Now wait a minute ... let's all get real here." Hefner T. Copeland drawled, as he lit up one of his Havana's, "Everyone knows the Russians have derelict nuclear vessels littered all over the Arctic," he didn't wait for a reaction, "all the way from Karelia to Kamchatka."

"That is true, but we are in the process of decommissioning all obsolete equipment," one of the Russian aides said indignantly, "and all our fissionable material is being made safe."

"Liar!" boomed Eshkol.

"These things take time..." a Russian naval officer shifted uneasily in his chair.

"And money!" his colleague demurred.

"This whole problem is far too complex," the Press Secretary commented, "It's not going to go away simply by throwing money at it."

"The man's right," Drew Dalton said, "This whole thing's going to take a lot of trust, technical co-operation and just downright common sense."

"*Precisely!*" Dyson raised his arms as if he was giving a benediction "This is not simply a Russian problem ... it would be naive of us to try and isolate it just like that. It is, after all, a global problem – and as such, one that will require global solutions. *That*, gentlemen, is *why* we are here!"

"OK, OK..." Copeland stood up and looked round at the delegates. "I am assuming that we've all been given full executive powers by our respective governments. Now let's just see if we can make a few responsible decisions! I can confirm that the American Delegation are under strict Presidential instructions to seek a satisfactory solution to this unfortunate problem … along the lines of the deal recently struck between the British Prime Minister and our own President." He turned to face the Russians. "Now, just how big is this problem – besides the one hundred and thirteen Northern Fleet submarines we already know about?"

The Russians momentarily exchanged eye contact with each other, before shuffling through their folders and pulling out sheaves of multi-coloured documents.

"There isn't really a large amount of…" a Kremlin aide stammered as he kneaded his brows in a bid for time.

"We won't get anywhere until you admit it!" Eshkol interrupted again with a resounding bang of his fist onto the table.

The Russian hypocrisy was astounding. A brief silence followed. The most senior naval officer picked up a faded pink document, cleared his throat, and got to his feet. "Moscow has given us authority to divulge that there are a further one hundred and sixty one warships of different classes, rotting away along our northern coastline." His stony expression didn't betray any hint of cynicism as he went on to outline the world's most terrifying dilemma to the assembled group.

"My God!" Drew Dalton exclaimed as he detected something worse. He suspected that the Russians were still relying upon the Western Powers to remain tolerant, whilst Russia tried to avoid her moral and legal obligations.

"Some have been tragically sunk…like the *Cherkassy*, the *K219*, the *Komsomolets* and the *Kursk*… whereas others have been beached, or remain semi-submerged. However, Moscow regrets to inform you that *all* are radioactive – and still contain fissionable material."

"But what about security?" Jeremy Sinclair enquired.

"Security?" The naval officer's mouth curled in a wry smile. "How do you police ten thousand kilometres of Arctic coastline?"

"Are you seriously trying to tell us this fissionable material could simply fall into the hands of anyone who just happens to drop by?"

"In theory, yes." The Russian flopped his papers onto the table and sat down.

Surprised and excited murmurs swept around the room. Outside, heavy squalls of rain from the leaden skies beat an incessant tattoo against the gothic windows and the ebbing spring tide had whipped up the Thames into a dull muddy colour. A huddled mass of early evening commuters making their way across Westminster Bridge towards Waterloo Station looked bent and dejected.

Urgent whispers reverberated around the historic walls of the meeting room – with the grandiose portraits of Pitt the Younger, flanked by Gladstone and Disraeli, silently looking down upon this international gathering. These doyens of the British Parliamentary System had borne silent witness to so many crisis gatherings over the years, but this one, however, was probably the most critical: The issues being debated were truly cataclysmic.

Adrian Dyson rose to the occasion. Adopting his most solemn pose, he soon brought the proceedings to order.

"Her Majesty's Government cannot ignore the commitments agreed in Washington. You will recall that Great Britain has demonstrated her total support for the Nuclear Non-Proliferation Treaty, by allowing a special consignment of highly enriched uranium from the former Soviet Republic of Georgia to be processed at Dounreay in Scotland as part of operation *Auburn Endeavour*'. The Government, on that occasion, was quick to realise that such a move had been essential to avoid this *sensitive* material falling into the unscrupulous hands of either Chechen rebels – or any other aspiring nuclear nation.

Gentlemen, remember, we have just had a very close call with the *Cherkassy* affair ... and what is even more disturbing, is the fact that we are still receiving alarming reports that confirm Iran has indeed acquired bomb-grade fuel from within the former Soviet Union."

Dyson was appalled at the continuing duplicity of the Russians, especially as the Western Powers were under such intense pressure to ensure the whole affair was handled discreetly. "We cannot leave this room without concluding a joint agreement, gentlemen." His voice remained sober "Something has to be done – and *we* are the ones who've got to do it!"

"But what *can* we do?" Benjamin Eshkol asked as he leaned forward and fixed Dyson with flashing eyes, as fiery as an avenging angel's. "Unscrupulous Russians are selling off bits of hardware even as we speak."

"That's true …" one of his Knesset advisors added, "Just about anyone can pick up the basic ingredients, know-how, personnel and technology to make a nuclear weapon these days."

"Apart from that, we must give very careful consideration to the enormous ecological ramifications," Drew Dalton jumped to his feet and joined the group haranguing each other. "The whole delicate balance of our global eco-system is under constant threat from these nuclear leakages. Not to mention the possibility of serious and irreversible mutation to the millions of species within our oceans"

Jeremy Sinclair was worried – but not just about the crisis under debate. He was concerned about Peter Lawrence. The agent was still deep under cover somewhere in Northern Ireland – and nobody had heard from him for some time.

Sinclair had convinced himself that everything must be all right. In any case, he had far more important things on his mind right now, especially as they were fast approaching a last chance to counsel with reason.

"Now let's not get *too negative*, gentlemen" Adrian Dyson growled "We have been entrusted to find a way forward and rest assured, I intend to see that we do it!"

"That's the spirit!" Senator Copeland clapped his hands with glee as he looked around the table and gestured for the Israelis to speak.

"Our first priority has to be to make the whole situation secure," Benjamin Eshkol advised. "Perhaps we could undertake joint patrols in the area – that is – if our Russian friends agree."

"We are not empowered to give such authority!" the senior naval officer replied "We will have to refer back to Moscow for official confirmation."

"Then do it!" roared Copeland. "Goddamit, I thought we all had executive powers for this summit?"

"It's not quite as simple as that..." a Russian aide added, "because of the new political situation in Russia, we cannot simply pick up a telephone and call someone for confirmation."

"Well? What are you stalling for?" Eshkol scoffed, "I find all this languorous indifference by the Russians to be totally depressing. We all know what's up there for Christ's sake. It's not a *secret* any more."

"Then how long will it take?" Drew Dalton asked softly, as he tried to defuse the situation.

"I don't know" the Russian hissed through clenched teeth as he shook his head. "Perhaps several days ... a week maybe."

"Very well," Adrian Dyson added, "just do it as quickly as possible."

"Next; we need to investigate the possibility of setting up a multinational decommissioning programme to make sure that all vessels and obsolete installations are safe."

Another of the Russian naval men added, with as much dignity as he could muster, "We do, of course, have the relevant expertise... but owing to the magnitude of the problem, we still need additional technical and personnel assistance."

"We can guarantee that on behalf of Her Majesty's Government," Dyson confirmed, "and I'm sure our American and Israeli colleagues, together with their French and German counterparts, would also be prepared to make any additional resources available."

Each delegate nodded and murmured his tacit approval, subject to ratification by their respective governments. To achieve a meaningful and lasting agreement would take nothing short of a political masterstroke. There were no sure-fire guarantees for success, and it was becoming increasingly apparent that full executive powers around this conference table didn't quite mean what they were supposed to mean. Nobody was prepared to put his head on the block.

Even the carefully drafted protocol had proved to be a masterpiece of improvisation, especially since everyone knew it would still require further sanctioning back in Washington, Paris, Bonn ... or even the House of Commons. Drew Dalton sighed. His worst suspicions and fears were being realised.

This whole summit *was* turning out to be just another talking shop. A sombre hush descended upon the gathering as they tried to contemplate the political consequences of inaction. Everyone knew that inaction was another name for failure. Decisions made today would inevitably be postponed, delayed and diluted. Political posturing and procrastination would be allowed to take the rightful place of positive action, whilst Russia's rotting and festering soup of radioactive poison continued to leak into the oceans of the world.

Hands were warmly shaken to emphasise the sincerity of their obligations as the meeting broke up with promises of aid, increased resources and co-operation.

Now that the more serious business had been dispensed with, conversations lightened and old acquaintances were re-established. Obsequious waiters circled with refreshments and the Press Secretary announced that a formal dinner had been arranged with the Prime Minister for later that same evening.

Drew Dalton glanced across at Jeremy Sinclair who was busily studying a plate of shortbread being offered by one of the waiters. Sinclair paused when he sensed Dalton's admonishing eyes levelled in his direction and delicately replaced the morsel on the tray. Both men shrugged their shoulders and rejoined their superiors in the *faire de l'esprit*.

Outside the rain-spattered window, a lone seagull could be seen screeching and reeling in the wintry sky…its raw flesh oozing with angry sores from featherless patches dotted over its emaciated body. The wildly disorientated bird had flown in from the North Sea, where it had recently feasted on fish offal thrown overboard from an unsuspecting trawler. With decks almost awash with their heavy load and thousands of shrieking gulls circling overhead, the fishing fleet chugged and wallowed as it made its way back to port, crammed full with a silvery harvest gathered from the Norwegian Sea. Fishing in the region had been particularly good during the past few months, with this bountiful catch being taken in record time from the Gulf Stream's faint meandering trail which makes its way across the Barents Sea…before fading out along Russia's inhospitable northern coastline.

The frightened and frustrated seagull instinctively turned towards the welcoming glow of lights coming from the Houses of Parliament and flew straight into the glass. The startled delegation quickly regained their composure, and some even pointed at the panicking bird as it squawked and hovered drunkenly for a moment, before plunging into the swirling river below. A foul greenish liquid seeped from the bird's bloodshot eyes as it twitched and struggled in its final death-throes… and sank beneath the choppy water.

End